COLORADO
RV PARKS
A Pictorial Guide

by

Hilton and Jenny Fitt-Peaster

Rocky Mountain Vacation Publishing, Inc.
Boulder, Colorado 80303-2799

Cover photo copyright by Stock Imagery, Inc./Nathan Bilow, Denver, Colorado. Back cover
photos (top to bottom): Golden's Scenic Rock RV Park, copyright by Juanita McNeill,
Golden, Colorado; Sugar Loafin' Campground, copyright by Freeman Studios, Carbondale, Colorado; Castle Lakes Campground Resort, copyright by Ed Harrington, Lake City,
Colorado

Cover design by Robert L. Schram, BookEnds, Boulder, Colorado.

Books by Hilton & Jenny Fitt-Peaster
  Colorado Cabins, Cottages & Lodges – Discover Scenic Vacation Hideaways
  Colorado RV Parks – A Pictorial Guide, Modern Facilities, Full Hookups & Pull Thru Sites

Library of Congress Catalog Card Number: 94-69174

Publisher's Cataloging in Publication
(Prepared by Quality Books, Inc.)
Fitt-Peaster, Hilton.
    Colorado RV parks : a pictorial guide : modern facilities /
Hilton & Jenny Fitt-Peaster.
    p. cm.
    Preassigned LCCN: 94-69174.
    1-883087-01-5.
    Includes index.

    1. Camp sites, facilities, etc.--Colorado 2. Recreational
vehicles--Colorado. I. Fitt-Peaster, Jenny. II. Title
GV198.L3.F58 1995 796.7'9'09788
                        QBI94-21114

This publication is a directory intended to provide information only, not recommendations, warranties, guaran-
tees, inducements or endorsements of any kind. The information contained herein was supplied by the individual
businesses. Although the publisher has prepared this directory with the information available as of March 15, 1995,
it does not assume any responsibility, and expressly disclaims any liability, for inaccuracies or errors regarding the
information contained herein. Readers are advised that prices and services are subject to change. The publisher
would appreciate notice that any information contained herein is no longer accurate.

Printed in the United States of America

10 9 8 7 6 5 4 3 2 1

Dedication

So you can enjoy worthwhile vacations, our business mission since 1977 has been to help people successfully purchase, operate and (later) sell their campground, cabin or lodge business. When our children were young, Jenny stayed home while Hilton spent each summer after 1980 traveling 8,000 miles around Colorado on eight mini-trips of about ten days each, visiting virtually all the family-operated campgrounds, cabins and lodges. On each trip he would take along one of our six children. Sometimes Jenny would go on a mini-trip, and occasionally Grandma would come along. As our children grew and left home, and our oldest child (Rebekah) joined our family firm to manage the office, Jenny graduated to full-time co-pilot. In October, 1994 our youngest child, Rachaell, died in an automobile accident at age 23. Now more than ever, we cherish the quality time our family spent together on vacations and on those many trips. We promise to continue our endeavor to provide information to help you create quality memories from wholesome vacations. This first edition of Colorado RV Parks is lovingly dedicated to Rachaell.

Foreword

Welcome to RV vacationing in Colorado. In this unique guide book, you'll find a comprehensive listing of the RV campgrounds and parks in our rugged state — The Camping Capital of America. Choose among sites near the major cities to ones tucked away by a snowcapped mountain peak. Whether you prefer high alpine get-a-ways or modern campgrounds with all the amenities, *COLORADO RV PARKS — A Pictorial Guide* has it all.

Taking an RV through the Rocky Mountains is my preferred way to travel. The authors, Hilton and Jenny Fitt-Peaster, feel similarly and it's obvious in how they have written their guidebook. The Fitt-Peasters personally visited all the RV parks and campgrounds on these pages many times and pass their observations onto you. The accompanying photographs conveniently give you the opportunity to see what waits at the end of the road.

In addition, the area descriptions include all the indoor and outdoor activities you'll want to participate in during your vacation. Spend your summer holiday whitewater rafting, fly fishing, canoeing, horseback riding, Golfing, hiking and mountain biking. During the winter, you can cross country and downhill ski, snowshoe, snowmobile, ice skate and ice fish. The possibilities are limitless. The RV accommodations cover the state and range from resort quality parks with recreation centers and health spas, to rustic sites deep in the mountains along trout laden streams. This guidebook, packed with useful information, will help you plan the ideal RV vacation in Colorado. Start reading and I'll see you on the trails!

Dennis Campbell
National President
Family Campers & RVers Association
(formerly National Campers & Hikers Association)

Table of Contents

Indexes to RV Parks

List of Towns

Map

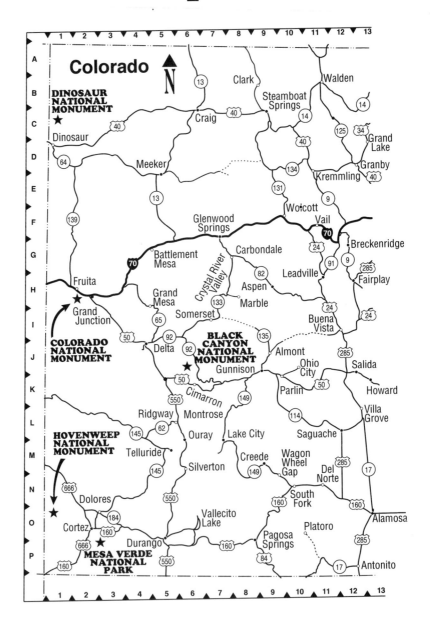

Map ix

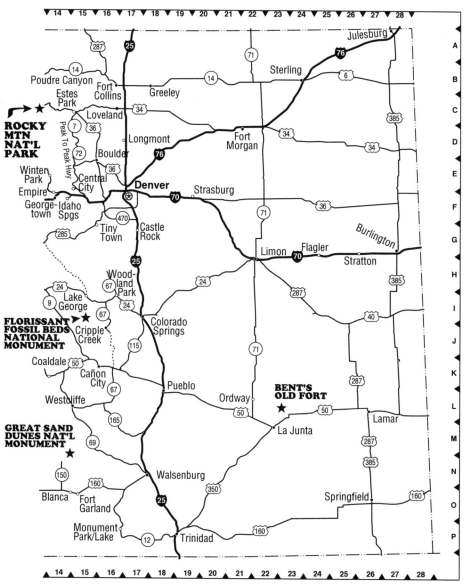

Note: not all highways, roads and towns appear on map

Preface

From snowcapped mountain peaks to high alpine meadows, past crystal streams through historic ghost towns, down lush valleys lined with spruce and aspen trees, Colorado is truly an outdoor paradise. Our beautiful state has it all: stunning scenery, Gold Medal fishing, clean, crisp air, and miles of trails. With 400% more RV parks and campgrounds in the mountains than any other state, Colorado is the Camping Capital Of America!

Many people mistakenly think the only way to reach Colorado's rugged wilderness is by hiking for two days with a backpack. Exploring Colorado is not arduous, however. Campgrounds catering to the RVer abound. Just imagine, when you return from frolicking in the sun, a hot shower and clean restroom await. Your RV can be hooked up to electricity, water, sewer and sometimes cable TV — all the comforts of home right at your site. When you step out your front door, you may be within walking distance to a pure mountain stream filled with rainbow trout. You'll wake to the soothing sounds of nature: birds chirping in the day and the breeze rustling the trees above your camper.

RV camping is the ideal way to see all the wonders Colorado has to offer. On top of that, the price is right. Less expensive than hotels and fancy ski resorts, more comfortable than backpacking, RVing is just right for you and your family. A campsite for two people a night averages $13.03 for no hookups, and $17.41 for full hookups. Additional people are usually $2.00 each. Now, with *COLORADO RV PARKS — A Pictorial Guide*, finding the RV park that meets your needs is easy because we've done all the work for you!

As executive directors of Colorado Association of Campgrounds, Cabins & Lodges since 1977, we drive over 8,000 miles each summer on Colorado's highways and back roads searching out and visiting owners of RV parks. Some of the properties in this book are out-of-the-way gems you won't find listed anywhere else.

No other book or directory has such comprehensive listings for each RV park. Park owner/operators around the state are eager to share their treasures. In writing *COLORADO RV PARKS — A Pictorial Guide*, we hope to bring owners and visitors together, helping fulfill your holiday dreams.

There are 201 RV parks and campground listed. No one paid to be listed in this book. All of them are professional members of the non?profit Colorado Association of Campgrounds, Cabins & Lodges.

We hope you find this book enjoyable, useful and rewarding. Feel free to give us your feedback or comments about this book — and be sure and tell the RV park and campground owners where you learned about their properties.

We wish to acknowledge the valuable services of the following people, without whom this book would never have been published: Rebekah Fitt-Peaster, our associate publisher (and daughter), Kathe Conti for expert and creative editing, Bob Quam for his editorial support, photo preparation and advise, Rodney Sauer of

RDD Consultants for computer layout design, Arthur Fitt of FittWare Consultants (and son) for making our computer database (he designed) talk with our word processing program, Tanya Devoll for proof reading, Bob Schram of BookEnds for cover design, and to all the RV park and campground owner/operator-hosts in this book who double checked the accuracy of their listings and (in some cases) supplied photos.

Thanks. Enjoy Colorado!

Hilton and Jenny Fitt-Peaster
Authors
March 1995

How To Use This Book

This guidebook features descriptions of a variety of RV parks, campgrounds and resorts along with fun things to do. It is organized A through Z by town/area to make it easy for you to find accommodations in particular areas of Colorado. Use the List of Towns to, locate the town or area you're interested in and then go to the page number listed for a description of RV parks in that area. Some towns are grouped together into a common area, so if you look up a particular town, you may find a cross reference directing you to a different area. The town and area headings all include map coordinates; use these to locate the town on the map in the front of this book or on the official Colorado state highway map. The town headings themselves may also refer you to other nearby areas for additional listings.

ACCOMMODATION DEFINITIONS
We realize you may not be familiar with all the terminology used throughout these pages, so we provide the following definitions for your convenience.

Campsite — Suitable for overnight camping for a family; usually has a fire ring or grill, picnic table, assessable to nearby drinking water, modern restrooms and hot showers. The site should be reasonably level and well drained. There are 12,422 campsites listed in this guidebook.

RV Site — A campsite for an RV (recreation vehicle) such as a motorhome, 5th wheel, camping (pop-up) trailer, travel trailer, pickup camper, or van. An RV site usually has utility hookups.

Tent Site — A campsite for a tent, pickup truck, van or car.

Full Hookup — An RV site with its own electrical, water and sewer connections. There are 7,297 full hookup RV sites listed in this book!

CHART DEFINITIONS
Accompanying each property listing is a chart with specifics about the campground. The following are the definitions for the chart terms.

VMAD — V = Visa (credit card), M = MasterCard, A = American Express, and D = Discover.

LP Gas — metered means that a fixed (non-removable) tank on a motorhome can be filled and the liquefied petroleum gas (LPG), is metered and sold by the gallon. Those with a meter can also fill removable bottles. Weight means that LPG is sold by weight only, and they don't have the equipment to fill a fixed tank, but can fill removable LPG tanks.

GLYPHS AT THE BOTTOM OF RV PARK PAGES :
Those for activities and facilities at the RV Park are:

 Coin operated Washer and Dryer.

 Some Meals served. (Breakfast, Lunch, Dinner or Snack)

 Well behaved Pets are okay on leash.

 Fishing. (free or for a fee)

 Hot Showers.

 Sanitary/Holding Tank Disposal or Dump Station.

 Campfires allowed (usually at each site, but may be only a central group campfire. Campfires allowed subject to weather conditions; prolonged dry weather can cause open fire bans. However fires in confined BBQ rings or pits may still be allowed.)

 Tent Sites.

 Cabins, or rustic Camper Cabins.(For more detailed information on cabins, we have written a book, *COLORADO CABINS, COTTAGES & LODGES — Discover Scenic Vacation Hideaways*, see order form at the end of this book.)

 Lodge or Motel Rooms.

 Swimming Pool.

Those for activities within a 15 minute drive or at RV Park are:

 Mountain Bike Trails.

 Rafting .

 Golf course.

 Horseback Riding (guided).

 Lake or Reservoir for boating or fishing.

RESERVATIONS, FACILITIES & FUN THINGS TO DO

Beware that reservations are recommended, sometimes months in advance especially for holiday weekends and during peak season (June 15th to August 20th) at popular destinations, particularly those within two hours of Denver. At other times of the year and in other areas of Colorado, reservations are usually not as necessary. Consider a fall, winter or spring vacation when rates can be lower, reservations easier, fewer people are around and the scenery even more spectacular.

When selecting places for your vacation, phone the owner/operator to double check what they offer: price, facilities, reservation deposit/refund policy, pet policy, and so on.

Facilities at commercial RV Parks and campgrounds often include a convenience store with some groceries, ice, firewood, camping and fishing supplies. The property may also offer a game room, recreation hall, gifts and souvenirs, pool, hot tub, playground, basketball, volleyball, miniature golf and a snack bar or restaurant. Best of all, the owner/operator lives on site — they care about your safety, security and serve as your personal hosts.

Activities may include fishing, guides and outfitters, nature walks, hiking, hay rides, water sports, pancake breakfasts, barbecue cookouts, potluck dinners, ice cream socials, campfire programs, movies, slide shows, whitewater raft trips, kayaking, four wheeling, square dancing, sightseeing, tours, gold panning, rock hounding and horseback riding. In the fall, viewing the aspen colors and hunting are the most popular Colorado events. Winter brings snowmobiling, cross-country and downhill skiing, ice fishing, sleigh and snow-cat rides. Inquire about rental equipment and instructions for wintertime activities. Season opening and closing dates may change, depending on the weather.

ALTITUDE AWARENESS

In Colorado's high country, the skies are bluer and the stars are brighter because of our altitude. The air is also thinner, with less oxygen, than at sea level, especially above 8,000 feet. Until your body adjusts, go easy on physical activity; drink more water than usual; minimize your intake of alcohol, caffeine and salty foods; and eat high-carbohydrate foods, such as grains, fruits and vegetables. There is less atmosphere to screen out ultraviolet rays, so remember to use sunscreen and sunglasses. If you adopt a proper attitude toward Colorado's altitude, you and your family will have the most enjoyable vacation experience possible.

RATES

RV site prices constantly change, both seasonally and annually, so instead of giving exact costs, we provide a price range. The 1995 rates for two people per night for a full hookup RV site are indicated this way: When planning where to stay, remember that some of the best RV parks are inexpensive. Weekly and monthly rates are common.

$$¢ \ = \ \text{Under } \$15$$
$$\$ \ = \ \$15 - \$25$$
$$\$\$ \ = \ \text{Over } \$25$$

Antonito & Conejos River Canyon

Includes Platoro. Map: P-13

This southern San Luis Valley city is rich in culture and history from the Ute Indians and the Spanish who called the valley home. Antonito lies between the Conejos and the San Antonio rivers at an elevation of 7,888 feet and is the gateway to the beautiful, 40-mile Conejos River Canyon where outdoor enthusiasts can fish, hunt and hike. The upper Conejos River offers excellent trout fishing and the lower part is good for rainbows, browns and the occasional northern pike. The Platoro Reservoir has wonderful fishing for browns, rainbows and some kokanee soon after the spring thaw and is stocked with rainbow trout in the summer. No matter the river or lake, fishermen will always have something biting their line near Antonito. This city was once the "mainline" of the infant Denver and Rio Grande railroads. Today, Antonito is the main station for the Cumbres & Toltec Scenic Railroad — the highest and longest narrow-gauge railroad in the North American continent — an authentic railroad trip to Chama, New Mexico, that brings Colorado history to the present day. Nearby the town of Conejos boasts the oldest church in Colorado, Our Lady of Guadeloupe Church. The Rio Grande National Forest offers rolling hills, river canyons, and thick pine and aspen forests to explore.

Fun Things to Do

- Cumbres & Toltec Scenic Railroad (719) 376-5483
- End of the Rail Clydesdale Rides & Gifts (719) 376-2042
- First Crossing Restaurant (800) 323-9469, (719) 376-5441
- Our Lady of Guadeloupe Church (719) 376-5985
- Rio Grande National Forest Headquarters (719) 852-5941

Conejos Cabins & Gold Pan Acres Campground

Near the Continental Divide, Conejos Campground has full hookup sites with campfire pits. Surrounded by mountains, the RV sites are near a river and gold mining town. The 23-mile road to this campground in Platoro is an easily-travelled gravel road.

Fish for trout on the Conejos River or the Platoro Reservoir. Rent a horse nearby or bring your own for a ride to the high mountain lakes in the surrounding area where the fishing is pristine.

Modern, furnished cabins with kitchens are available right on the beautiful Conejos River.

Location: Located West of Antonito, exit Highway 17 at milepost 17 and travel North 23 miles on the gravel road.

Total RV sites: 20	Pull thru sites: 20	Open: Memorial Day to 10/2
Full hookup sites: 20	45+ foot long sites: 10	Bob, Dixie & Troy Peterson, Owners
Water & elec. sites: 0	Slideout sites: 10	PO Box 519
Elec. only sites: 0	Licenses sold: None	Antonito, Colorado 81120-0519
50 amp sites: 0	LP Gas: None	719/376-2547 Cabins
Hookup sites open in Fall: 0	Credit Cards: VM	719/376-2246 Gold Pan
Winter hookup sites: 0	Elevation: 9750	
RV site cost: ¢		

Within 15 minutes:

At RV Park:

Conejos River Campground

Bordering the Rio Grande National Forest and the Conejos River (Spanish for rabbits), this ideal location is an angler's dream. The campground has all level pull thrus with 20, 30 and 50 amps full hookups near the foothills and the river. Small trees are scattered between sites which are equipped with campfire pits and picnic tables. Lean-tos on some sites provide shade at this great family campground. Look for elk, deer, rabbits and occasional big horn sheep that frequent the area while you take the beautiful walk to the river.

A hot tub and 9-hole miniature golf are new additions near the heated pool. A recreation room with board and video games, a large playground and small convenience store with snacks are on the property. Anglers will want to test their lines in the Platoro Reservoir or along the Conejos River, flowing southeast from the reservoir, for rainbow and brown trout. In the fall, hunters will find numerous elk and deer. Hiking and mountain biking trails are nearby.

Location: Borders the Rio Grande National Forest and Conejos River, off Highway 17, 12 miles West of Antonito.

Total RV sites: 58
Full hookup sites: 29
Water & elec. sites: 26
Elec. only sites: 3
50 amp sites: 15
Hookup sites open in Fall: 58
Winter hookup sites: 15
RV site cost: ¢

Pull thru sites: 58
45+ foot long sites: 58
Slideout sites: 58
Licenses sold: None
LP Gas: None
Credit Cards: VM
Elevation: 8400

Open: 5/15 to 11/15
Bud & Norma Evans, Owners
26714 Hwy 17
Antonito, Colorado 81120-0386
719/376-5943

Within 15 minutes:

At RV Park:

Josey's Mogote Meadow

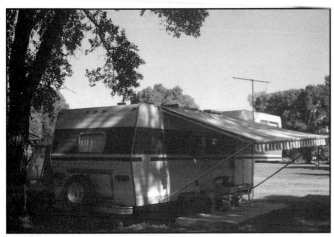

Placed among seven acres of green grass and shady cottonwood trees, Josey's has spacious full hookup sites (30 amps); most with cement patios. There are laundry and hot shower facilities available at this friendly, family atmosphere campground in a mountain meadow.

Beautiful and relaxing, the campground offers fishing nearby. Mountain bike trails and horseback riding are minutes away. Fish the Conejos River and nearby lakes. Join the nightly campfire and bring something for the Wednesday night pot luck dinners. On Sundays, enjoy a pancake breakfast. Josey's sits right by the Los Caminos Antiguos Scenic Byway which runs southwest over La Manga and Cumbres pass, both over 10,000 feet in elevation. Within an easy day trip are the Red River, Wolf Creek Pass, and Taos and Chama in New Mexico.

Cabins and an outdoor, group meeting area are also available.

Location: On Highway 17, 5 miles West of Antonito.

Total RV sites: 44	Pull thru sites: 10	Open: 5/1 to 10/20
Full hookup sites: 44	45+ foot long sites: 44	Bob & Anne Josey, Owners
Water & elec. sites: 0	Slideout sites: 44	34127 Hwy 17
Elec. only sites: 0	Licenses sold: None	Antonito, Colorado 81120
50 amp sites: 0	LP Gas: metered	719/376-5774
Hookup sites open in Fall: 44	Credit Cards: None	
Winter hookup sites: 0	Elevation: 8066	
RV site cost: Not available		

Within 15 minutes:

At RV Park:

Narrow Gauge Railroad Inn & RV Park

Within easy walking distance of the Cumbres & Toltec Scenic Railroad depot, the park has full hookup sites. Begin and end your ride on this historic railroad which twists its way to Chama, New Mexico, by staying here. The train's whistle, the hiss of steam and the pungent smell of coal smoke linger along with your pleasant memories of staying in this lush, photogenic countryside.

This is a bare bones RV. Breakfast, lunch and dinner are served at the First Crossing Restaurant. Wagon and horse rides are available a short stroll away. Rivers to fish and trails to mountain bike are nearby.

Motel lodging and an indoor, group meeting area are also available. Overnight packages include a train trip and be sure to ask about the group rates.

Location: South of Antonito at the junction of Highway 285 and Colorado 17.

Total RV sites: 8	Pull thru sites: 0	Open: 5/1 to 10/31
Full hookup sites: 8	45+ foot long sites: 6	Ray & Joyce Francis, Owners
Water & elec. sites: 0	Slideout sites: 6	PO Box 636
Elec. only sites: 0	Licenses sold: None	Antonito, Colorado 81120-0636
50 amp sites: 0	LP Gas: None	719/376-54411
Hookup sites open in Fall: 8	Credit Cards: VMAD	800/323-9469
Winter hookup sites: 0	Elevation: 8000	
RV site cost: Not available		

Within 15 minutes:

At RV Park:

Ponderosa Campground

The combination of pine trees, cottonwood trees and the Conejos River make this a beautiful campground. All sites have electricity (30 amp) and water with campfire pits. Gather firewood in the area. Camp along the river where the gravel pads are surrounded by large cottonwoods, pines, firs and willows. A place for leisure with its clean, crisp mountain air, the campground includes one mile of access along the rushing Conejos River and rests at the foot of the scenic Cumbres Pass. In the summertime, the climate is dry in the day and cool at night.

A game room with board games, pool table and video games and a playground are on the property. With the river just steps away, fishing opportunities abound. Mountain bike trails are a short distance away. Kayaking and rafting is excellent here in June.

Cabins and an indoor, group meeting area are also available.

Location: 20 miles West of Antonito on Highway 17.

Total RV sites: 32	Pull thru sites: 7	Open: 5/26 to 10/1
Full hookup sites: 0	45+ foot long sites: 4	Managers
Water & elec. sites: 32	Slideout sites: 10	19600 Hwy 17
Elec. only sites: 0	Licenses sold: Fishing	Antonito, Colorado 81120
50 amp sites: 0	LP Gas: None	719/376-5857
Hookup sites open in Fall: 32	Credit Cards: V	
Winter hookup sites: 0	Elevation: 8500	
RV site cost: Not available		

Within 15 minutes:

At RV Park:

Twin Rivers RV Park & Cabins

Away from the hustle and bustle, at the mouth of the beautiful Conejos Canyon where the fishing and hunting are excellent, Twin Rivers' full hookups sites are in a shade tree lined meadow. All sites are level and open; some are pull thru and grassy with 20 and 30 amps. Pick your own site; many have a picnic table.

Fly fish right at your doorstep in the park's two stocked streams or cast your line in nearby reservoirs, mountain lakes, rivers and streams. A tackle and gift shop are close by. A game room and playground are on the property. Eat a complimentary Sunday morning pancake breakfast before exploring mountain bike trails near the park. Guest horses are allowed. Four-wheel drivers will find rugged, mountain trails just 5 minutes away. The Rio Grande National Forest and San Juan Mountains, within 10 miles, have countless hiking trails to explore. Or sit in the clubhouse and enjoy your relaxing vacation at Twin Rivers.

Modern cabins, an indoor, group meeting area, group activities and catering are available.

Location: Located 5 miles West of Antonito, on Highway 17, at the mouth of Conejos Canyon

Total RV sites: 38	Pull thru sites: 11	Open: 5/1 to 11/15
Full hookup sites: 38	45+ foot long sites: 11	Barbara Jordan, Owner
Water & elec. sites: 0	Slideout sites: 38	34044 Hwy 17
Elec. only sites: 0	Licenses sold: None	Antonito, Colorado 81120
50 amp sites: 0	LP Gas: None	719/376-5710
Hookup sites open in Fall: 38	Credit Cards: D	800/376-5710
Winter hookup sites: 0	Elevation: 8000	
RV site cost: Not available		

Within 15 minutes:

At RV Park:

Black Canyon Area

Includes Cimarron, Delta and Montrose.
See also Grand Mesa Area and Gunnison. Map: J-4, K-5 & 6

Located in southwestern Colorado amid three national forests, the Black Canyon of the Gunnison National Monument, Curecanti National Recreation Area and the San Juan Mountains, this is the gateway to the San Juan Skyway and the Ridgway State Recreation Area. Take a scenic day trip to Telluride, Ridgway, Grand Mesa, Blue Mesa Reservoir, Owl Creek Pass, Marrow Point Reservoir and Silver Jack Reservoir. The Black Canyon is the most stunning day trip of all: as deep as 2,700 feet and as narrow as 1,300 feet, the canyon was shaped by the churning waters of the Gunnison River. A 50-mile long chasm, the Black Canyon's sheer, shadowy rock walls drop more than a half mile to the river creating a somber and memorable site. The area offers some of the best fishing in Colorado on the Gunnison, San Miguel, Cimarron and Dolores rivers. Keep an eye out for the many golden eagles, red-tailed hawks, prairie falcons and great horned owls that live here. The many recreation areas provide boating, fishing, swimming and sunning opportunities. To the northwest lies Escalante Canyon where, with a short walk, you can see Ute petroglyphs, dinosaur digs and old homesteads. The mild climate and fertile soil make this an outstanding fruit-producing area; many tourists arrive in late summer to pick peaches, apples, sweet-and-sour cherries, pears, apricots and plums.

Fun Things to Do

- Black Canyon of the Gunnison National Monument (970) 249-7036
- Curecanti National Recreation Area (970) 641-2337

Flying A Motel & Campground

The campground sits behind the motel, along the Gunnison River. Sites are level, grassy and open. Full hookups (30 and 50 amps) with TV hookup are available. Relax on the lawn, under the shade of tall, globe willow trees after a day of adventures in Delta County.

Kids will like the playground with swings, horseshoes and volleyball. A walking trail and dog run border the campground along the river. From here, you are within walking distance to Delta's shops and restaurants. Just down the road, bordered by the Uncompahgre and Gunnison rivers are miles of hiking and biking trails around ponds and Confluence Park Lake where you can boat, swim and fish for trout and bass. Flying A has its own boat dock and you can book a river trip down the Escalante and Dominguez canyons from here. Both the Black Canyon of the Gunnison National Monument and Grand Mesa are within driving distance.

Motel rooms with kitchens are available. Ask about the daily, weekly, monthly and seasonal rates.

Location: Located on the West side of US Highway 50, ½ mile North of the junction of Highway 50 and 92 at the North end of the Gunnison River bridge.

Total RV sites: 33	Pull thru sites: 9	Open: All Year
Full hookup sites: 25	45+ foot long sites: 13	Don & Danette Nolan &
Water & elec. sites: 3	Slideout sites: 25	Kenneth & Gail Rigdon, Owners
Elec. only sites: 0	Licenses sold: None	676 Hwy 50 N
50 amp sites: 19	LP Gas: metered	Delta, Colorado 81416
Hookup sites open in Fall: 25	Credit Cards: VMAD	970/874-9659
Winter hookup sites: 25	Elevation: 5000	
RV site cost: ¢–$		

Within 15 minutes:

At RV Park:

Mountain View RV Park

On the eastern edge of Montrose, beneath large shade elm trees, Mountain View RV Park has shaded sites along Cedar Creek. The full hookup (20 and 30 amps) sites are pull thrus with picnic tables, patios, barbecue grills and 30-channel cable TV hookup.

Not only can you play miniature golf right on the campground, but Mountain View has horseshoes. Make this your headquarters for visiting Montrose, the Black Canyon of the Gunnison National Monument, Ouray, Delta, and Ridgway Reservoir. An 18-hole public golf course is only four blocks away. The Montrose area has fishing, four-wheel driving, mountain biking, horseback riding and even whitewater raft trips.

Reservations are recommended in the summer. Ask about the daily, weekly and monthly rates.

Location: At the junction of US Highways 50 and 550, travel East 1 1/3 miles on US Highway 50 to Gibson's or from East US Highway 50, turn left at the 1st traffic light. The park is behind Gibson's.

Total RV sites: 42	Pull thru sites: 42	Open: All Year
Full hookup sites: 26	45+ foot long sites: 20	Duane & Charlene Kirby, Owners
Water & elec. sites: 10	Slideout sites: 10	126 Rose Lane
Elec. only sites: 6	Licenses sold: None	Montrose, Colorado 81401
50 amp sites: 1	LP Gas: None	970/249-3884
Hookup sites open in Fall: 42	Credit Cards: VM	
Winter hookup sites: 18	Elevation: 5800	
RV site cost: Not available		

Within 15 minutes:

At RV Park:

Pleasant Valley Campground & Cabins

A good place to vacation and relax, Pleasant Valley has shaded sites along Little Cimarron River on the western slopes of the Colorado Rockies. All sites are full hookups and have campfire pits and picnic tables. A clean, quiet, friendly haven, this is a great retreat for families.

The convenience store, in addition to groceries, hunting and fishing licenses, has a wide selection of antiques and collectibles. Pleasant Valley is close to major attractions such as the Black Canyon of the Gunnison National Monument and Blue Mesa Reservoir. Try your hand at the excellent trout fishing on the property or nearby. Hunt in some of the best deer and elk areas in the state, explore four-wheel drive roads or browse among the antiques. Horseback riding is minutes away and guest horses are welcome.

Cabins with kitchenettes are available.

Location: On US Highway 50 at milepost 115, 3 miles East of Cimarron.

Total RV sites: 13
Full hookup sites: 10
Water & elec. sites: 0
Elec. only sites: 0
50 amp sites: 0
Hookup sites open in Fall: 10
Winter hookup sites: 0
RV site cost: ¢

Pull thru sites: 0
45+ foot long sites: 6
Slideout sites: 13
Licenses sold: Fish & Hunt
LP Gas: metered
Credit Cards: VMD
Elevation: 7500

Open: 5/1 to 12/1
Larry & Linda Griffin, Owners
84100 E Hwy 50
Box 127
Cimarron, Colorado 81220-0127
970/249-8330

Within 15 minutes:

At RV Park:.

RV Camperland

Just 2 ½ miles west of the entrance to the Black Canyon of the Gunnison National Monument, RV Camperland sits on the shores of a deep blue, private lake. All sites are full hookups with campfire pits. With a view of the snow-capped San Juan Mountains in the distance, the sites are large and many are shady. This is the closest RV park with hot showers to the Black Canyon.

Fish in the lake without a state license for trout, catfish and perch. The antique store has Indian artifacts and souvenirs. Rent horses nearby or bring your own to ride through the picturesque Black Canyon country. Explore the unique countryside on your mountain bike or with a four-wheel drive vehicle.

Daily, weekly and monthly rates are available.

Location: Located 3 miles East of Montrose. Exit Highway 50 at milepost 98 and travel 2 ½ miles West of the entrance to Black Canyon of the Gunnison National Monument.

Total RV sites: 24	Pull thru sites: 9	Open: 5/1 to 11/1
Full hookup sites: 24	45+ foot long sites: 24	Paul & Shirley Donovan, Owners
Water & elec. sites: 0	Slideout sites: 24	69905 Hwy 50
Elec. only sites: 0	Licenses sold: None	Montrose, Colorado 81401
50 amp sites: 2	LP Gas: None	970/249-8314
Hookup sites open in Fall: 24	Credit Cards: VM	
Winter hookup sites: 10	Elevation: 6800	
RV site cost: Not available		

Within 15 minutes:

At RV Park:

Breckenridge

Map G-12

Charmingly restored, gingerbread Victorian houses lining its streets earned Breckenridge a National Historic District designation. Set amidst mountain splendor and the Continental Divide for a backdrop, this former mining town was established in an 1859 gold rush — the first permanent settlement on Colorado's Western Slope. Named in honor of Vice President John C. Breckenridge (in order to get a post office more easily), the town, when the Civil War broke out and the vice president supported the Confederacy, was re-named Breckenridge. In addition to the diverse terrain on the ski resort's three mountains, Breckenridge, at an elevation of 9,603 feet, has the only Jack Nicklaus-designed municipal golf course, renown musical organizations, and miles of hiking trails. Surrounded by Arapaho National Forest, the city has fishing on the Upper Blue River or the nearby Mohawk Lakes and, of course, skiing and snowboarding at the resort's specially designed park. A popular summer pastime is riding on the paved bike trail that encircles Breckenridge and connects to the extensive Summit County bike path system of 47 trails! Four 14ers (mountain peaks 14,000-feet and higher in elevation) can be climbed nearby. The closest peak to Breckenridge is Quandry Peak, 5 miles south of town. Be sure and check out the human maze at Peak 8 — a fun place to get lost! Visit and find out why locals say, "winters are why we come, summers are why we stay."

Fun Things To Do:

- Alpine Slide (970) 453-5000
- Breckenridge Activity Center (970) 453-5579
- Breckenridge Golf Club (970) 453-9104
- Breckenridge National Historic District (970) 453-6018
- Breckenridge Ski Area (970) 453-5000
- Dillon Ranger District Office, Silverthorne (970) 468-5400
- Frisco Historical Park, Frisco (970) 668-3428
- Peak 8 Human Maze (970) 453-7262
- Summit Historical Society Tours (970) 453-9022

Tiger Run Resort

Snug in a scenic fork of the pristine Blue and Swan rivers, Tiger Run is an RV enthusiasts' paradise with paved sites, full hookups with cable TV which can be rented by day, week or month. The level sites, with 20, 30 and 50 amps available, are landscaped by a river with mountains for a scenic backdrop.

In the summertime, you can sail on Lake Dillon, river-raft, hike, horseback ride, bike, fish, play tennis, golf, and ride a train or a hot air balloon! Local Jeep tours will take you to deserted mining camps, through breath-taking fields of high alpine wildflowers above timberline at 13,000 feet. In the winter, downhill and cross country ski at Breckenridge and Vail, ice skate, sleigh ride, and ice fish. There are groomed snowmobile trails that lead to high meadows with fantastic, scenic vistas. After a day of activity, relax in the indoor, heated pool and hot tub in the luxurious clubhouse.

Quaint mountain chalets, indoor and outdoor meeting areas are also available.

Location: North of Breckenridge on Highway 9.

Total RV sites: 125	Pull thru sites: 3	Open: All Year
Full hookup sites: 125	45+ foot long sites: 125	Russell, Lisa, & Jack, Jeannette Whitt
Water & elec. sites: 0	Slideout sites: 125	85 Tiger Run Rd (CR 315)
Elec. only sites: 0	Licenses sold: None	Box 815
50 amp sites: 125	LP Gas: metered	Breckenridge, Colorado 80424-0815
Hookup sites open in Fall: 0	Credit Cards: VM	970/453-9690
Winter hookup sites: 0	Elevation: 9300	
RV site cost: $$		

Within 15 minutes:

At RV Park:

Buena Vista

Includes Nathrop. Map: I-12

This small town, nestled at the base of the Collegiate and Sawatch Mountain Ranges, is named for its "good view." Located in the Upper Arkansas River Valley, Buena Vista and its surroundings were once home to the Ute Indians. Lt. Zebulon Pike, who passed through in 1806, found evidence of some 3,000 Utes who had lived here. Like other Colorado towns, miners came when they learned of gold strikes in the area and ranchers eventually followed. The city has a rowdy past, once hosting 36 bars, a hanging judge and two of the state's most notorious madams. Now Buena Vista is the jumping off point for some of the best river rafting in Colorado. Brown's Canyon, 8 miles south, is often called the whitewater capital of the state. The impressive Collegiate Range, which lies to the west and is the most concentrated number of peaks above 14,000 feet in Colorado, abounds with hiking trails and mountain bike trails. The valley and surrounding mountains are riddled with ghost towns. Be sure and visit the numerous art galleries in town. Another feature that brings people to the Buena Vista area are the natural hot springs where you can soothe your body while gazing up at majestic, snow-topped peaks.

Fun Things to Do

- Buena Vista Family Horseback Riding (800) 621-9960, (719) 395-8318
- Buena Vista Heritage Museum/Model Railroad Display (719) 395-8458
- Buena Vista Recreational River Park (719) 395-8643
- Buffalo Joe River Trips (800) 356-7984, (719) 395-8757
- Collegiate Peaks Golf Course (719) 395-8189
- Crazy Horse Jeep Rentals & Horseback Riding (800) 888-7320
- River Runners Ltd. (800) 525-2081

Arkansas River Rim Campground & RV Park

On a bluff overlooking the Arkansas River these large, open and shaded sites with campfire pits have spectacular mountain views. Many of the level sites are gravel pull thrus and most have full hookups with 30 and 50 amps.

River fishing and a playground are on the easily accessible property. Four-wheel driving, horseback riding and world class river rafting are minutes away. The impressive Collegiate Range has many peaks above 14,000 feet and has countless hiking trails and picturesque ghost towns.

Location: At the junction of Highway 285 and 24. 4 ½ miles North of the town stoplight, take Highway 24 North 7 ¼ miles.

Total RV sites: 38	Pull thru sites: 6	Open: 5/1 to 9/15
Full hookup sites: 38	45+ foot long sites: 15	Bob & Nancy Totten & Bev Coggins
Water & elec. sites: 0	Slideout sites: 15	33198 Hwy 24 North
Elec. only sites: 0	Licenses sold: None	PO Box 1170
50 amp sites: 7	LP Gas: None	Buena Vista, Colorado 81211-11701
Hookup sites open in Fall: 0	Credit Cards: None	719/395-8883Arkansas River Rim Camp-
Winter hookup sites: 0	Elevation: 8000	ground & RV Park
RV site cost: Not available		

Within 15 minutes:

At RV Park:

Bergstrom's Court & Campsites

Convenient to the city with beautiful mountain views, Bergstrom's grassy, shaded sites have full hookups (20, 30 and 50 amps) and some pull thrus. Barbecue grilling is permitted.

The recreational hall where you can play board games has a kitchen. Camper storage is available. Nearby activities include fishing, four-wheel driving, rafting and horseback riding. Relax in the mountain sunshine and play a game of horseshoes with your family.

Bergstrom's caters to groups and family reunions. An indoor group meeting area is available.

Location: Approximately 1 ¼ miles North of Buena Vista on Highway 24 near milepost 209.

Total RV sites: 42	Pull thru sites: 25	Open: All Year
Full hookup sites: 42	45+ foot long sites: 25	Art & Mary Bergstrom, Owners
Water & elec. sites: 3	Slideout sites: 42	30430 North Hwy 24
Elec. only sites: 0	Licenses sold: None	Buena Vista, Colorado 81211
50 amp sites: 12	LP Gas: None	719/395-8481
Hookup sites open in Fall: 45	Credit Cards: None	
Winter hookup sites: 45	Elevation: 8000	
RV site cost: ¢		

Within 15 minutes:

At RV Park:

Brown's Campground

Named for Brown's Canyon, often called the whitewater capital of Colorado, this campground has shady, quiet sites under big trees along Chalk Creek. All sites have electricity and some are full hookups. Let a campfire at night warm you while you lean back and count the stars above. This is a paradise for camera bugs and rock hounds. Be sure to check out the numerous, natural hot springs that are a unique part of any visit to Buena Vista.

Children will enjoy the playground, game room and video games. Fish on the property's Chalk Creek or hike and four-wheel drive nearby. Don't forget to try a memorable whitewater raft trip down the Arkansas River. Rafting and kayaking facilities across the road. Horseback riding is minutes away. Motorbikes are welcome.

An indoor, group meeting area is available.

Location: On US Highway 285 at County Road 197, 18 miles North of Salida and 8 miles South of Buena Vista.

Total RV sites: 40	Pull thru sites: 6	Open: 5/1 to 10/15
Full hookup sites: 15	45+ foot long sites: 15	Weldon & Frances Ratliff, Owners
Water & elec. sites: 0	Slideout sites: 12	11430 County Rd 197
Elec. only sites: 29	Licenses sold: None	PO Box 39
50 amp sites: 0	LP Gas: None	Nathrop, Colorado 81236-0039
Hookup sites open in Fall: 40	Credit Cards: VM	719/395-8301
Winter hookup sites: 0	Elevation: 7900	
RV site cost: ¢–$$		

Within 15 minutes:

At RV Park:

Buena Vista Family Campground & Resort

With a view of the highest peaks in Colorado, the Buena Vista Family Campground has campfire pits in open and shaded level sites. All sites have 20 and 30 amps, and many are full hookups with private pull thrus. You'll enjoy cool evenings, fabulous sunsets, and a friendly western atmosphere.

Kids will love the video games and hayrides — not to mention the ice cream socials! While they frolic, adults can relax in the hot tub on the sun deck. From the pavilion, you can view the snow-capped Collegiate Peaks. The cook-shack offers full breakfast and dinner menus, from hotdogs to steaks. Guest horses reside at the "horse motel" and the stables offer daily sunset steak rides. Adventures in the Arkansas River Valley include gold panning, trekking through ghost towns and four-wheel driving in the Sawatch Mountain Range. For those who like to get wet, there's always a whitewater ride down the Arkansas River. Motorcycle trail riders are welcomed and will enjoy the trails on adjacent BLM and US Forest Service land.

Indoor and outdoor group meeting areas, rustic log cabins, and remote group RV and tent sites are also available.

Location: On US Highways 285 and 24, 4 miles Southeast of Buena Vista, ¾ miles East of Johnson Village and the Arkansas River.

Total RV sites: 66	Pull thru sites: 46	Open: All Year
Full hookup sites: 21	45+ foot long sites: 60	Mike & Ruth Simpson, Owners
Water & elec. sites: 40	Slideout sites: 60	27700 CR 303
Elec. only sites: 7	Licenses sold: None	Buena Vista, Colorado 81211
50 amp sites: 0	LP Gas: metered	719/395-8318
Hookup sites open in Fall: 66	Credit Cards: VM	800/621-9960
Winter hookup sites: 11	Elevation: 8000	719/395-2192 Fax
RV site cost: Not available		

Within 15 minutes:

At RV Park:

Crazy Horse Camping Resort

Formerly a stagecoach stop, Crazy Horse Camping Resort puts you at the foot of the mountains in a terraced, family-oriented campground. All sites have electricity and campfire pits; some are shaded, others open. Hot showers, coin laundry room with a soap machine, and a convenience store are all on the property.

You can be picked up here for raft trips and four-wheel drive tours. Or explore on your own as this is the only campground in the area that rents Jeeps. In your rental Jeep, travel to high mountain lakes and see the real Colorado — historic ghost towns, remote beaver ponds, mineral rock hounding sites and wildlife in pristine meadows. Satisfy your hunger at the Saturday barbecue dinners and Sunday morning pancake breakfasts. Rent or bring your own horse on trail rides which include breakfast, dinner and moonlight tours. Play miniature golf or volleyball and swim in the heated pool. Other activities include square dancing, horseshoes and ice cream socials.

Rustic camper cabins are also available and groups are heartily welcomed.

Location: On Highway 24 at milepost 205, 5 miles North of Buena Vista.

Total RV sites: 89	Pull thru sites: 6	Open: 4/15 to 10/01
Full hookup sites: 34	45+ foot long sites: 34	Jim & Jeannine Bettes, Owners
Water & elec. sites: 32	Slideout sites: 34	33975 US Highway 24
Elec. only sites: 20	Licenses sold: Fishing	Buena Vista, Colorado 81211
50 amp sites:	LP Gas: metered	719/395-2323
Hookup sites open in Fall: 86	Credit Cards: VMD	800/395-2323
Winter hookup sites: 0	Elevation: 8300	719/395-9288 fax
RV site cost: Not available		

Within 15 minutes:

At RV Park:

Fisherman's Bridge Campground

This rafting-oriented campground for the young-at-heart sits on the shores of the best whitewater rafting and kayaking river in Colorado: the Arkansas River. Most sites have electricity, campfire pits, and several are full hookups. Camp along the river in a terraced site with a view of the majestic mountains. The famous Brown's Canyon, where you're guaranteed a wild, wet ride, is just downstream from Fisherman's Bridge.

Raft trips and all-day Jeep tours leave daily from Fisherman's Bridge. Play volleyball or horseshoes on the playground after a day of fun in Colorado. Fish right along the river's banks for trout. Mountain bike trails and horseback rides are nearby.

Location: On US Highway 285, 5 miles South of Buena Vista.

Total RV sites: 12	Pull thru sites: 0	Open: 5/15 to 9/15
Full hookup sites: 6	45+ foot long sites: 8	Jerry Brag, Manager.
Water & elec. sites: 6	Slideout sites: 6	24070 County Rd 301
Elec. only sites: 0	Licenses sold: None	Buena Vista, Colorado 81211
50 amp sites: 2	LP Gas: None	719/539-8207
Hookup sites open in Fall: 0	Credit Cards: VMAD	800/539-2144
Winter hookup sites: 0	Elevation: 7500	
RV site cost: ¢		

Within 15 minutes:

At RV Park:

Cañon City Area

Includes Coaldale, Cotopaxi, Penrose and Texas Creek. Map: K-19; K-14

Considered the climate capital of Colorado, Cañon City's natural setting protects it from harsh weather. Once a favorite camping area of the Ute Indians, both dinosaur bones and oil were discovered here. Five miles north of the city is the Garden Park Monument commemorating the 1877 dinosaur find. In the early 1900s, Cañon City offered a new treasure, a prime location for making movie westerns. The Arkansas River, flowing through the city and offering great fishing west of town, formed one of the most spectacular attractions in the state — the Royal Gorge, 8 miles west. The world's highest suspension bridge hangs a dizzying 1,053 feet above the rushing river, offering unforgettable vistas of the 8 mile canyon in the city's largest park. Next to viewing the bridge, rafting the Arkansas River is the most popular reason for vacationing here. Cotopaxi and Coaldale are also popular launching pads to rafting the Arkansas River. The Colorado Territorial Prison, built in 1868, is the only prison museum located next to a currently operating prison. Several scenic byways lead out of Cañon City, including one through Phantom Canyon on its way to Cripple Creek. Other activities include hiking and horseback riding.

Fun Things to Do

- Arkansas Headwaters Recreation Area (719) 539-7289
- Buckskin Joe Park & Railway (719) 275-5149, (719) 275-5485
- Buffalo Joe River Trips (800) 356-7984, (719) 395-8757
- Echo Canyon River Expeditions, Inc. (800) 748-2953
- El Carma Rock Shop, Texas Creek (719) 275-6169
- Hidden Valley Trail Rides & Fee Fishing (800) 320-4171,
- Indian Springs Ranch National Natural Landmark (719) 372-3907
- Lazy J Rafting Company (800) 678-4274, (719) 942-4274
- Raven Rafting & Adventure Trips (800) 332-3381
- River Runners Ltd. (800) 525-2081
- Royal Gorge Bridge Park (719) 275-7507
- Royal Gorge Scenic Railway (719) 275-5485
- Shadow Hills Golf Course (719) 275-0603

Arkansas River KOA & Loma Linda Motel

Make Loma Linda KOA in Cotopaxi your base camp for family reunions. Bounded by scenic Highway 50 and the Arkansas River, you'll find a whole new world to roam and unwind in. Most of the open and shaded sites along the river have electricity (20 and 30 amps) and water. Several sites are full hookups and pull thrus. Sit back and listen to the roar of the raging river while you gaze at the red rocks and snow-tipped peaks of southern Colorado. Every night you'll have starry, starry skies and wide open spaces filled with fresh air.

From here you can fish on the beautiful Arkansas or scramble along its picturesque banks, rock hunting. On-site summertime activities include miniature golf, free nightly movies, shuffleboard, and hay rides. Nearby you can pan for gold, hike, hunt, whitewater raft or horseback ride. After it all, take a dip in the heated swimming pool or challenge your family to a video game in the recreation room.

Indoor and outdoor group meeting areas, guest motel rooms with kitchenettes, and camping cabins are available.

Location: Off Highway 50 at milepost 247, between Cañon City and Salida.

Total RV sites: 49
Full hookup sites: 29
Water & elec. sites: 20
Elec. only sites: 0
50 amp sites:
Hookup sites open in Fall: 49
Winter hookup sites: 0
RV site cost: $

Pull thru sites: 49
45+ foot long sites: 49
Slideout sites: 49
Licenses sold: Fish & Hunt
LP Gas: weight
Credit Cards: VMD
Elevation: 6300

Open: 4/1 to 11/1
Jerry & Jeanne Holdren, Owners
21435 US Hwy 50
PO Box 387
Cotopaxi, Colorado 81223-0387
719/275-9308

Within 15 minutes:

At RV Park:

Floyd's RV Park

Camp in the quiet among piñon pines and grassy flatlands where the full hookup, pull thru sites have excellent TV reception and soft city water. Large rigs are welcomed. Most sites are gravel and have 20 and 30 amps.

Just down the road is the Pueblo Reservoir which sits on semi-arid plains encircled by limestone cliffs and buttes. Whether fishing along this man-made lake's 60 miles of shoreline or boating across its cool, clear waters, you'll enjoy the mountain vistas to the north of Pikes Peak and to the west of the Wet Mountains. Four-wheel driving and raft trips are also nearby. Horseback riding is minutes away and your horse is welcome to camp with you at Floyd's. After a day of fun, challenge your family to a game of horseshoes. From here, it's a convenient day trip to visit Cripple Creek. The open pavilion with a fireplace is ideal for groups.

Location: 17 miles East of Cañon City on US Highway 50 at milepost 293.

Total RV sites: 30
Full hookup sites: 22
Water & elec. sites: 8
Elec. only sites: 0
50 amp sites: 0
Hookup sites open in Fall: 30
Winter hookup sites: 0
RV site cost: ¢

Pull thru sites: 28
45+ foot long sites: 30
Slideout sites: 30
Licenses sold: None
LP Gas: weight
Credit Cards: VM
Elevation: 5400

Open: 4/1 to 10/31
Floyd & Iletta Fields, Owners
1438 Hwy 50
Penrose, Colorado 81240
719/372-3385

Within 15 minutes:

At RV Park:

Fort Gorge Campground & RV Park

With a view of the Royal Gorge Bridge, these spacious, open and some shaded sites are in a pretty mountain setting. Off of the highway, most sites are away from traffic noise. The pull thru sites have electricity (20, 30 and 50 amps), water, and some have sewer.

The Royal Gorge Bridge, one of the most spectacular attractions in Colorado, is the world's highest suspension bridge hanging at an awesome 1,053 feet above the rushing Arkansas River.

A small store and video game room are at the campground. Right across the street you can whitewater raft. Trips range from rollicking rides through Raintree Falls, Sharks Tooth and Double Dip rapids, to twilight dinners floating while you feast on char-broiled steak. Horseback rides (your horse is welcome at Fort Gorge) and helicopter tours are also available. Or rent a mountain bike and tour the countryside. Stay here and visit Cripple Creek for a change-of-pace day trip.

Camper cabins and an outdoor, group meeting area is available.

Location: Located 7 miles West of Cañon City, on Highway 50, ¼ mile East of the Royal Gorge Bridge Exit.

Total RV sites: 54
Full hookup sites: 10
Water & elec. sites: 44
Elec. only sites: 0
50 amp sites: 4
Hookup sites open in Fall: 54
Winter hookup sites: 0
RV site cost: Not available

Pull thru sites: 54
45+ foot long sites: 10
Slideout sites: 54
Licenses sold: None
LP Gas: M
Credit Cards: VM
Elevation: 6330

Open: 5/1 to 11/1
Dave & Robert Anderson, Owners
45044 US Hwy 50
Cañon City, Colorado 81212
719/275-5111

Within 15 minutes:

At RV Park:

Hidden Valley Campground

The majestic Sangre de Cristo mountains are the backdrop to this family resort adjacent to ponds and Cottonwood Creek. Many of the level, pull thru sites are full hookups (20 and 30 amps) with picnic tables and fire pits. Kids will like the cute farm animals on the property. A quarter of a mile off the main highway, Hidden Valley offers peace and quiet.

Fish for rainbow trout on the nearby Arkansas River or in the private, stocked ponds. There's no charge to fish license-free for the trophy trout; you only pay by the inch caught. If you reel in one over 4 pounds, it's half price! Try one of the on-site hiking and mountain bike trails or play horseshoes, basketball and volleyball. Enjoy a guided breakfast and/or an evening steak dinner horseback ride into the mountains. Other rides are also available. Whitewater raft trips and four-wheel drive trails are minutes away and can be arranged through the campground's hosts. A jacuzzi, sauna and weight room are available. Enjoy weekend summer cookouts, western dancing and movie nights. For your convenience, a camp store, gift shop, video rentals and snack bar on the property.

Camper cabins and a lodge with a fireplace for group meetings, family reunions, dances and potluck suppers, are also available.

Location: In Coaldale, ¼ mile South of Highway 50, off City Road 40.

Total RV sites: 46	Pull thru sites: 28	Open: All Year
Full hookup sites: 25	45+ foot long sites: 20	Lee & Dee Bates & John Engle, Owners
Water & elec. sites: 21	Slideout sites: 25	0340 City Rd 40
Elec. only sites: 0	Licenses sold: None	PO Box 220
50 amp sites: 5	LP Gas: metered	Coaldale, Colorado 81222
Hookup sites open in Fall: 46	Credit Cards: VM	719/942-4171
Winter hookup sites: 11	Elevation: 6900	800/320-4171
RV site cost: ¢–$		719/942-4685 fax

Within 15 minutes:

At RV Park:

Indian Springs Ranch

Camp where Indians used to at this quiet destination campground, great for groups and family reunions. Just off the Phantom Canyon Road, Indian Springs Ranch is a registered National Natural Landmark spread over 2,700 acres. A historical, hand-hewn log cabin and old stage-

coach road are on this quiet and peaceful working ranch. Phantom Canyon is a scenic and historic byway that passes granite tunnels between sheer cliff walls on its way to Cripple Creek. All sites are full hookups, shaded, and in wooded foothills with panoramic views.

Swim in the ranch's heated pool or search for Indian arrow heads and fossils. While hiking the beautiful surroundings you may see hummingbirds, deer, coyotes, rabbits, and even wild turkeys. Ride a horse from their stables or bring your own — out here there's plenty of room to roam! Try fishing at the ranch's pond or at the nearby Brush Hollow and Beaver creeks.

Indian Springs specializes in custom event planning and an indoor, enclosed pavilion group meeting area is available.

Location: Approximately 5 miles East of Cañon City on US Highway 50, 4 miles North on Highway 67 (Phantom Canyon Road). Turn left at sign and proceed 3 miles. *apr 1 - Sept. 15*

Total RV sites: 30	Pull thru sites: 0	Open: 4/1 to 10/31
Full hookup sites: 30	45+ foot long sites: 0	Carlie Henry, Ina Finch & Bennie Thorson
Water & elec. sites: 0	Slideout sites: 0	3251 CR 67
Elec. only sites: 0	Licenses sold: None	PO Box 405
50 amp sites: 0	LP Gas: None	Cañon City, Colorado 81215-0405
Hookup sites open in Fall: 0	Credit Cards: None	719/372-3907
Winter hookup sites: 0	Elevation: 5800	
RV site cost: Not available		

Within 15 minutes:

At RV Park:

Lazy J Resort & Rafting Company

Camp in the valley solitude of the Lazy J Resort which sits on the banks of the Arkansas River. With beautiful views of the Sangre de Cristo mountains, these full hookup (20 amps), level sites have nearby large, grassy lawns for children to play and families to relax on and enjoy. Choose between open or shady sites; all have barbecue grills.

A full-service restaurant specializing in sandwiches and Mexican food is on the property, a playground and heated swimming pool are other on-site amenities. Whitewater raft trips for every level, run by the resort, are Lazy J's specialty. Take a wild and wet half or full-day trip. Overnight or custom journeys can be arranged. "Saddle and Paddle" combination trips includes both horses and rafts. If you prefer river fishing, cast your line from the resort, or hike to one of the many nearby fishing areas.

Indoor and outdoor group meeting areas, modern motel rooms, and log cabins are also available.

Location: On US Highway 50 at milepost 242, just 70 miles West of Pueblo and Colorado Springs or 30 miles West of Royal Gorge.

Total RV sites: 25	Pull thru sites: 25	Open: 4/15 to 11/1
Full hookup sites: 7	45+ foot long sites: 3	Jeff Jeffries, Owner
Water & elec. sites: 18	Slideout sites: 25	16373 Hwy 50
Elec. only sites: 0	Licenses sold: None	PO Box 109
50 amp sites: 0	LP Gas: None	Coaldale, Colorado 81222-0109
Hookup sites open in Fall: 25	Credit Cards: VMAD	719/942-4274
Winter hookup sites: 0	Elevation: 6200	800/678-4274
RV site cost: Not available		

Within 15 minutes:

At RV Park:

Mountain View Campground

In a lovely, wooded mountain setting, these shaded sites are full hookups (30 amps) with campfire pits. Enjoy panoramic views from your grassy site. Sites have picnic tables, fire pits and large shade trees.

Browse at the Trading Post and southwest gift shop. Ice, groceries and firewood are also for sale. A cafe serving breakfast and lunch, and a raft company are at the campground. Guest horses are permitted and horseback riding and fishing are minutes away. A nice playground is provided for children and the owners speak Polish, Spanish and German. Bring your favorite two-wheeler as Mountain View is located on a bike route.

A rustic, southwestern style cabin and indoor, group meeting area are also available. Ask about the two tepees for rent.

Location: Off Highway 50, 7 miles West of Cañon City, near the Royal Gorge Bridge.

Total RV sites: 38
Full hookup sites: 18
Water & elec. sites: 5
Elec. only sites: 6
50 amp sites: 12
Hookup sites open in Fall: 14
Winter hookup sites: 14
RV site cost: Not available

Pull thru sites: 2
45+ foot long sites: 21
Slideout sites: 21
Licenses sold: None
LP Gas: None
Credit Cards: VM
Elevation: 6323

Open: All Year
Alfreda & Ty Schoenholtz, Owners
45606 Hwy 50 West
Cañon City, Colorado 81212
719/275-7232

Within 15 minutes:

At RV Park:

Royal Gorge Camp Eight Eighty

These open and shaded sites have a view of the Royal Gorge Bridge only 4 miles away. Long pull thru, level sites are available and all have electricity (20, 30 and 50 amps). Most sites also have campfire pits. The sites' picnic tables are sheltered. Located on 10 acres, most sites are away from the road. The Royal Gorge Bridge is the world's highest suspension bridge hanging at an incredible 1,053 feet above the churning Arkansas River.

A heated, 9-foot deep swimming pool, playground, and video game room are at the camp. Within walking distance is a restaurant. The property store sells Indian jewelry, T-shirts, souvenirs, ice and firewood. Rent a horse from the stables across the street and explore the numerous area trails. River rafting and river fishing are minutes away. A scenic railway and old west town are also close.

A camper cabin, group tent sites, and indoor, group meeting area are available.

Location: Proceed 8 miles West of Cañon City on Highway 50 to the Royal Gorge Bridge Exit, South to CR 3A.

Total RV sites: 36
Full hookup sites: 16
Water & elec. sites: 13
Elec. only sites: 4
50 amp sites: 2
Hookup sites open in Fall: 32
Winter hookup sites: 0
RV site cost: ¢–$

Pull thru sites: 20
45+ foot long sites: 23
Slideout sites: 20
Licenses sold: None
LP Gas: None
Credit Cards: VMD
Elevation: 6300

Open: 4/15 to 10/15
Richard & Gloria Hanson, Owners
0030 CR 3-A
Cañon City, Colorado 81212-9729
719/269-3211

Within 15 minutes:

At RV Park:

Royal View Campground

With a spectacular view of the Royal Gorge Bridge, this country-quiet campground off of the highway has open sites and some sites with shade trees. All sites are full hookups (20, 30 and 50 amps), level pull thrus and have picnic tables. You'll feel right at home with the pancake, all-you-can-eat breakfasts and tasty barbecue dinners.

The fenced swimming pool with a large deck has a slide for kids of all ages. Play with the family on a fun hayride. Your hosts can help arrange a half or full-day whitewater raft trip down the popular Arkansas River. In the evening, watch one of the nightly movies and morning cartoons are shown by request. During the day, tour the Royal Gorge Bridge, Cripple Creek, the Garden Park Fossil area, and the Colorado Territorial Prison Museum. Or take a horseback ride through a scenic area; guest horses are permitted. The campground has all the amenities to make your vacation worry-free: an on-site store with limited groceries, RV supplies and ice, club room, game room, miniature golf, volleyball and basketball. You can exercise your pet on the pet walk.

Camper cabins and RV storage are also available.

Location: Go 1 mile West of Highway 50's Royal Gorge Bridge Exit, (South side).

Total RV sites: 29	Pull thru sites: 30	Open: 3/15 to 11/15
Full hookup sites: 27	45+ foot long sites: 9	Joe & Myrtle Manning, Owners
Water & elec. sites: 3	Slideout sites: 15	0227 8-Mile Hill
Elec. only sites: 0	Licenses sold: None	Cañon City, Colorado 81212
50 amp sites: 9	LP Gas: metered	719/275-1900
Hookup sites open in Fall: 32	Credit Cards: VMD	
Winter hookup sites: 5	Elevation: 6250	
RV site cost: ¢–$		

Within 15 minutes:

At RV Park:

RV Station Campground

On the edge of Cañon City, the RV Station Campground has large, grassy, open sites in a pleasant rural setting near entertainment and restaurants. Shopping is walking distance away. Half of the level sites are full hookups (20 and 30 amps) and all are pull thrus with city water. Some sites have a picnic table and shade trees. The sites have a meadow atmosphere.

The gravel, interior roads make for easy driving. Fishing, horseback rides and raft trips are all nearby. Be sure to explore the Royal Gorge Bridge, Pikes Peak and Cripple Creek for a scenic day trip.

Rent overnight, for the week or month.

Location: Off Highway 50 on East edge of Cañon City.

Total RV sites: 50
Full hookup sites: 20
Water & elec. sites: 27
Elec. only sites: 0
50 amp sites: 0
Hookup sites open in Fall: 47
Winter hookup sites: 47
RV site cost: ¢

Pull thru sites: 47
45+ foot long sites: 6
Slideout sites: 20
Licenses sold: None
LP Gas: weight
Credit Cards: None
Elevation: 5300

Open: All Year
John & Conney Palmer
3120 East Main
Cañon City, Colorado 81212
719/275-4576

Within 15 minutes:

At RV Park:

Whispering Pines Resort

The roaring Arkansas River runs for a mile right through Whispering Pines Resort in Texas Creek. On the south side of the river, the level, pull thru, full hookup sites have a breathtaking view of the Rocky Mountains from the river's banks.Large rigs have plenty of room as most sites are 45 feet long.

Kick back in the shade at this newest park in the area and watch the rafters paddle past.

It almost goes without saying that the trout fishing is excellent and the whitewater rafting is great — all right from the campground. Nearby, you can horseback ride, golf, visit tourist attractions, and get all your groceries, camping supplies and fishing tackle in the shops.

Motel rooms and rustic camper cabins are also available.

Location: On Highway 50 near Texas Creek

Total RV sites: 32
Full hookup sites: 20
Water & elec. sites: 0
Elec. only sites: 0
50 amp sites: 0
Hookup sites open in Fall: 20
Winter hookup sites: 0
RV site cost: ¢–$

Pull thru sites: 32
45+ foot long sites: 28
Slideout sites: 9
Licenses sold: None
LP Gas: None
Credit Cards: VM
Elevation: 7200

Open: 4/1 to 10/30
Hal & Mary Davenport, Owners
24871 Hwy 50
Texas Creek, Colorado 81223
719/275-3827

Within 15 minutes:

At RV Park:

Yogi Bear's Jellystone Park Camp Resort

A true family campground, Yogi Bear's Jellystone Park Camp is among 23-acres of shady pine covered sites with a view of the Royal Gorge Bridge. Some sites are full hookups (30 amps) with pull thrus and all have campfire pits and picnic tables. Several sites have decks to admire the mountain views while grilling dinner. The spacious sites give you plenty of elbow room and piñon pine, cedar and elm trees to relax under. Yogi Bear may even visit your site.

On-site entertainment includes nightly family movies, morning cartoons and hayrides with Yogi and Ranger Smith. The kids will like the large playground, volleyball, basketball, horseshoes and whiffleball games. Spend the day of fishing, horseback riding, and whitewater rafting nearby. Enjoy theme weekends and special meals throughout the year. The camp store sells camping supplies, assorted groceries and Yogi souvenirs. After a day of Royal Gorge adventures, relax in the heated, 9-foot deep swimming pool or soak in the hot tub and rest on the large sun deck.

Ask about RV storage. The enclosed pavilion with a kitchen is ideal for group meetings. Rental trailer and camper cabin are also available.

Location: 9 miles West of Cañon City at the junction of US Highway 50 and CO Highway 9.

Total RV sites: 43	Pull thru sites: 19	Open: All Year
Full hookup sites: 8	45+ foot long sites: 21	Jan & Lee Massey, Owners
Water & elec. sites: 35	Slideout sites: 35	43595 Hwy 50
Elec. only sites: 0	Licenses sold: None	PO Box 1025
50 amp sites: 0	LP Gas: metered	Cañon City, Colorado 81215-1025
Hookup sites open in Fall: 35	Credit Cards: VMD	719/275-2128
Winter hookup sites: 8	Elevation: 6350	719/275-0019 Fax
RV site cost: ¢–$		

Within 15 minutes:

At RV Park:

Central City

Map: M-12

Once known as the richest square mile on earth, Central City is again enjoying a boom. A historic mining town where fortunes were made and lost, this mountain city now has legal gambling mixed in with Victorian houses, the fanciest opera house in the west and abandoned mines. Most of the gold unearthed from the mountains during Colorado's gold rush was discovered here. The entire city, just a mile up the road from Black Hawk, is part of a National Historic District. Because Central City attracted more than 20,000 people in the 1860s, it became a cultural center for Colorado. The Central City Opera House, which opened in 1878, still runs a nationally renown summer season. Gambling has brought people back in droves and the city is once again filled with dance hall music and the clink of coins. Along with numerous casinos, Central City still offers a glimpse into a rowdy, exciting past. Hiking around Central City and Black Hawk, however, is not recommended because the hillsides are dotted with abandoned mine shafts. Take a tour instead at the Lost Gold Mine and see how early settlers lived at the Thomas House. Or drive the scenic Peak-to-Peak highway which begins here and stretches all the way north to Rocky Mountain National Park with unforgettable mountain vistas along the way.

Fun Things To Do

- Central City Opera House (303) 292-6700
- Gilpin County Arts Association (303) 582-5574
- Gilpin County Historical Society Museum (303) 582-5283
- Lost Gold Mine (303) 582-5913
- Teller House & Tours (303) 582-3200
- Thomas House (800) 582-5283

Central City/Dory Hill KOA

Just five miles north of historic Black Hawk's and Central City's gambling saloons, clean and friendly Central City/Dory Hill KOA is next to the scenic Peak-to-Peak highway. The only KOA in the mountains near Denver, most sites have electricity, water, grills and campfire pits. Cable TV hookup is available at a few sites. Some of the open and shady sites are pull thrus. You'll find the wooded sites ideal for a restful mountain vacation.

The campground has a heated swimming pool, video game room, playground, video rentals, store and package liquors. Exercise your pet in the dog walk area before a game in the horseshoe pit. Nearby you can fish, mountain bike, pan for gold, or take a mine and ghost town tour. This area is rich in history, outdoor recreation and scenery — from Central City/Dory Hill KOA you can experience it all from the Denver Zoo to high county casinos to Rocky Mountain National Park in Estes Park.

Camper cabins and weekly rates are available.

Location: Take I-70 to US Highway 6, North to Highway 119 to Route 46 or go South from Nederland on Highway 119 to Route 46, and milepost 12 ½ then East for ½ mile.

Total RV sites: 20	Pull thru sites: 10	Open: All Year
Full hookup sites: 0	45+ foot long sites: 5	KNC, INC
Water & elec. sites: 15	Slideout sites: 5	661 Hwy 46
Elec. only sites: 5	Licenses sold: None	Golden, Colorado 80403
50 amp sites: 8	LP Gas: metered	303/582-9979
Hookup sites open in Fall: 20	Credit Cards: VMD	
Winter hookup sites: 5	Elevation: 9230	
RV site cost: $–$$		

Within 15 minutes:

At RV Park:

Colorado Springs Area

Includes Cascade, Falcon, Fountain, Green Mountain Falls, Manitou Springs, Monument and Woodland Park. Map: I-17

Catch the excitement of Pikes Peak purple mountain majesty and see why Katharine Lee Bates was inspired to write "American the Beautiful" when she stood on the mountains overlooking Colorado Springs. From a morning ride on the Pikes Peak Cog Railway to the dramatic 14,110-foot summit, to the sunny charm of an afternoon hike through an alpine forest near Manitou Springs, the Colorado Springs area offers a myriad of activities. Visit the out-of-this-world natural red rock formations of the Garden of the Gods or tour the US Air Force Academy. Explore Old Colorado City, the original site of Colorado Springs, where restored late-1800s architecture made it a registered National Historic District. Fish for Rocky Mountain trout and enjoy the fresh, pine-scented air of this high-country region.

Fun Things to Do

- Apple Tree Golf Course (719) 382-3649
- Broadmoor Golf Club (719) 577-5790
- Cheyenne Mountain Zoo & Will Rogers Shrine (719) 475-9555
- Flying W Ranch (800) 232-FLYW or (719) 598-4000
- Fountain Creek Nature Center (719) 520-6745
- Garden of the Gods (719) 578-6640
- Ghost Town (719) 634-0696
- John May Museum Center: Natural History & Space Exploration (800) 666-3841, (719) 576-0450
- Pikes Peak Highway (719) 684-9383
- Pro Rodeo Hall of Fame (719) 528-4764
- Rainbow Falls Trout Fishing & Stable (719) 687-9074
- Swiss Miss Shop (800) 521-GIFT, (719) 684-9679
- United States Air Force Academy (719) 472-2555
- US Olympic Complex (719) 578-4644/4618
- Ute Pass Historical Society, Woodland Park (719) 687-3041
- Valley Hi Golf Course (719) 578-6925
- Western Museum of Mining & Industry (719) 488-0880
- White House Ranch Historic Site (719) 578-6777

Campground at Woodland Park

In the mountains close to Colorado Springs and all its attractions, the Campground at Woodland Park has lots of shade and views. The large, spacious sites are nestled on a hillside, surrounded by aspen trees. All sites are full hookups (15 and 30 amps) and campfires are allowed. An adult-oriented park, this campground caters to seniors with special senior discounts.

Relax in the heated swimming pool or play 18-hole miniature golf. Children will enjoy the playground and in the video game room. Evening activities include chuckwagon suppers and free nightly movies. Chow down on a hearty, chuckwagon breakfast before setting out to fish, four-wheel drive or horseback ride nearby. Rent a mountain bike and explore the bike trail beginning at the entrance to the campground. Shuttle vans run to historic Cripple Creek's casinos. Ask about the discount casino coupons.

Camper cabins, tepees, an outdoor, group meeting area and group tent sites are available.

Location: On Highway 67, 16 miles West of Colorado Springs, ½ mile North of the junction of US Highway 24 and Highway 67, 3 blocks West on Bowman Avenue.

Total RV sites: 90	Pull thru sites: 8	Open: 5/1 to 9/20
Full hookup sites: 55	45+ foot long sites: 10	Craig & Karen Stewart, Owners
Water & elec. sites: 37	Slideout sites: 20	1125 West Bowman Ave
Elec. only sites: 0	Licenses sold: None	PO Box 725
50 amp sites: 0	LP Gas: None	Woodland Park, Colorado 80866-0725
Hookup sites open in Fall: 92	Credit Cards: VMD	719/687-7575
Winter hookup sites: 0	Elevation: 8500	800/808-CAMP Reserve. Only
RV site cost: $		

Within 15 minutes:

At RV Park:

Coachlight RV Park, Campground & Motel

Up in the quiet mountains with tall pine and spruce trees for nice shady sites, Coachlight has a lovely view of Pikes Peak. The terraced sites are full hookups with 15, 30 and 50 amps and phone hookup is available. Most sites have a picnic table, patio, fire ring and grill.

One of the main attractions here is loafing — sit in the sun or the shade, stare at the blue sky, listen to the trees grow, read a treasured book or just take a nap. Kids can play in the game room with both board and video games. Fishing, four-wheel driving, mountain biking and horseback riding are all nearby. Open all year, Coachlight is brightened in the fall by aspens turning yellow and gold. Ski, snow mobile or ice skate in the crisp winter air and sunshine.

Remodeled housekeeping motel rooms and a camper cabin are available. Coachlight RV Park is easily accessible off of US Highway 24.

Location: On Highway 24, 1 mile East of Woodland Park and 17 miles West of Colorado Springs.

Total RV sites: 36
Full hookup sites: 36
Water & elec. sites: 0
Elec. only sites: 0
50 amp sites: 4
Hookup sites open in Fall: 36
Winter hookup sites: 15
RV site cost: ¢–$

Pull thru sites: 4
45+ foot long sites: 10
Slideout sites: 36
Licenses sold: None
LP Gas: None
Credit Cards: VM
Elevation: 8400

Open: All Year
Marshallson Investments Corp
19253 Hwy 24
Woodland Park, Colorado 80863
719/687-8732 CG

Within 15 minutes:

At RV Park:

Diamond Campground & RV Park

Set amidst pine-tree covered mountains at the foot of Pikes Peak, Diamond Campground on 18-acres is a true alpine retreat. Fireplace grill and picnic tables are at each site. All sites are full hookups with 20, 30 and 50 amps; many are pull thrus.

The adult clubhouse is ideal for clubs, rallies and reunions. A playground with badminton and horseshoes is provided for the kids. Fishing areas, riding stables, hiking and biking trails are all nearby. From here, day trips can be made to all the attractions in the Pikes Peak region: Cripple Creek, Royal Gorge, old ghost-mining towns and some of the most beautiful back country in Colorado. Come and enjoy the warm days and cool nights.

On-site rental trailers and indoor and outdoor group meeting areas are available.

Location: From US Highway 24, 18 miles West of Colorado Springs, take Highway 67½ mile North of Woodland Park.

Total RV sites: 145	Pull thru sites: 35	Open: 5/10 to 10/1
Full hookup sites: 145	45+ foot long sites: 25	Jan Anderson, Owner & Red & Doris
Water & elec. sites: 3	Slideout sites: 30	Halverson, Managers
Elec. only sites: 0	Licenses sold: None	900 North Hwy 67
50 amp sites: 6	LP Gas: None	Woodland Park, Colorado 80863-9724
Hookup sites open in Fall: 0	Credit Cards: VMD	719/687-9684
Winter hookup sites: 0	Elevation: 8600	
RV site cost: $		

Within 15 minutes:

At RV Park:

Falcon Meadow Campground

Located just east of Colorado Springs near Falcon, this campground is a great place to stop for your first or last night in the Pikes Peak region. The large, grassy pull thru sites have a wonderful view of the towering Pikes Peak. Many of the level, open sites are full hookups with 20 and 30 amps. Phone hookups are available for monthly campers.

Children can romp on the campground's 7 acres or play basketball, horseshoes and volleyball. The air-conditioned recreation room has video games and a pool table. Guest horses are permitted and within a half hour there are horseback rides, fishing areas, and mountain bike trails. A complete convenience store and a Phillips 66 gas station are on-site.

Low cost daily, weekly, and monthly rates are available all year. Ask about the indoor, group meeting area.

Location: On US Highway 24, 15 miles East of I-25, between mileposts 319 and 320, 1 mile Southwest of Falcon and 60 miles Southwest of Limon.

Total RV sites: 20	Pull thru sites: 15	Open: All Year
Full hookup sites: 8	45+ foot long sites: 17	Jim, Delia & Leona Ozburn, Owners
Water & elec. sites: 10	Slideout sites: 20	11150 Hwy 24
Elec. only sites: 2	Licenses sold: None	Falcon, Colorado 80831
50 amp sites: 0	LP Gas: metered	719/495-2694
Hookup sites open in Fall: 20	Credit Cards: VMAD	
Winter hookup sites: 20	Elevation: 6800	
RV site cost: ¢		

Within 15 minutes:

At RV Park:

Golden Eagle Ranch Campground

Camp at the foot of the mountains among shady trees with easy access to on-site reservoirs and trout fishing. Sites have electricity (15, 20, 30 or 50 amps) and water; most are full hookups. These shaded and open sites are in a rolling, semi-wooded area with campfire pits and a natural, lake side setting.

Fish along the frequently stocked lakes' 3,000 feet of shoreline for rainbow trout; no state license required. Explore 8 miles of hiking trails around Golden Eagle on foot or mountain bike. As you meander through the terrain look for the three golden eagles that nest here annually as well as the foxes, coyotes, mule deer, wild turkeys, and jack rabbits. Four-wheel drive tours and horseback riding are nearby. The campground is on the grounds of the May Natural History Museum which has 7,000 of the world's most colorful and unusual tropical invertebrates. The Museum of Space Exploration, also at Golden Eagle, includes photographs taken by planetary space craft and models of space machines supplied by NASA.

Large group and rally area, 5,000 square foot pavilion, and small shelters for small groups are available.

Location: Exit I-25 at exit 135, go West to Highway 115 (Nevada Avenue, South) then South 5 miles.

Total RV sites: 450	Pull thru sites: 450	Open: 5/1 to 10/1
Full hookup sites: 200	45+ foot long sites: 400	John & Frances May, Owners
Water & elec. sites: 130	Slideout sites: 300	710 Rock Creek Canyon
Elec. only sites: 0	Licenses sold: None	Colorado Springs, Colorado 80926
50 amp sites: 40	LP Gas: metered	719/576-0450
Hookup sites open in Fall: 20	Credit Cards: None	800/666-3841
Winter hookup sites: 0	Elevation: 6200	
RV site cost: ¢		

Within 15 minutes:

At RV Park:

Goldfield Campground

Midway between Colorado Springs and Manitou Springs, Goldfield is known for its friendliness, cleanliness and service. These shaded, semi-wooded sites, with pull thrus and picnic tables, are in a metro area adjacent to US Highway 24. The gravel sites have electricity (15, 20 or 30 amps) and water, many are full hookups.

A video game room is on the property. A swimming pool, four-wheel drive trails, fishing areas and horseback riding stables are nearby. Stock up at the small convenience store before taking one of the many scenic tours of the Pikes Peak area that leave from here. Two city parks and the restored, historic Old Colorado City, with its shops and restaurants, are within walking distance. Or dine at the restaurant right across the street.

Daily, weekly and seasonal rates are available.

Location: Midway between Colorado Springs and Manitou Springs, West on US Highway 24 (I-25 Exit 141) to 26th St. (Gold Camp Road) and turn left.

Total RV sites: 71	Pull thru sites: 19	Open: All Year
Full hookup sites: 36	45+ foot long sites: 10	Don & Alice Beverly, Owners
Water & elec. sites: 35	Slideout sites: 5	411 S 26th St.
Elec. only sites: 0	Licenses sold: None	Colorado Springs, Colorado 80904
50 amp sites: 0	LP Gas: None	719/471-0495
Hookup sites open in Fall: 36	Credit Cards: VMD	
Winter hookup sites: 36	Elevation: 6500	
RV site cost: ¢–$		

Within 15 minutes:

At RV Park:

KOA Colorado Springs South

Located along Fountain Creek with a scenic view of the 14,110-foot Pikes Peak, this KOA offers you a carefree vacation in the Colorado Springs area. The long, pull thru sites have 50 amps service, water and phone hookups; most of the sites are full hookups.

Return from a day's adventure at Pikes Peak, Fort Carson, the US Air Force Academy, Cripple Creek casinos, the Garden of the Gods, Cave of the Winds, or the Royal Gorge Bridge to relax in the luxurious, indoor, heated swimming pool and hot tub. While you soak, the kids can play in the video game room or on the playground. Campground activities include 18-hole miniature golf, horseshoes, basketball, hayrides, nightly movies, and weekend pancake breakfast in the summer. Gray Line tours leave daily from the property.

Modern camper cabins and large, grassy areas for group camping are also available.

Location: South of Colorado Springs, exit I-25 at milepost 132.

Total RV sites: 203	RV site cost: $	Open: All Year
Full hookup sites: 126	Pull thru sites: 126	Jack & Joanne McGill, Managers
Water & elec. sites: 83	45+ foot long sites: 126	8100 S Bandley Drive
Elec. only sites: 0	Slideout sites: 126	Fountain, Colorado 80817
50 amp sites: 15	Licenses sold: None	719/382-7575
Hookup sites open in Fall:	LP Gas: metered	
209	Credit Cards: VMD	
Winter hookup sites: 60	Elevation: 6012	

Within 15 minutes:

At RV Park:

Lake of the Rockies Retreat & Camping Resort

Nestled in the foothills of the Rocky Mountains in the tiny town of Monument, this resort has open and shaded, grassy sites adjacent to Monument Lake and Fountain Creek. A majority of the large, level sites are full hookups (20 and 30 amps) and pull thrus with picnic tables and barbecue grills.

Fish for trout in 44-acre lake, frolic in its cool waters or canoe across its glassy surface. Row and paddle boats are also available for rent. Other amenities include a country store, playground, basketball, volleyball, shuffleboard, frisbee golf and miniature golf. End the day with a soothing visit to the heated swimming pool, whirlpool and wading pool.

Ask about the group sites for tents, indoor and outdoor group meeting areas and RV storage.

Location: Exit I-25 at milepost 161, South of Colorado Springs in Monument.

Total RV sites: 200	RV site cost: $–$$	Open: 4/1 to 11/1
Full hookup sites: 200	Pull thru sites: 24	Bonnie & Ernie Biggs, Owners
Water & elec. sites: 0	45+ foot long sites: 200	99 Mitchell Rd
Elec. only sites: 0	Slideout sites: 200	Monument, Colorado 80132
50 amp sites: 5	Licenses sold: None	719/481-4227
Hookup sites open in Fall: 200	LP Gas: None	800/429-4228 Reservations.
Winter hookup sites: 0	Credit Cards: VMD	
	Elevation: 6500	

Within 15 minutes:

At RV Park:

Lone Duck Campground

Hidden in the beautiful Ute Pass mountain valley, Lone Duck sits on the alpine-fed Fountain Creek. Each of the grassy sites are cool under the shade of numerous trees and have campfire pits. All sites have electricity (20, 30 and some 50 amps) and several are full hookups in this family oriented campground.

Swim in the new heated pool or fish in the campground's pond, no license required. Kids will like the new, extra large, log playground and. Groups will enjoy the family recreation room with video games and a fireplace. Gather around for the delicious pancake breakfasts served every morning. Horseback rides are nearby. Around dusk, join in the nightly duck feeding or rent a video from next door. Although Lone Duck is close to city attractions, it's refreshing and quiet, and far from the city lights.

Location: Get off I-25 at Exit 141, go West on Highway 24 for 12 miles, make a U-turn at 1st Green Mountain Falls Exit and proceed East on Highway 24 for 250 yards.

Total RV sites: 36	Pull thru sites: 0	Open: 5/15 to 9/15
Full hookup sites: 8	45+ foot long sites: 4	Lisa & Steve Mack, Owners
Water & elec. sites: 7	Slideout sites: 5	8855 W Hwy 24
Elec. only sites: 21	Licenses sold: None	Box 25
50 amp sites: 5	LP Gas: None	Cascade, Colorado 80809-0250
Hookup sites open in Fall: 36	Credit Cards: VM	719/684-9907
Winter hookup sites: 0	Elevation: 7500	800/776-KWAK (5925)
RV site cost: ¢–$		

Within 15 minutes:

At RV Park:

Pikes Peak RV Park & Campground

The nearest campground to the Cog Railway, Pikes Peak RV Park rests under tall shade trees along Fountain Creek which runs through the property. The large, gravel sites are full hookups with cement patios. The paved driveway makes for easy access for large RVs and motor homes. Walk from your RV site to Manitou Springs city parks, olympic-sized pool, water slide and the stunning Garden of the Gods.

Four-wheel drive trails, mountain bike trails and horseback riding stables are near this centrally located campground. Buy gifts and RV supplies at the small shop here. Relaxing, site-seeing bus tours leave hourly to the Pikes Peak region — tickets are available at the RV park. Or rent a car on-site to visit the Royal Gorge and Cripple Creek area, only an hour's drive away.

Location: Exit I-25 at milepost 141, travel 4 miles West on US Highway 24 to the Manitou Avenue Exit and go 2 blocks West.

Total RV sites: 59	Pull thru sites: 0	Open: 4/1 to 10/31
Full hookup sites: 56	45+ foot long sites: 0	Allen & Jackie Branine, Hosts
Water & elec. sites: 3	Slideout sites: 6	320 Manitou Ave
Elec. only sites: 0	Licenses sold: None	Manitou Springs, Colorado 80829
50 amp sites: 12	LP Gas: None	719/685-9459
Hookup sites open in Fall: 59	Credit Cards: VM	
Winter hookup sites: 0	Elevation: 6400	
RV site cost: Not available		

Within 15 minutes:

At RV Park:

Rainbow Falls Park

Bring your family to relax at Colorado's first trout hatchery, established in 1871. Camp on 25 acres by crystal-clear lakes or streams and fry your freshly caught trout for breakfast at your campsite. Best of all, this is no license fishing! The waters are brimming with rainbow, brook, cutthroat, golden and brown trout. The level, pull thru RV sites are full hookups (20 amps) with campfire pits.

Other activities include hatchery tours, hayrides, and a taste of the West with chuckwagon suppers. Guided horseback rides will take you through majestic pine forests and mountain meadows with a view of the towering, north side of Pikes Peak. The more adventurous will want to explore with their mountain bikes or go climbing. A complete fishing store with snacks and playground are also on-site. Discover a Ute Indian cave, explore a gold mine or hike into the Rampart Range.

Cabins overlooking the lakes and an outdoor, group meeting area are also available.

Location: Exit I-25 at milepost 141, at Colorado Springs, go West on Highway 24 to Woodland Park, then North 10 miles on Highway 67

Total RV sites: 35	Pull thru sites: 8	Open: All Year
Full hookup sites: 35	45+ foot long sites: 4	Christine & Larry Posik, Owners
Water & elec. sites: 0	Slideout sites: 35	PO Box 9062
Elec. only sites: 0	Licenses sold: None	Woodland Park, Colorado 80866-9062
50 amp sites: 0	LP Gas: None	719/687-9074
Hookup sites open in Fall: 35	Credit Cards: VM	
Winter hookup sites: 0	Elevation: 7440	
RV site cost: Not available		

Within 15 minutes:

At RV Park:

Town & Country Resort

In a wooded, mountain setting, these large, spacious sites are level with some pull thrus. All are full hookups complete with concrete pads. The sites are nestled on a hillside, surrounded by aspen and pine trees. Individual men's and women's shower rooms are heated and have ceramic tile showers and dressing rooms. New 50 amp sites are planned for 1995 as are new cabin suites.

Town & Country Resort caters to seniors with special senior discounts. Partake in game nights, potlucks and poker nights at this adult-oriented park. The country store has everything you need from snacks to fishing supplies to gifts. Shuttle vans to the Cripple Creek Casinos and discount coupons are available. In the heart of Pikes Peak country, you'll find the nights cool and quiet, the days sunny, and your vacation perfect.

Daily, weekly and monthly rates are available.

Location: Exit Highway 67 at milepost 77.

Total RV sites: 50	Pull thru sites: 10	Open: All Year
Full hookup sites: 50	45+ foot long sites: 0	Gwen Collins, Manager
Water & elec. sites: 0	Slideout sites: 25	510 N Hwy 67
Elec. only sites: 0	Licenses sold: None	PO Box 368
50 amp sites: 6	LP Gas: None	Woodland Park, Colorado 80866
Hookup sites open in Fall: 50	Credit Cards: VM	719/687-9518
Winter hookup sites: 14	Elevation: 8500	800/600-0399
RV site cost: $		

Within 15 minutes:

At RV Park:

Creede

Also see South Fork and Wagon Wheel Gap areas. Map: M9

Isolated and picturesque, Creede, at 8,854 feet, is in Mineral County where 95 percent of the land is national forest or wilderness. Prospector Nicholas Creede discovered silver here in 1889 and one of his mines, the Amethyst, produced $2 million one year. What attracted hundreds of miners also brought crooks: "Soapy" Smith opened the Orleans Club to separate miners from their riches. He was eventually banned from Creede which was also home to other famous westerners, including Calamity Jane and Bob Ford, the man who shot Jesse James in the back. Today, the old mining town atmosphere still exists in restaurants, shops and the Creede Repertory Theater. The Wheeler Geologic Area, 24 miles northeast, is a photographer's dream: unusual volcanic rock formations have earned it the name City of Gnomes. From the Rio Grande Reservoir, 30 miles away, to Creede, people raft and fish for the plentiful German brown trout along the Rio Grande headwaters. The Bachelor Historic Loop, a 17-mile ride through the unique silver mining district and two ghost towns, and the Silver Thread Scenic Byway, which runs from South Fork through Creede east to Lake City, are two ways to enjoy the backcountry without crowds. Along the Silver Thread Scenic Byway, state highway 149, are some of the most majestic valleys in all of Colorado — the distances between mountain peaks appears vast and mesmerizing.

Fun Things to Do

- Broadacres Stables (719) 658-2291
- Creede Museum (800) 327-2102
- Creede Ranger District (719) 658-2556
- Creede Repertory Theater (719) 658-2540
- Creede Underground Firehouse (719) 658-2600
- Rio Grande National Forest & Weminuche Wilderness (719) 658-2556
- The Wood Gallery (719) 658-2423
- Underground Mining Museum (719) 658-0406

Broadacres Guest Ranch

A heavenly place to relax, Broadacres Ranch is a 600-acre working cattle ranch. With picture-perfect scenery, the sites take RVs up to 45 feet long. Each pull thru site has a cement pad, fire ring and is a full hookup (30 and 50 amps). A quarter mile off the highway on the river, Broadacres isn't visible  from the road and has level, open sites. Register at the ranch office and look forward to quiet, cool nights away from it all.

Fish in the stocked Rio Grande River, in nearby streams or at a private lake for the abundant German brown trout. Take guided horseback rides along scenic mountain trails — the ranch borders National Forest lands. Four-wheel driving, mountain biking and whitewater river rafting are nearby.

Modern cottages are also available.

Location: Five miles Southwest of Creede, ¼ mile off Highway 149 between mileposts 25 and 26 (not visible from highway).

Total RV sites: 20
Full hookup sites: 20
Water & elec. sites: 0
Elec. only sites: 0
50 amp sites: 20
Hookup sites open in Fall: 20
Winter hookup sites: 0
RV site cost: ¢–$

Pull thru sites: 19
45+ foot long sites: 20
Slideout sites: 20
Licenses sold: None
LP Gas: None
Credit Cards: None
Elevation: 8887

Open: 5/26 to 10/15
Bea Collerette, Owner
HCR 70
PO Box 39
Creede, Colorado 81130-0039
719/658-2291

Within 15 minutes:

At RV Park:

Clear Creek Guest Ranch

This 38-acre campground, homesteaded in 1904, has high mountain views and is surrounded by National Forest. Camp on Rocky Mountain grassland among wildflowers, aspen, bristol cone pines and spruce trees. Sites are full hookups with campfire pits. Halfway between the old mining towns of Creede and Lake City, the ranch is less than two miles off the state highway on a well-kept country road.

Crisscrossing the ranch's meadows are North Clear Creek and numerous smaller creeks and springs. These and the nearby stocked rivers and reservoirs are great for fishing. Take a hike into the backcountry where you'll find untouched, seldom fished beaver ponds. Mountain biking and river rafting are nearby. Bring your horse or rent one at close by stables for a trip into the wilderness area. You'll frequently see bear, moose, elk and deer as you explore the wilderness that encompasses the ranch.

Two modern and three rustic log cabins are also available. Ask about the daily, weekly, and monthly rates.

Location: Off Highway 149 at milepost 44, halfway between Creede and Lake City, and proceed 2 miles on North Clear Creek Rd.

Total RV sites: 17	Pull thru sites: 5	Open: 5/26 to 9/15
Full hookup sites: 17	45+ foot long sites: 17	Jerry & Karen Fleming, Owners
Water & elec. sites: 0	Slideout sites: 17	1786 Forest Service Rd 510
Elec. only sites: 0	Licenses sold: None	Creede, Colorado 81130
50 amp sites: 2	LP Gas: None	719/658-2491
Hookup sites open in Fall: 17	Credit Cards: None	
Winter hookup sites: 0	Elevation: 9500	
RV site cost: Not available		

Within 15 minutes:

At RV Park:

Cripple Creek

Map: I-16

Nestled in an extinct volcano crater riddled with gold fields, Cripple Creek and its surroundings eventually produced $600 million in gold (that's more than $12 billion today). Streets are still paved in gold, low grade gold ore that is. Some 30 miners became millionaires during Cripple Creek's and Victor's gold rushes. Cripple Creek's casino gambling, in this historic mining town located in a remote region on the backside of Pikes Peak, once again offers the opportunity to strike it rich. Along with trying your hand at slot machines, visit an old mining camp, or stroll historic Bennett Avenue. Nearby, the town of Victor was the home of renown world-traveling journalist Lowell Thomas who was the first news commentator. One gold field in Victor, uncovered when a hotel foundation was being built, eventually yielded $5.5 million in gold. The Phantom Canyon Scenic Byway begins in Victor and travels to Cañon City. Fifteen miles from Cripple Creek is Florissant Fossil Beds National Monument where palm trees, redwoods, and thousands of insects are preserved in volcanic beds. Hike either of the three trails to prehistoric wonders. Outdoor enthusiasts will find abundant fishing and hiking in the adjoining 3 million acres of Pike National Forest.

Fun Things to Do

- Cripple Creek & Victor Narrow Gauge Railroad (719) 689-2640
- Cripple Creek District Museum (719) 689-2634
- Cripple Creek Golf Course (719) 689-2531
- Florissant Fossil Beds National Monument (719) 748-3253
- Imperial Melodrama (719) 689-7777
- Mollie Kathleen Gold Mine (719) 689-2466
- Mueller State Park (719) 687-2366
- The Old Homestead Parlour House Museum (719) 689-3090
- Victor-Lowell Thomas Museum, Victor (719) 689-2766

Cripple Creek Gold Campground

Conveniently located just around the bend from the Old West town of Cripple Creek and next to a national forest, this campground is a great way to visit the former gold-mining town which has been newly revitalized by casino gambling. The large, rustic sites are in secluded woods of tall aspen trees and have electrical (15, 20 and 30 amps) hookups. Barbecue grills, fire rings and firewood (charge) are provided. This is a family-oriented campground with no additional charge for a third or fourth person on a site.

Facilities include a playground, with horseshoes and volleyball, and video game room. The campground store has groceries and camping supplies. Nondenominational outdoor Sunday services are offered throughout the summer. Hike or horseback ride in nearby Pike National Forest. Guest horses are welcome to join you. Elk, deer, mountain sheep and antelope can be seen from time to time short distances from your site. A visit to historic Cripple Creek is a must. Museums, mine tours, train rides and gambling casinos abound in this living legend of the old American West.

Camper cabins are also available.

Location: Off Highway 67 near milepost 58, 6 miles North of Cripple Creek and 12 miles South of Divide.

Total RV sites: 12	Pull thru sites: 3	Open: 5/15 to 10/15
Full hookup sites: 0	45+ foot long sites: 10	William & Linda Buckhanan, Owners
Water & elec. sites: 0	Slideout sites: 4	12654 Hwy 67 North
Elec. only sites: 12	Licenses sold: None	PO Box 601
50 amp sites: 0	LP Gas: None	Cripple Creek, Colorado 80813-0601
Hookup sites open in Fall: 12	Credit Cards: None	719/689-2342
Winter hookup sites: 0	Elevation: 10200	
RV site cost: ¢		

Within 15 minutes:

At RV Park:

Cripple Creek Travel Park & Hospitality House

This is truly a unique travel park and campground adjacent to an awarding winning restored Victorian county hospital which has been converted into a gracious guest house. Set amidst the mountain splendor of the Pikes Peak region, the charming, red-brick house with sunshine yellow columns takes you back to Teller County's glory days. The open, dry, grassy sites behind the classic architecture of the hospital have picnic tables and grills. Pull thrus for 40-foot RVs and a covered picnic area are also available. All sites are full hookups with 20, 30 and some 50 amps. Handicap restrooms are provided.

Amenities include a children's playground and a family recreation room with cable television. Enjoy the on-site beauty shop and new hot tub. In the adjoining 3 million acres of Pike National Forest, you'll find plenty to do from abundant fishing to horseback riding to hiking. And, of course, Cripple Creek offers every thing from slot machines to live theater. Take an easy stroll to the downtown museums and casinos or a free shuttle.

Rooms in the elegant historic inn, and indoor and outdoor group meeting areas are also available.

Location: Exit Highway 67 at milepost 52 and go West on Bennett Avenue to B Street, then North 6 blocks.

Total RV sites: 48	Pull thru sites: 34	Open: 5/1 to 10/31
Full hookup sites: 48	45+ foot long sites: 18	Steve & Bonnie Mackin, Operators
Water & elec. sites: 0	Slideout sites: 14	600 N "B" St.
Elec. only sites: 0	Licenses sold: None	Box 577
50 amp sites: 2	LP Gas: None	Cripple Creek, Colorado 80813-0577
Hookup sites open in Fall: 48	Credit Cards: VMD	719/689-2513
Winter hookup sites: 0	Elevation: 9500	800/500-2513
RV site cost: $		

Within 15 minutes:

At RV Park:

Lost Burro Campground

You'll find a genuine Western wilderness experience in this campground located in a beautiful, grassy mountain valley. Enjoy the scenic view and cool, quiet nights in the rolling hills of Lost Burro where the sites are open and shaded by pine trees. Sites have electricity (20 amps) and all have fire rings. Deer frequently roam the property.

A fire-warmed lodge serving tasty meals is a short distance from Lost Burro as is a golf course. You can try your hand at gold panning in a clear, cold mountain stream near your private site. Children will enjoy dog-sledding rides on-site in the winter. Hike in the shade of Colorado pines and aspens along the same trails used by Ute Indians and prospectors of yesteryear. The Florissant Fossil Beds are just down the road, awaiting your exploration. Lost Burro is wilderness camping with all the modern conveniences and is an excellent base for all your daily excursions.

Location: Exit Highway 67 at milepost 52, Northwest of historic Cripple Creek on County Road 1.

Total RV sites: 14	Pull thru sites: 5	Open: All Year
Full hookup sites: 0	45+ foot long sites: 7	Jim & Mary Eddleman, Owners
Water & elec. sites: 0	Slideout sites: 14	4023 Teller County Road 1
Elec. only sites: 14	Licenses sold: None	Box 614
50 amp sites: 0	LP Gas: None	Cripple Creek, Colorado 80813-6140
Hookup sites open in Fall: 14	Credit Cards: None	719/689-2345
Winter hookup sites: 14	Elevation: 8800	
RV site cost: ¢		

Within 15 minutes:

At RV Park:

Prospectors RV Park

The closest RV park to historic downtown Cripple Creek, Prospectors has level, gravel sites. Many RV sites have full hookups and all have campfire pits. Several sites accommodate extra large rigs and are pull thru. Keep an eye out for the occasional burros that wander through the campground.

Your pet can vacation with you at Prospectors. Walk two and half blocks to the casinos or take a frequent free shuttle that stops at the park. The large convenience store on site has all the vacation supplies you need. Located on a scenic highway, this campground is within minutes of fishing, horseback riding, golfing and mountain biking in the summer. In the winter try snowmobiling, ice fishing, cross country skiing and hunting on your own or with a guide. In town, visit the museums and explore historic sites between casino stops. This is a good area for collecting rock and mineral specimens. A high quality turquoise mine is nearby.

Reservations are recommended in the summer.

Location: Off Highway 67 between mileposts 51 and 52.

Total RV sites: 36	Pull thru sites: 8	Open: All Year
Full hookup sites: 16	45+ foot long sites: 8	RV Park Manager
Water & elec. sites: 0	Slideout sites: 36	202 E May
Elec. only sites: 10	Licenses sold: None	PO Box 1237
50 amp sites: 0	LP Gas: None	Cripple Creek, Colorado 80813-0976
Hookup sites open in Fall: 26	Credit Cards: None	719/689-2006
Winter hookup sites: 26	Elevation: 9494	719/577-4908 Fax
RV site cost: $–$$		

Within 15 minutes:

At RV Park:

RNK Park and Camp

Camp in open sites with a scenic view of Pikes Peak. A majority of the sites have electricity (30 amps), fire pits, TV and phone hookups. Facilities are handicap accessible. At RNK Park, big rigs will find easy access.

A convenience grocery store with souvenirs and entertainment room with video games are on the property. Kids will enjoy the soda fountain on-site. A swimming pool, mountain bike trails and horseback rides are minutes away. Free shuttles by appointment are available to Cripple Creek.

Daily, weekly and monthly rates are available. Ask about the group rates and tent rentals.

Location: Just 3 ½ miles Northeast of Cripple Creek on Highway 67S.

Total RV sites: 18	Pull thru sites: 6	Open: All Year
Full hookup sites: 0	45+ foot long sites: 18	Wayne Delabarre & Rachael Letch
Water & elec. sites: 0	Slideout sites: 18	10702 Hwy 67 S
Elec. only sites: 12	Licenses sold: None	PO Box 190
50 amp sites: 4	LP Gas: M	Cripple Creek, Colorado 80813-0190
Hookup sites open in Fall: 12	Credit Cards: None	719/689-3371
Winter hookup sites: 12	Elevation: 10050	
RV site cost: ¢		

Within 15 minutes:

At RV Park:

Crystal River Valley

Includes Carbondale and Marble. Also see Glenwood Springs Area Map: G-8 and H- 8.

The towering Mount Sopris, its peak reaches 12, 953 feet, dominates the charming Crystal River Valley. Carbondale, the former stagecoach stop on the 40 mile run to Aspen, takes pride in its specialty shops, local arts and crafts and fine restaurants. Meander through town, exploring art galleries and eating lunch on a patio with a view of Mount Sopris. Tucked away in the pristine Crystal River Valley, Marble is surrounded by cliffs and mountain peaks. Marble stone helped the area survive the coal mining era and prosper into the early 1900s. Visit the Marble Quarry where you can still see the mountain of pure white marble which supplied stone for the Tomb of the Unknown Soldier and the Lincoln Memorial. Crystal Mill, 6 miles above town, is perhaps the most photographed structure in Colorado. Great mountain bike trails and four-wheel drive jeep trails lead out of town into the White River National Forest. Anglers should try Beaver Lake which is heavily stocked with rainbow and brook trout or the Crystal River where there are plenty of fish. Today, people come to this quiet valley to enjoy the Colorado outdoors and some of the most spectacular scenery in the state.

Fun Things to Do

- Crystal Glass Studio (970) 963-3227
- Main Street Gallery (970) 963-3775
- Main Street Nursery & Gifts (970) 963-2497
- Marble Museum (970)963-0358
- Mount Sopris Historical Society Museum (970) 963-2889
- Roaring Forge (970) 963-1930
- The Colorado Artisan's Boutique (970) 963-0467

B-R-B Crystal River Resort

Rocky Mountain splendor at its finest! Located at the base of Mount Sporis on the lively Crystal River which has some of the best fishing in Colorado, the resort has 10 acres of shady, grass sites with electricity and water hookups, picnic tables and fire pits. Come for the tranquil mountain scenery, stay for all the outdoor recreation. Numerous trees surround the sites and you'll be lulled to sleep at night by the steady, soothing sounds of the Crystal River.

On-site, play horseshoes, basketball, volleyball, badminton, ping pong, and tether ball at the playground. The main lodge has an adult game room, small grocery store and gift shop. Local hunting and fishing are some of the best in the country. Horseback riding, four-wheel drive and mountain bike trails and river rafting are nearby. The open-air hot tub and swimming pool are a welcome retreat after a day of adventuring. The Glenwood Springs natural hot springs pool is only 18 miles away. History buffs will want to tour the historic towns of Marble and Redstone just up the road.

Modern log cabins with fireplaces, and indoor/outdoor group meeting areas are also available.

Location: Off Highway 133 near milepost 62, 6 miles South of Carbondale.

Total RV sites: 22	Pull thru sites: 2	Open: 5/15 to 10/31
Full hookup sites: 0	45+ foot long sites: 18	Dick & Marianne Fedderman, Owners
Water & elec. sites: 18	Slideout sites: 18	7202 Hwy 133
Elec. only sites: 0	Licenses sold: None	Carbondale, Colorado 81623
50 amp sites: 0	LP Gas: metered	970/963-2341
Hookup sites open in Fall: 18	Credit Cards: VMD	800/963-2341
Winter hookup sites: 0	Elevation: 6200	
RV site cost: $–$$		

Within 15 minutes:

At RV Park:

Meri Daes RV Park

Camp in the shade along the beautiful Crystal River. The level RV sites at Meri Daes have electricity (20 and 30 amps) and water hookups. Lots of tall spruce trees and Ponderosa pines abound in this campground decorated by slabs of marble. Relax at your site to the soothing sounds of the river.

The campground has a general store and horseshoes. The Crystal River has excellent trout fishing and lakes are nearby for those who prefer casting from shore or a boat. Explore the relatively untouched back country via four-wheel drive or on horseback. Bring your hiking boots and mountain bikes, because trails through the forests to alpine meadows and snow-capped peaks are everywhere. Marble is the only white marble dump station in Colorado — and perhaps the world. Glenwood Springs and Aspen, with all their amenities, are a short drive away.

Location: In Marble, turn off Highway 133 near milepost 46.

Total RV sites: 15	Pull thru sites: 6	Open: 6/1 to 10/15
Full hookup sites: 0	45+ foot long sites: 8	Dave & Meri Jones, Owners
Water & elec. sites: 15	Slideout sites: 8	220 West Park
Elec. only sites: 0	Licenses sold: None	Marble, Colorado 81623
50 amp sites: 0	LP Gas: None	970/963-1831
Hookup sites open in Fall: 15	Credit Cards: VM	
Winter hookup sites: 0	Elevation: 8000	
RV site cost: ¢		

Within 15 minutes:

At RV Park:

Denver Area

Includes Aurora, Brighton, Broomfield, Castle Rock, Golden, Morrison, Tiny Town, Strasburg and Wheat Ridge. Map: F-17

The Queen City of the Plains, Denver is a mile above sea level. With a mild climate of only 15 inches of precipitation a year and more annual hours of sunshine than Miami or San Diego, the city has a variety of attractions, including free walking tours, the US Mint, the Denver Art Museum (which has the world's greatest collection of Indian art), the 16th Street Mall downtown, specialty shops in Cherry Creek and the 20-mile long Platte River Greenway. Denver has parks and gardens, museums, shopping, night life, restaurants from casual to elegant, theater and sporting events. There's something for everyone in Colorado's capital.

Fun Things to Do

- Children's Museum (303) 433-7444
- Colorado History Museum (303) 866-3682
- Denver Art Museum (303) 640-2793
- Denver Botanical Gardens (303) 331-4000
- Denver City Park Golf Course (303) 295-2095
- Denver History Museum (303) 620-4933
- Denver Museum of Miniatures, Dolls & Toys (303) 322-3704
- Denver Museum of Natural History (303) 322-7009
- Denver Zoological Gardens (303) 331-4100
- Echo Lake Lodge Restaurant (303) 567-2138
- El Rancho Restaurant ((303) 526-0661
- Grant-Humphreys Museum (303) 894-2506
- Harvard Gulch Golf Course (303) 698-4078
- Molly Brown House (303) 832-4092
- Mountain View Golf Course (303) 694-3012
- Overland Park Golf Course (303) 777-7331
- Park Hill Golf Course (303) 333-5411
- United States Mint (303) 844-3332
- Wellshire Golf Course (303) 757-1352
- Willis Case Golf Course (303) 455-9801

Barr Lake Campground

Northeast of Denver near Denver International Airport — the newst airport in America, these large, level, grassy pull thrus sites have 20, 30 and 50 amps, TV hookups and picnic tables under limited shade.

A playground and pool will keep the kids busy. Groceries, snacks and ice are available on-site. This campground is just 2 ½ miles from Barr Lake State Park which has good fishing and an excellent bird sanctuary. Bald eagles nest here and an additional 400 kinds of birds use the sanctuary on their migratory paths. The state park has a nature center, wildlife watches plus free, fun, hands-on programs for children. You may also sail on Barr Lake with low horsepower boats. A short half-hour drive away from the campground is the foot of the majestic Rocky Mountain National Park.

Location: 15 miles Northeast of Denver on I-76, take Exit 20 at 136th Avenue, or 3 miles East of Brighton and Highway 85 on 136th Avenue.

Total RV sites: 94
Full hookup sites: 72
Water & elec. sites: 15
Elec. only sites: 2
50 amp sites: 37
Hookup sites open in Fall: 87
Winter hookup sites: 87
RV site cost: $–$$

Pull thru sites: 94
45+ foot long sites: 68
Slideout sites: 45
Licenses sold: None
LP Gas: weight
Credit Cards: VM
Elevation: 5000

Open: All Year
Rusty & Lori Komar, Owners
17180 E 136th Ave
Brighton, Colorado 80601
303/659-6180

Within 15 minutes:

At RV Park:

Castle Rock KOA

Halfway between Denver and Colorado Springs, Castle Rock is in the foothills with beautiful views of the mountains. All the shady, spacious sites have electricity (15, 20 and 30 amps), barbecue grills, and many are full hookups and pull thrus. A colorful red caboose from yesteryear is easy to spot as you approach the secluded, 24-acre campground.

The campground has a heated swimming pool, wading pool, video game room, convenience and gift store. Enjoy the playground with basketball, volleyball, horseshoes and shuffleboard. Free video rentals are available. Headquarter here to see Pike's Peak, Garden of the Gods, the US Mint, Coors Brewery and other Denver and Colorado Springs attractions. Fishing, mountain biking and horseback riding are all nearby. The Castle Rock area is home to the summer Colorado Renaissance Festival in nearby Larkspur and an international golf tournament in Castle Pines. Enjoy shopping at the factory outlets.

Camper cabins and an indoor, group meeting area are available. Ask about the weekly, monthly and groups rates.

Location: On I-25, 7 miles South of Castle Rock at Exit 174.

Total RV sites: 81	Pull thru sites: 28	Open: 3/15 to 10/31
Full hookup sites: 24	45+ foot long sites: 50	Doug & Ruth Ann, Douglas & Shawna Dick,
Water & elec. sites: 40	Slideout sites: 41	Owners
Elec. only sites: 6	Licenses sold: None	6527 South I-25
50 amp sites: 0	LP Gas: metered	Castle Rock, Colorado 80104
Hookup sites open in Fall: 70	Credit Cards: VMD	303/681-3169
Winter hookup sites: 0	Elevation: 6200	
RV site cost: Not available		

Within 15 minutes:

At RV Park:

Chief Hosa Lodge & Campground

At Denver's closest mountain campground the buffalo still roam through beautiful Genesee Park. The park is on the National Register of Historic Places. The lodge, constructed by stone masonry, was built in 1918 as a forested, foothills getaway for Denver residents. Lovely, shaded sites on 56 acres with views of the breathtaking Continental Divide are yours for the taking. Numerous sites are hookups with campfire pits and picnic tables.

From your campsite, explore numerous nature hiking trails past grazing buffalo and elk herds. Play volleyball, basketball or horseshoes in the athletic area or cruise around on your mountain bike. Rafting trips, fishing, four-wheel driving and horseback riding are all nearby as are Denver's big city amenities. For your peace of mind, Chief Hosa has a security gate. After a day of fun, put the kids in their own wading pool while you soak in the heated outdoor swimming pool.

The picturesque, historic lodge is open all year for weddings, family reunions and special events.

Location: Located 20 miles West of Denver, Exit I-70 at milepost 253.

Total RV sites: 150
Full hookup sites: 3
Water & elec. sites: 45
Elec. only sites: 0
50 amp sites: 0
Hookup sites open in Fall: 0
Winter hookup sites: 0
RV site cost: Not available

Pull thru sites: 6
45+ foot long sites: 10
Slideout sites: 49
Licenses sold: None
LP Gas: None
Credit Cards: VM
Elevation: 7700

Open: Memorial Day to Labor Day
David & Jane Christie, Owners
27661 Genesee Dr.
Golden, Colorado 80401
303/526-0364

Within 15 minutes:

At RV Park:

Delux RV Park

In Denver, minutes from downtown, Delux RV Park has shaded, level and landscaped sites with gravel. All sites are full hookups (20, 30 and 50 amps) and have TV hookup. From greeting you with a sincere smile to sharing their first-hand knowledge of Denver's restaurant, shops and other attractions, they'll make you feel right at home.

A swimming pool, bowling alley and shopping center, are within 10 minutes from this city RV park. The mile high city offers a variety of attractions, including free walking tours, the US Mint, the Denver Art Museum, the downtown 16th Street Mall, Coors Field baseball stadium, specialty shops in Cherry Creek and the 20-mile long Platte River Greenway.

Location: From the junction of I-25 and I-70 go West on I-70 for 2 miles (Exit 272), then ¾ miles North on Federal Boulevard on the East side of Federal. From I-76 (Exit 3), go South 1 ½ blocks on Federal.

Total RV sites: 29	Pull thru sites: 5	Open: All Year
Full hookup sites: 29	45+ foot long sites: 0	Gulshan & Sadru Shariff, Owners
Water & elec. sites: 0	Slideout sites: 20	5520 N Federal
Elec. only sites: 0	Licenses sold: None	Denver, Colorado 80221
50 amp sites: 5	LP Gas: None	303⁄433-0452
Hookup sites open in Fall: 29	Credit Cards: VM	
Winter hookup sites: 29	Elevation: 5200	
RV site cost: $		

Within 15 minutes:

At RV Park:

Denver East/Strasburg KOA

A campground dotted with shade trees, Denver East/Strasburg KOA has pull thru sites with full hookups (30 and 50 amps). All sites have picnic tables and many have barbecue grills. The old-fashioned bakery next door will wake you with the tantalizing aroma of fresh baked breakfast goodies.

On-site amenities include a playground, large video game room, heated swimming pool, and free nightly movies. A large meeting room is ideal for groups of up to 70. Take your pet on the dog walk for daily exercise. The camp store has groceries, pop, ice, camping supplies and souvenirs. Let your hosts help plan a visit to all of the nearby Denver attractions, including the zoo and Museum of Natural History. Check out the local Comanche Crossing Museum in Strasburg, with its restored train depot, 1904 schoolhouse, 1910 homestead and over 3,000 artifacts.

Camper cabins are also available. Groups are encouraged and welcomed.

Location: Located 35 miles East of Denver, on I-70 at milepost 310.

Total RV sites: 62	Pull thru sites: 52	Open: All to Year
Full hookup sites: 23	45+ foot long sites: 60	Jim & Sharon Strange, Owners
Water & elec. sites: 39	Slideout sites: 40	1312 Monroe St.
Elec. only sites: 0	Licenses sold: None	PO Box 597
50 amp sites: 6	LP Gas: metered	Strasburg, Colorado 80136-0597
Hookup sites open in Fall: 62	Credit Cards: VMAD	303/622-9274
Winter hookup sites: 13	Elevation: 5380	
RV site cost: $		

Within 15 minutes:

At RV Park:

Denver Meadows RV Park & Camper Cabins

Centrally located for seeing Denver and the Rockies and near to city buses and shopping centers, Denver Meadow's sites are partially shaded. The sites have full hookup (30 and 50 amp), TV hookup and border a small stream. Private showers and laundry facilities are also available.

The park sports a swimming pool and a hot tub. The playground has swings for the children. Exercise your pet on the dog walk around the park. If you're interested in sight-seeing tours, just ask your hosts to arrange them. Denver Meadows is right on the road to great Colorado adventures.

Camper cabins are also available. Ask about the daily, weekly and monthly rates.

Location: 9 miles East of Denver at Exit I-225, at East Colfax (US Highway 40 and 287). Go 200 yards West then 3 blocks North on Potomac.

Total RV sites: 278	RV site cost: ¢–$$	Open: All Year
Full hookup sites: 278	Pull thru sites: 100	Shawn Lustigman, Teddy Cline &
Water & elec. sites: 0	45+ foot long sites: 0	Ralph Shaoul, Owners
Elec. only sites: 0	Slideout sites: 278	2075 Potomac St.
50 amp sites: 278	Licenses sold: None	Aurora, Colorado 80011
Hookup sites open in Fall: 278	LP Gas: M	303/364-9483
Winter hookup sites: 0	Credit Cards: VM	303/366-7289 fax
	Elevation: 5280	

Within 15 minutes:

At RV Park:

Denver North Campground

In a quiet, countryside location, yet centrally located for Denver and Boulder area attractions, the pull thru, level sites are full hookups (20, 30 and 50 amp) with barbecue grills and picnic tables. The local TV reception is excellent. Large trees shade most of the grassy sites with gravel driveways. Vaca-

tion with a view of the snow-capped Front Range of the Rockies at Denver North Campground. Denver North Campground is convenient for trips to Boulder and the University of Colorado.

The grocery store on-site has ice, snacks, souvenirs and RV supplies. A video game room and playground with horseshoes and basketball will please the kids. Yummy pancake breakfasts are served six days a week during the summer. The heated swimming pool is a great way to relax after a day of mile high fun. Denver North is a good location from which to see Denver, Boulder and the Rocky Mountains.

Camper cabins, an indoor and outdoor group meeting room are also available.

Location: Fifteen miles North of I-70, on I-25, at Exit 229.

Total RV sites: 104
Full hookup sites: 80
Water & elec. sites: 31
Elec. only sites: 15
50 amp sites: 8
Hookup sites open in Fall: 126
Winter hookup sites: 70

RV site cost: $
Pull thru sites: 72
45+ foot long sites: 25
Slideout sites: 25
Licenses sold: None
LP Gas: metered
Credit Cards: VMD
Elevation: 5280

Open: All Year
Jerry, Sue & Ken, Debbie Maloney, Owns.
16700 North Washington
Broomfield Colorado 80020
303/452-4120

Within 15 minutes:

At RV Park:

Golden's Scenic Rock RV Park

This campground in Denver's suburbs is exclusively designed for RVs. The long, pull thru, grassy sites are all full hookups (20, 30 and 50 amp) with TV hookup and paved drives. The park is enclosed by an 8-foot privacy fence and is backed by a natural, red rock outcropping which is great for nature hikes and picnics. From the Scenic Rock RV Park, you'll have a spectacular, panoramic view of Denver and the Front Range.

Park amenities include a picnic area and a country store with groceries, snacks, beer and gifts. Kids will like the playground, video game room and pool tables. The luxurious, air-conditioned lounge with TV and fireplace has a group meeting room. There are also pet exercise areas, basketball courts, and horseshoe pits.

Near the campground are Central City's gambling casinos, the Coors Brewery, Buffalo Bill's Grave and Red Rocks Park. You are just minutes away from a world of recreational activities — swim, fish, sail, ski, hike, bike or visit a health club. Just ask your hosts for directions.

Safe, police-protected RV and boat storage is also available.

Location: From the intersection of US Highway 40 and I-70, go 2 miles West on US Highway 40 (Colfax Avenue).

Total RV sites: 141	RV site cost: $–$$	Open: All Year
Full hookup sites: 141	Pull thru sites: 88	Dean & Sue Reese, Resident Manager
Water & elec. sites: 0	45+ foot long sites: 80	17700 West Colfax
Elec. only sites: 0	Slideout sites: 80	Golden, Colorado 80401
50 amp sites: 141	Licenses sold: None	303/279-1625
Hookup sites open in Fall: 141	LP Gas: M	800/398-1625
Winter hookup sites: 141	Credit Cards: VMD	
	Elevation: 6000	

Within 15 minutes:

At RV Park:

Mountain Air Ranch — Family Nudist Resort

Located on 150 secluded acres, Mountain Air Ranch is a family *nudist* resort 3 miles south of Tiny Town in the mountains. All the RV sites are in a meadow and have electricity and water. The only Colorado member of the American Sunbathing Association (AANR), Mountain Air Ranch has had a safe, congenial family atmosphere since 1935.

The hot tub and sauna will help you relax after playing volleyball, paddle tennis, horseshoes, shuffle board or hiking on 10 miles of trails located on the property. Family activities throughout the year include bingo, card games, carnival and field days. Kids will enjoy the large playground with a merry-go-round and sand box. The Club House, when not used for monthly dances, is ideal for board games, ping pong, billiards and family gatherings. The restaurant serves meals on summer weekends or visitors can use the community kitchen. Annual events include pool parties with live entertainment, a luau, a western weekend, chili cookoffs, a kid's July 4th parade, a family video night, steak fries and sport tournaments.

Location: Off Highway 285, 3 miles South of Tiny Town, 30 minutes Southwest of Denver.

Total RV sites: 10	Pull thru sites: 4	Open: 5/1 to 10/1
Full hookup sites: 0	45+ foot long sites: 4	Ron Earthman, Public Comm. Chairman
Water & elec. sites: 10	Slideout sites: 4	950 Macon St.
Elec. only sites: 0	Licenses sold: None	Aurora, Colorado 80010
50 amp sites: 0	LP Gas: None	303/697-4083
Hookup sites open in Fall: 0	Credit Cards: VM	
Winter hookup sites: 0	Elevation: 7000	
RV site cost: Not available		

Within 15 minutes:

At RV Park:

Prospect RV Park

Prospect Park is adjacent to a city park with many recreational facilities. The level, pull thru sites are open and shady with full hookups (20, 30 and 50 amp). The gravel sites are separated by split rail fences for privacy. Private bathrooms for individuals and families are also available. A quiet RV park, Prospect has very clean and modern facilities. Enjoy grassy areas under trees with picnic tables at dinner time.

An RV repair and maintenance shop is right on the site. Prospect Park is next door to fishing, hiking and biking paths. Area attractions, shops, restaurants are all nearby as are local bus routes. Take a shuttle to Central City and try your hand at modern casinos in historical buildings.

Location: In West Denver, take I-70 to Exit 266 (West bound Ward Rd, East bound 44th Avenue) and proceed East on 44th.

Total RV sites: 70	Pull thru sites: 32	Open: All Year
Full hookup sites: 47	45+ foot long sites: 30	Nancy Laird & Kay & Warren Johnson
Water & elec. sites: 23	Slideout sites: 56	11600 W 44th Ave
Elec. only sites: 0	Licenses sold: None	PO Box 626
50 amp sites: 26	LP Gas: None	Wheat Ridge, Colorado 80033-0626
Hookup sites open in Fall: 70	Credit Cards: VM	303/424-4414
Winter hookup sites: 35	Elevation: 5400	800/344-5702
RV site cost: Not available		

Within 15 minutes:

At RV Park:

Stage Stop Campground

An old fashioned campground with hot showers and flush toilets on 60 wooded acres in the mountains outside of Denver, the Stage Stop is a secluded campground just down the hill off the main highway. Because of the steep entrance, only RVs with a max of 30 feet are allowed. Camp

under shady pine trees at sites with electrical hookup, picnic tables and campfire pits. The abundant shrubbery between sites affords you lots of natural privacy.

From the campground, you'll have views of the nearby foothills and will be surrounded by trees: Ponderosa pines, fir, spruce, scrub oak and shimmering aspen. The new pavilion is ideal for group meetings and kids will like the playground. Horseback riding is minutes away and your horse is welcomed at Stage Stop. Mountain bike trails and fishing area are also nearby.

Weekly rates and senior citizens discounts are available.

Location: Just 25 miles from the Southwest center of Denver, 9 miles Southwest of Red Rocks Park or 5 miles East of Conifer on US Highway 285 at milepost 241.

Total RV sites: 15	Pull thru sites: 6	Open: Memorial Day to Labor Day
Full hookup sites: 0	45+ foot long sites: 0	Harry & Ann Lax, Owners
Water & elec. sites: 0	Slideout sites: 0	8884 South US Hwy 285
Elec. only sites: 16	Licenses sold: None	Morrison, Colorado 80465
50 amp sites: 0	LP Gas: None	303/697-4901
Hookup sites open in Fall: 0	Credit Cards: None	
Winter hookup sites: 0	Elevation: 7600	
RV site cost: ¢–$		

Within 15 minutes:

At RV Park:

Dolores

See also Mesa Verde Area. Map: O-3

Dolores has it all, from mountain scenery to the second largest lake in Colorado, McPhee Lake. Completely filled for the first time in 1987, McPhee's sloping, timbered shore makes for interesting views. Fish from a boat for large and small-mouth bass, blue gills and crappies. Or try the Dolores River, named by two Spanish friars in honor of "Our Lady of Sorrows," where the nutrient-rich waters are teaming with rainbow, brown, cutthroat and brook trout. This area also has excellent hunting, with an abundance of wildlife and big game. You can see the area's beautiful archeology in the nearby Anasazi Heritage Center which has over 2 million artifacts of the "ancient ones," and educational and participatory exhibits. The Escalante Ruins, overlooking McPhee Lake, is named for the one of the friars who passed this way in 1776. Enjoy outdoor recreation at its finest: hike, jeep, or horseback ride in the San Juan National Forest, from the Dolores River Valley to 14,000-foot peaks in the Mount Wilson Primitive Area. Or take the scenic byway that goes northeast to Telluride on Highway 145 or southeast to Durango. The drive from Dolores to Telluride is especially magnificent.

Fun Things to Do

- Anasazi Heritage Center (970) 882-4811
- Conquistador Golf Course, Cortez (970) 565-9208
- Crow Canyon Archeological Center (800) 422-8975
- Dolores River Line Camp (970) 882-4158
- Galloping Goose Museum & Dolores Visitor Center (970) 882-4018
- Mesa Verde Cortez Information Center (800) 346-6528
- Outfitter Sporting Goods & Mercantile (970) 882-7740
- San Juan National Forest, Dolores District (970) 882-7296

Cozy Comfort RV Park

Located in downtown Dolores, Cozy Comfort has full hookup sites. Half of the sites are pull thrus.

There is a playground for children. The scenic San Juan Highway starts right here. Nearby, you can fish, golf, visit museums and historic sites, mountain bike, snowmobile, ice fish and hunt. Both cross-country and downhill skiing and rentals are close.

Ask about vehicle and boat storage.

Location: Downtown Dolores on Central Avenue near the junction of Highway 184 and 145.

Total RV sites: 11
Full hookup sites: 11
Water & elec. sites: 11
Elec. only sites: 11
50 amp sites: 0
Hookup sites open in Fall: 11
Winter hookup sites: 11
RV site cost: ¢–$

Pull thru sites: 5
45+ foot long sites: 2
Slideout sites: 2
Licenses sold: None
LP Gas: None
Credit Cards: VM
Elevation: 6900

Open: All Year
Kelly & Jeannie Pryor, Owners
1501 Central Ave
PO Box 1327
Dolores, Colorado 81323
970/882-2483

Within 15 minutes:

At RV Park:

Dolores River RV Park & Cabins

You'll find large, level, pull thru, full hookup (30 and 50 amps) sites at this RV park. Along the Dolores River in a valley, the sites have barbecue grills and firewood is available. Pick among open or wooded sites by the tumbling river. Ask about the cable TV and phone hookups. Come here to simply relax.

Fish right on the river, at the pond or down the road at McPhee Reservoir. The the playground is great for the kids while the adults can enjoy the game room with exercise equipment, card tables and color TV. The lounge and commercial kitchen are ideal for family reunions. Exercise your best friend at the pet walk and then exercise yourself along the picturesque river walk. Nearby, you can take a four-wheel drive tour, horseback ride, whitewater raft, golf and mountain bike. End the day with a visit to the soda fountain for a refreshing drink and snack.

Weekly and month rates are available. Groups are welcomed. Ask about the camper cabins, housekeeping cabins and on-site trailers.

Location: From the junction of Highway 184 & 145 between mileposts 13 and 14, go 14 miles East on Highway 145, 2 ½ miles North of Dolores.

Total RV sites: 80	Pull thru sites: 20	Open: All Year
Full hookup sites: 63	45+ foot long sites: 80	Harold & Steve Horten, Owners & Managers
Water & elec. sites: 24	Slideout sites: 60	18680 Hwy 145
Elec. only sites: 0	Licenses sold: None	Dolores, Colorado 81323
50 amp sites: 60	LP Gas: metered	970/882-7761
Hookup sites open in Fall: 80	Credit Cards: VMD	
Winter hookup sites: 20	Elevation: 7200	
RV site cost: $		

Within 15 minutes:

At RV Park:

McPhee Mobile Home & RV Park

Across from the entrance to McPhee Reservoir and its 50 miles of shoreline, this RV park is on top of a mesa with a 360 degree view. The extra-long, pull thru and back-in sites have room for your RV, boat and a personal vehicle. Sites have full hookups (20, 30 and 50 amp) with TV and phone hook-ups and rural drinking water available. Sites have a barbecue pit, picnic table and grassy lawn. Clean restrooms, hot showers and laundry facilities are provided.

Fishing, mountain biking and horseback riding are nearby. McPhee Reservoir is the second largest lake in Colorado and has, rainbow trout, kokanee, large and small-mouth bass, blue gills and crappies. From here, enjoy all the sites southwestern Colorado has to offer — Mesa Verde National Park, the Anasazi Heritage Center, and the San Juan Scenic Byway.

Location: Across from the McPhee Reservoir, take Highway 184 and exit at mile-post 4.

Total RV sites: 28	Pull thru sites: 11	Open: All Year
Full hookup sites: 28	45+ foot long sites: 28	Dan Cline, Owner
Water & elec. sites: 0	Slideout sites: 28	24990 Hwy 184 W #10
Elec. only sites: 0	Licenses sold: None	Dolores, Colorado 81323
50 amp sites: 14	LP Gas: None	970/882-4901
Hookup sites open in Fall: 28	Credit Cards: None	
Winter hookup sites: 10	Elevation: 6800	
RV site cost: $–$$		

Within 15 minutes:

At RV Park:

Outpost Motel & RV Park

Breathe in cool mountain air at the Outpost campground along the sparkling Dolores River. Surrounded by tall shade trees, all sites are full hookups (20 and 30 amps) with TV hookup. Phone hookups are available. Relax on the grassy lawn during your barbecue picnic.

Fish right from Outpost's spacious deck overlooking the Dolores River. Or try for some of the best bass and trout in Colorado at McPhee Reservoir. If fishing isn't your game, try water skiing, boating, sailing or jet skiing on the reservoir. In the surrounding national forest you can hike, hunt and four-wheel drive. For those who like to get wet, try a river rafting trip or inner tubing down the Dolores. After a day of Colorado fun, guests can sit on the deck overlooking the Dolores River. The restaurants in town are walking distance away.

Rustic, cozy cabins, motel rooms with kitchens and seasonal rentals are available.

Location: In Dolores, 10 miles North of Cortez on Highway 145 or from Durango, go West on US Highway 160, then Northwest on Highway 184.

Total RV sites: 14	Pull thru sites: 0	Open: All Year
Full hookup sites: 14	45+ foot long sites: 14	Ray & Darlene LeBlanc, Owners
Water & elec. sites: 0	Slideout sites: 5	1800 Hwy 145
Elec. only sites: 0	Licenses sold: None	PO Box 295
50 amp sites: 0	LP Gas: None	Dolores, Colorado 81323-0295
Hookup sites open in Fall: 14	Credit Cards: VMAD	970/882-7271
Winter hookup sites: 14	Elevation: 6900	800/382-4892
RV site cost: Not available		970/882-7194 Fax

Within 15 minutes:

At RV Park:

Priest Gulch Campground & RV Park

Stay in an idyllic, 10-acre setting in the lovely Dolores River valley for a beautiful getaway. The wooded and open sites are large and level with full hookups (20, 30 and 50 amps). Bordered by national forest, tall spruce, ponderosa pines and aspen trees landscape the campground. The Dolores River runs through it.

A well-stocked camp and gift store and game room are on-site. If you feel chilly or have a hankering to roast marshmallows, ask for free firewood. Local activities include trout fishing, elk hunting, and hiking in the 14,000-foot peaks of the San Juan National Forest. Horseback riding is nearby and your horse is welcomed near Priest Gulch. Explore four-wheel drive roads or pan for gold — your hosts will even lend you a gold pan to try your luck! Be sure to photograph the kaleidoscope of autumn colors during the spectacular fall months. Priest Gulch is on the San Juan Scenic Byway which covers 236 miles of paved highway. From your vehicle, experience the amazing diversity of the area, including rivers, mountains, valleys, desert plateaus, rolling vistas, wildlife, and ancient ruins of Indian country.

This is a destination park. Advance reservations are recommended in the summer. Deluxe cabins and an indoor, group meeting area are also available.

Location: Located 35 miles Northeast of Cortez on Highway 145 between mileposts 35 and 36.

Total RV sites: 71	Pull thru sites: 17	Open: 4/15 to 11/15
Full hookup sites: 63	45+ foot long sites: 60	Ernie & Margaret Allsup, Owners
Water & elec. sites: 8	Slideout sites: 65	26750 Hwy 145
Elec. only sites: 0	Licenses sold: Fish & Hunt	Dolores, Colorado 81323
50 amp sites: 5	LP Gas: metered	970/562-3810
Hookup sites open in Fall: 71	Credit Cards: VM	
Winter hookup sites: 0	Elevation: 8100	
RV site cost: ¢–$		

Within 15 minutes:

At RV Park:

Stoner Creek RV Park, Cafe & Store

Relax and enjoy the mountain grandeur on this quiet 5 ½-acre site, lush with tall pines in the heart of the Dolores River valley. Shaded and open sites with full hookups are available. Nestled at the mouth of Stoner Canyon, this campground is on the San Juan Scenic Byway.

A store and gift shop are among Stoner Creek's amenities. The cafe serves home-cooked breakfast, lunch and dinner. Basketball, volleyball and horseshoes will make the sports-oriented camper happy. Fish the Dolores River, McPhee Reservoir and miles of nearby mountain streams, or hunt deer and elk in the wooded areas. The hiking in the picturesque San Juan National Forest is memorable. At the end of the day, gather around the nightly campfire and share tall tales of your adventures.

Ask about the housekeeping cabins and mobile homes for rent and the indoor, group meeting area for reunions.

Location: On Highway 145, 25 ½ miles Northeast of Cortez.

Total RV sites: 34	Pull thru sites: 0	Open: 5/16 to 10/20
Full hookup sites: 30	45+ foot long sites: 30	Tura & Pete Peterson, Owners
Water & elec. sites: 0	Slideout sites: 28	25113 Hwy 145
Elec. only sites: 0	Licenses sold: None	Dolores, Colorado 81323
50 amp sites: 0	LP Gas: metered	970/882-2204
Hookup sites open in Fall: 30	Credit Cards: VM	
Winter hookup sites: 0	Elevation: 7500	
RV site cost: Not available		

Within 15 minutes:

At RV Park:

Durango & Vallecito Lake

Includes Bayfield. Also see Mesa Verde Area. Map: P-5

A city created by the railroad, Durango retains a Frontier West feeling. Surrounded by the San Juan Mountains, this town bustles with activity. Take a walk through living history down Main Street, Durango's National Register Historic District. The famous Durango-Silverton Narrow Gauge Railroad is the country's only coal and-steam-powered train operating daily. Chug along sheer cliffs, criss-crossing the Animas River on the 45 mile trip to Silverton. The Animas River, or River of Lost Souls, has wild whitewater rafting during spring run-off and settles down in the summer for family jaunts. Rent a bike for a day and discover why this area is so popular with mountain bikers. Fish for rainbow, kokanee, German brown trout and northern pike at Vallecito Lake 23 miles northeast. Only 6 miles north is the Trimble Hot Springs where heated water from the La Plata Mountains arrives at the resort at a toasty 119° F. Set amidst reddish, sandstone bluffs, Durango is 25 miles north of Purgatory Ski Resort which offers the unpretentious skiing of the southwest.

Fun Things to Do

- Animas Ranger District (970) 247-4874
- Animas School Museum (970) 259-2402
- Bar D Chuckwagon Suppers (970) 247-5753
- Durango Area Chamber Resort Association (800) GO-DURANGO
- Durango National Historic Districts (970) 247-0312
- Durango-Silverton Narrow Gauge Railroad (970) 247-2733
- Five Branches Boat Rentals (800) 582-9580, (970) 884-2582
- Hillcrest Golf Course (970) 247-1499
- Mesa Verde National Park (970) 529-4421
- Mountain Waters Rafting (800) 748-2507, (970) 259-4191
- Old Hundred Gold Mine Tour (800) 872-3009
- Tamarron Golf Course (970) 259-2000

Alpen-Rose RV Park

A friendly, family place in the scenic Animas Valley with good gravel interior roads, the park has a grassy picnic area with barbecue grills near the pool. All sites are large, full hookups (30 and 50 amps) with free cable TV hookup. Many of the shady sites are 50-foot pull thrus. The Alpen-Rose offers complete camping comfort.

Swim in the heated pool, play in the arcade or relax in the lounge. The stocked trout pond requires no license for fishing. The store has limited groceries and ice. Play basketball, volleyball, horseshoes, or croquet on-site. Ask about the VCR movie rentals. There's a separate pet area to exercise your dog. Four-wheel drive tours, mountain bike trails and horseback rides are nearby. Or just sit under the ample shade trees and watch the clouds go by.

Tipi lodges, daily and monthly rates are available.

Location: Two miles North of Durango on US Highway 550 near milepost 27.

Total RV sites: 100	RV site cost: $	Open: 4/15 to 10/15
Full hookup sites: 100	Pull thru sites: 70	Jim & Shari Dale, Owners
Water & elec. sites: 10	45+ foot long sites: 70	27847 US Highway 550 N
Elec. only sites: 0	Slideout sites: 100	Durango, Colorado 81301
50 amp sites: 17	Licenses sold: None	970/247-5540
Hookup sites open in Fall: 110	LP Gas: None	
Winter hookup sites: 0	Credit Cards: VMAD	
	Elevation: 6700	

Within 15 minutes:

At RV Park:

Blue Spruce RV Park & Campground

Nestled under tall spruce and pine trees, Blue Spruce RV Park borders the national forest northeast of Durango at Vallecito Lake. Pick among the numerous full hookup (50 amp) RV sites. The shaded, RV sites have campfire pits, patios and phone hookup is available. Several sites are pull thrus, with room for slideouts and have more than 45 feet of space for your comfort. Hot showers, clean restrooms and laundry are also available. The roads to the park are gravel.

Amenities include a country store on-site, an ice cream parlor and full cafe. Spend your days hiking and four-wheel driving in this lovely part of Colorado. Fish on the stream or the close by lake. Use the meeting room/recreation hall for family reunions. Winter activities include cross-country skiing on-site, sleigh rides, snowmobiling and hunting nearby.

Tent sites, motel rooms with kitchens and trailer rentals are also available. Daily, weekly, monthly and seasonal rates are available.

Location: 25 miles Northeast of Durango at Vallecito Lake. From Highway 160 take Vallecito Lake Exit in Bayfield, on County Road 500.

Total RV sites: 125	Pull thru sites: 20	Open: 5/1 to 10/1
Full hookup sites: 125	45+ foot long sites: 16	Bill & Bic Eudy, Owners
Water & elec. sites: 0	Slideout sites: 25	1875 County Rd 500
Elec. only sites: 0	Licenses sold: None	Bayfield, Colorado 81122
50 amp sites: 125	LP Gas: W	970/884-2641
Hookup sites open in Fall: 4	Credit Cards: None	
Winter hookup sites: 0	Elevation: 7800	
RV site cost: $		

Within 15 minutes:

At RV Park:

Butch's Beach RV Park

Butch's Beach RV Park is on a scenic location with a small "beach" along Lightner Creek. All the large, level and open sites have electricity (20 and 30 amps), pull thrus and are adjacent to the creek. A 1,000 feet of creek frontage and small sandy beach is yours for the taking. A laundry and clean restrooms with hot showers are also available.

Butch's is close to downtown Durango and the Durango/Silverton Narrow Gauge Railroad. Nearby you can whitewater raft, horseback ride, mountain bike, hike, hunt and golf. Stream fishing on Lightner Creek could yield delicious rainbow trout.   Horseshoes and   volleyball are on the playground.

Location: 1.7 miles West of Durango, on Highway 160.

Total RV sites: 20	Pull thru sites: 20	Open: 5/1 to 11/1
Full hookup sites: 0	45+ foot long sites: 20	Butch Keller & Joe Wilson, Owners
Water & elec. sites: 10	Slideout sites: 20	20310 Hwy 160 W
Elec. only sites: 10	Licenses sold: None	Durango, Colorado 81301
50 amp sites: 0	LP Gas: None	970/247-3404
Hookup sites open in Fall: 20	Credit Cards: None	
Winter hookup sites: 0	Elevation: 6500	
RV site cost: ¢–$		

Within 15 minutes:

At RV Park:

Cottonwood Camper Park

The closest RV park to downtown Durango, Cottonwood Camper Park is within walking distance of the Durango/Silverton Narrow Gauge Railroad and shopping district. The open and shaded sites on Lightner Creek have gravel pad. Some are pull thru. All are full hookups (20, 30 and some  50 amps) with picnic tables. The roads are gravel and easy to drive. This is a "plain jane" overnight RV park for those who want to save money and walk to town.

You'll be able to fish nearby on the Animas River for a dinner of fresh rainbow trout. Mountain biking, horseback riding and whitewater rafting are among the area's outdoor attractions.

Location: On US Highway 160, 1/3 miles West of US Highway 550.

Total RV sites: 73	Pull thru sites: 2	Open: All Year
Full hookup sites: 73	45+ foot long sites: 12	Robert A. Johnson, Sr., Owner
Water & elec. sites: 0	Slideout sites: 12	21636 US Highway 160
Elec. only sites: 0	Licenses sold: None	Durango, Colorado 81301
50 amp sites: 5	LP Gas: None	970/247-1977
Hookup sites open in Fall: 73	Credit Cards: None	
Winter hookup sites: 5	Elevation: 7000	
RV site cost: Not available		

Within 15 minutes:

At RV Park:

Durango East KOA™

The closest KOA to Durango, these sites are in a rolling, semi-wooded area high on the Mesa with panoramic views. Most open and shady sites have electricity (20 and 30 amps) and some have free cable TV hookups. All sites have picnic tables and grills. Large, pull thrus are available. The abundant piñon pines provide shade and the distinct aroma of southwestern Colorado.

You'll love the daily feast of delicious pancake breakfasts served between Memorial Day and Labor Day. Soak in the heated swimming pool before watching a free nightly movie. Enjoy ice cream socials throughout the summer. Take advantage of the miniature golf course and the video game room. The camp store has souvenirs, snacks and groceries. Exercise your pet on the dog walk that follows the creek running through the campground. Some popular area attractions are the Durango & Silverton Narrow Gauge Railroad, Mesa Verde National Park, Vallecito Lake, Durango Pro Rodeo, the Million Dollar Highway and Trimble Hot Springs. Of course, you can always explore the terrain on a mountain bike or on horseback. Whitewater raft on the Animas River.

Ask about the Camper Cabins and the outdoor pavilion for group meetings.

Location: East of US Highway 550 on Highway 160 at milepost 91.

Total RV sites: 88
Full hookup sites: 39
Water & elec. sites: 28
Elec. only sites: 0
50 amp sites: 0
Hookup sites open in Fall: 67
Winter hookup sites: 0
RV site cost: $

Pull thru sites: 27
45+ foot long sites: 25
Slideout sites: 25
Licenses sold: None
LP Gas: None
Credit Cards: VMD
Elevation: 7000

Open: 4/15 to 10/15
Jay & Carol Coates, Owners
30090 US Hwy 160
Durango, Colorado 81301-8289
970/247-0783

Within 15 minutes:

At RV Park:

Durango North Ponderosa KOA

Next to the Animas River in the majestic mountains, amid lush oak trees and towering ponderosa pines, this is a vacation paradise. A majority of the sites have electricity (20 and 30 amp), water and TV hookup. A family campground, Durango North has scenic open and shaded sites with

campfire pits along the river. Summers here boast pleasantly warm days and cool nights. Fall brings dazzling autumn colors to the mountain foliage and nights range from cool to cold.

On-site facilities include a large recreation hall with video games, a playground and a heated swimming pool. The large, open air Ponderosa Cafe serves big breakfasts, lunch and tasty dinners. After your evening meal, enjoy the free, nightly movie. Fish right on the property in the stocked pond or try your line in the tumbling Animas River. The cafe will even cook up your trout for an unforgettable, fresh dinner! Horseback riding tours are adjacent to the campground. Local activities include four-wheel driving, mountain biking, and hiking. The more daring should check out the thrilling alpine slide nearby. Take advantage of the free bus to the Durango/Silverton Narrow Gauge Train Depot.

Camper cabins are also available.

Location: Ten miles North of Durango on US Highway 550, exit County Road 250.

Total RV sites: 140
Full hookup sites: 41
Water & elec. sites: 68
Elec. only sites: 17
50 amp sites: 0
Hookup sites open in Fall: 126
Winter hookup sites: 0

RV site cost: $–$$
Pull thru sites: 49
45+ foot long sites: 45
Slideout sites: 30
Licenses sold: Fish & Hunt
LP Gas: metered
Credit Cards: VMAD
Elevation: 7000

Open: 5/1 to 10/15
John & Adeline Harvey, Owners
13391 CR 250
Durango, Colorado 81301-8687
970/247-4499

Within 15 minutes:

At RV Park:

Five Branches Camper Park

Snug among 20 acres of tall pine trees, the campground is on the picturesque Vallecito Lake and the roaring Pine River. Across the covered, wooden bridge, you'll find full hookup sites in the shade with grass surroundings and a view of clear blue water backed by snow-capped peaks.

Take a breakfast horseback ride into the San Juan Mountains or an evening lake cruise as the setting sun casts colorful images onto the rippling water. Guest horses are welcomed here. Four-wheel drive tours and mountain bike trails start at Five Branches. There's plenty of river and lake fishing for avid anglers and you can rent a pontoon or motor boat from the park. Side trips to Silverton and Ouray are great for those who like to explore. A video game room and playground will keep the kids busy. The camp store has groceries and snacks for last minute shopping. Planned activities include bingo, horseshoes, volleyball, movies and potluck suppers.

An outdoor, group meeting area is available.

Location: On Vallecito Lake, 25 miles East of Durango off Highway 160 or 20 miles North of Bayfield on County Road 501-A.

Total RV sites: 95	Pull thru sites: 2	Open: 5/1 to 10/1
Full hookup sites: 95	45+ foot long sites: 2	Robert & Kay Binckes, Owners
Water & elec. sites: 2	Slideout sites: 70	4677 County Rd 501-A
Elec. only sites: 0	Licenses sold: Fish & Hunt	Bayfield, Colorado 81122-9701
50 amp sites: 0	LP Gas: weight	970/884-2582
Hookup sites open in Fall: 96	Credit Cards: VM	800/582-9580
Winter hookup sites: 0	Elevation: 7650	
RV site cost: $		

Within 15 minutes:

At RV Park:

Hermosa Meadows Camper Park

Hermosa Meadows offers shaded, grassy sites along the Animas River with red mountains for a backdrop. The full hookup, level sites have 20, 30 and 50 amps and TV hookup is available. Many sites are pull thrus and have campfire pits. The 50-acre park has a secluded, spacious feeling and sits next to

1,270 feet of river frontage. The meadows are flourishing with tall, shady, cottonwood trees. If you look very closely, you just might glimpse the rare native Colorado orchids which have been seen here.

Toss a line into the no-license needed, stocked trout fishing pond in the park or fish in the Animas River (license required). The video game room and playground with basketball, badminton, horseshoes and volleyball, will please kids of all ages. Rent a bike and explore the numerous mountain trails. Try the free hay wagon ride which leaves every morning to meet the narrow gauge train when it passes Hermosa Meadows' crossing near the highway. Golf, hot springs and other tourist attractions are nearby.

A pavilion for group meetings is provided. Groups and family reunions are welcomed.

Location: On US Highway 550, 7 miles North of Durango, near milepost 31, ½ miles East on Hermosa Meadows Road.

Total RV sites: 90	Pull thru sites: 28	Open: All Year
Full hookup sites: 59	45+ foot long sites: 40	Mike & Janet Francis, Owners
Water & elec. sites: 14	Slideout sites: 75	31420 Hwy 550 #24
Elec. only sites: 17	Licenses sold: None	Durango, Colorado 81301-6879
50 amp sites: 12	LP Gas: metered	970/247-3055
Hookup sites open in Fall: 90	Credit Cards: VMD	800/748-2853
Winter hookup sites: 30	Elevation: 6600	
RV site cost: ¢–$		

Within 15 minutes:

At RV Park:

Lightner Creek Campground

This 27-acre family resort sits beside a clear mountain stream. Exactly 1 ½ miles north of US Highway 160, you'll find abundant peace and quiet here. Many of the shaded and open, level sites are pull thrus with full hookups (20 and 30 amps), picnic tables and campfire pits. At night, fall asleep to the gentle, bubbling flow of Lightner Creek which winds through the campground.

Lightner Creek Campground features a heated swimming pool, a playground with a basketball court, horseshoes, dust-free paved roads, a video game room and a grocery store. Situated only minutes from the Durango/Silverton Narrow Gauge Railroad and downtown, this is an excellent base camp to the area's numerous attractions. Visit the Aztec Ruins National Monument, the San Juan Scenic Byway, and numerous hiking and biking trails.

Camper cabins and an outdoor, group meeting area are also available.

Location: Take Highway 160 West of Durango 3 ½ miles to Lightner Creek Road (CR 207) then North 1 ½ miles.

Total RV sites: 58	Pull thru sites: 17	Open: 5/1 to 9/30
Full hookup sites: 32	45+ foot long sites: 30	Joe & Cheryl Amorelli, Owners
Water & elec. sites: 26	Slideout sites: 30	1567 County Rd 207
Elec. only sites: 0	Licenses sold: None	Durango, Colorado 81301
50 amp sites: 0	LP Gas: weight	970/247-5406
Hookup sites open in Fall: 58	Credit Cards: VM	
Winter hookup sites: 0	Elevation: 7200	
RV site cost: $		

Within 15 minutes:

At RV Park:

Riverside RV Park

Between Durango and Pagosa Springs, in the beautiful Pine River Valley, Riverside RV Park has large, pull thru, full hookup (20 and 30 amps) sites among cottonwood trees. The free cable TV hookup offers 20 channels. The large, open, grassy and shaded sites sit on the Los Piños River with picnic tables and barbecue grills.

This park caters to and offers special monthly rates for senior citizens.

Fish steps away from your site on the sparkling Riverside Creek or Rainbow Pond. From here, it's a short drive to Salmon and Aztec Indian ruins, Vallecito, Lemon and Navajo Lakes and historic Durango. Come for the big game hunting in the fall. Nearby, friendly Bayfield has all the conveniences needed, including restaurants and shops.

Daily, weekly and monthly rates are available.

Location: North of Bayfield on Highway 160 at milepost 107, 18 miles East of Durango and 54 miles West of Pagosa Springs.

Total RV sites: 80	Pull thru sites: 60	Open: 4/1 to 10/31
Full hookup sites: 66	45+ foot long sites: 60	Al & Brenda Sullivan, Owners
Water & elec. sites: 13	Slideout sites: 80	41743 US Highway 160
Elec. only sites: 0	Licenses sold: None	PO Box 919
50 amp sites: 0	LP Gas: None	Bayfield, Colorado 81122-0919
Hookup sites open in Fall: 80	Credit Cards: None	970/884-2475
Winter hookup sites: 0	Elevation: 6900	
RV site cost: ¢–$		

Within 15 minutes:

At RV Park:

United Campground of Durango

A deluxe campground, located on the north edge of Durango, the United Campground has the famous Durango/Silverton Narrow Gauge train huffing and puffing right through it! This is an ideal place to observe and photograph the historic train. The rolling, terraced campground has shaded sites near the scenic Los Animas River. Many of the level sites are grassy, full hookups (20, 30 and 50 amps) and pull thru with free cable TV hookups. The campground is on 78 acres of mountain meadows, a golden opportunity to reacquaint you with fresh air and Mother Nature.

A convenience store with groceries, gifts, and RV supplies and a laundromat are on-site. Other amenities include a recreation room with video games, a heated swimming pool, and horseshoe pits. Fishing on the Los Animas River is great. Hiking trails abound. Bring your horse along or rent one nearby. Four-wheel drive tours, mountain bike trails and whitewater raft trips are only minutes away. Purgatory Ski Area has a thrilling alpine slide during the summer. The putting and chipping greens planned for 1995 will satisfy every golf fan.

Group camping sites are available.

Location: North of Durango on US Highway 550 near milepost 25 ½ on Animas Drive.

Total RV sites: 103	RV site cost: $–$$	Open: 4/1 to 10/31
Full hookup sites: 77	Pull thru sites: 42	Tim & Sherry Holt, Owners
Water & elec. sites: 24	45+ foot long sites: 41	1322 Animas View Dr.
Elec. only sites: 0	Slideout sites: 41	Durango, Colorado 81301
50 amp sites: 41	Licenses sold: None	970/247-3853
Hookup sites open in Fall: 103	LP Gas: None	
Winter hookup sites: 0	Credit Cards: VM	
	Elevation: 6512	

Within 15 minutes:

At RV Park:

Vallecito Resort RV Park & Cabins

There's something for everyone in the cool pines of Vallecito Resort. The RV sites are all full hookups. The grassy, shaded sites nestled in tall ponderosa pine trees are quiet and restful.

You'll find everything you need here, from a beauty salon, grocery store and playground to a recreation hall, card room, library and craft room. Bring your square dance attire for the exciting evening dances: square (plus-C3), round (all phases), line and country swing. Vallecito Resort boasts national square dance and round dance callers. Weekly activities at the resort include Sunday church services, potlucks, poker, aerobics and bonfires. Fish for state-record trout in the Pine River or take a short drive to Vallecito and Lemon lakes.

Cabins of all sizes, an indoor and an outdoor group meeting area are also available. Ask about off-season special rates.

Location: North of Bayfield on County Road 501, south of Vallecito Lake.

Total RV sites: 200	RV site cost: ¢	Open: 5/1 to 10/5
Full hookup sites: 210	Pull thru sites: 5	Rex & Jeannie Hornbaker, Owners
Water & elec. sites: 0	45+ foot long sites: 25	13030 CR 501
Elec. only sites: 0	Slideout sites: 75	Bayfield, Colorado 81122
50 amp sites: 0	Licenses sold: Fishing	970/884-9458
Hookup sites open in Fall: 210	LP Gas: weight	800/258-9458
Winter hookup sites: 0	Credit Cards: None	
	Elevation: 7600	

Within 15 minutes:

At RV Park:

Estes Park

Includes Drake. Map: C-14

Longs Peak, at a dizzying 14, 255 feet, towers over this picturesque mountain town. The gate to Rocky Mountain National Park, Estes Park, at 7,522 feet, started when Joel Estes and his family moved to the valley in 1859. After a particularly harsh winter, Estes sold out for $50 or a yoke of oxen (no one is sure which). The public soon learned about the high mountain valley surrounded by snow capped peaks when a journalist wrote about scaling Longs Peak. Crowds made their way here to visit the park and stay at the famous Stanley Hotel, build in 1909. Rocky Mountain National Park has 415 glacially-carved square miles covered with lakes, wildlife and wild flowers. Trail Ridge Road, the highest continuous paved road in the United States, traverses the park and crosses the Continental Divide. From Estes Park, you can drive through the Big Thompson Canyon east to Loveland or tour the Peak-to-Peak Scenic Highway which travels 55 miles to Central City through Arapaho and Roosevelt National Forests. In town, stroll along the streets, sampling the numerous candy stores and craft shops, play golf, horseback ride or sail.

Fun Things to Do

- Aerial Tramway (970) 586-3675
- Barleen Family Country Music Dinner Theatre Summer: (800) 586-5741, (970) 586-5749
- Dick's Rock Museum (970)586-4180
- Enos Mills Cabin (970) 586-4706
- Estes Park Area Historical Museum (970) 586-6256
- Estes Park Golf Course (970) 586-8146, (970) 586-8176
- Lyons Redstone Museum (303) 823-6692
- MacGregor Ranch (970) 586-3749
- Moraine Park Visitor Center (970) 586-3777
- Rock'N River Trout Pond Fishing (800) 448-4611
- Rocky Mountain National Park (970) 586-2371

7 Pines Campground & Cabins

Located in the spectacular Big Thompson Canyon, 7 Pines' RV sites all border the churning whitewaters of the snow-fed Big Thompson River. Rest in the shade trees by each site. During the cool evenings, roast marshmallows over your campfire and enjoy the solitude of the Rocky Mountains. All sites are full hookups with gravel pads and picnic tables. Modern, clean restrooms and hot showers are provided. A small, cozy campground, it's perfect for a private getaway.

The campground is close to lakes, streams, hiking trails, fine restaurants, downtown Estes Park — you name it. Challenge your family to a game of horseshoes on the playground. Anglers can fish on the river from the campground. Horseback riding stables are nearby.

Cabins with fireplaces and seasonal rates are also available.

Location: In Big Thompson Canyon, 7 miles East of Estes Park on US Highway 34 near milepost 70 ½.

Total RV sites: 23	Pull thru sites: 0	Open: 5/15 to 9/18
Full hookup sites: 23	45+ foot long sites: 0	Doug & Marty Walker, Managers
Water & elec. sites: 0	Slideout sites: 8	2137 Big Thompson Canyon
Elec. only sites: 0	Licenses sold: None	Drake, Colorado 80515
50 amp sites: 0	LP Gas: None	970/586-3809
Hookup sites open in Fall: 23	Credit Cards: None	
Winter hookup sites: 0	Elevation: 7300	
RV site cost: $		

Within 15 minutes:

At RV Park:

Manor RV Park & Motel

Camp with unspoiled mountain views encircling your site. All sites are full hookups (30 amps) with cable TV hookup. The landscaped, grassy sites with paved pads are along the Big Thompson River in this activity-oriented campground. Each site has a picnic table and concrete patio to make your barbecue dinners easy to prepare and comfortable to enjoy. Lush green grass and unforgettable mountain vistas are plentiful.

The pavilion and club house are great for group potlucks. On-site activities include shuffleboard, bingo, bridge and horseshoes. Fishing the mighty Big Thompson for the BIG one is a challenge not to be missed. Take a trolley shuttle to Estes Park where you can golf, bowl, boat, square dance, four-wheel drive or loaf. Quaint hobby shops line the streets of the Bavarian-style town and the majestic Rocky Mountains are a nature lover's paradise.

Ask about the motel rooms in the log house and RV storage. Weekly, monthly and seasonal discounts are available.

Location: In Estes Park take Highway 36, turn South on Crags Drive and West on Riverside Drive.

Total RV sites: 110	RV site cost: $	Open: 5/7 to 9/30
Full hookup sites: 110	Pull thru sites: 10	Creighton & Marianne Lake, Owners
Water & elec. sites: 0	45+ foot long sites: 20	815 E Riverside Dr.
Elec. only sites: 0	Slideout sites: 80	Moraine Rt
50 amp sites: 0	Licenses sold: None	Estes Park, Colorado 80517-9801
Hookup sites open in Fall: 110	LP Gas: weight	970/586-3251
Winter hookup sites: 0	Credit Cards: None	
	Elevation: 7800	

Within 15 minutes:

At RV Park:

Mary's Lake Campground

At Mary's Lake, you'll find spacious sites with panoramic views. Across from a cool, clear mountain lake, this campground has open and shaded sites. Most sites are full hookups (20, 30 and 50 amps) with cable TV hookups; all have campfire pits and picnic tables. You'll have fantastic views of rugged peaks that seem just beyond your finger tips.

At the camp store pick up your fishing license, tackle and bait before crossing the road to cast your line into Mary's Lake. The store also carries groceries, firewood, camping and RV supplies. Families will like the horseshoe pits, basketball court, playground and video game room. A convenient trolley service shuttles you to and from Estes Park. After shopping in town or traversing Rocky Mountain National Park, relax in the heated swimming pool. Close to it all and fun for everyone, Mary's Lake Campground remains a quiet vacation, high in the breath-taking Colorado Rockies. Visit in September and watch and listen to the elk bugling in their mating rituals.

Location: In Estes Park take Highway 36 to Mary's Lake Road or Highway 7 to Peak View Drive to Mary's Lake Road.

Total RV sites: 110	Pull thru sites: 10	Open: 5/12 to 9/30
Full hookup sites: 60	45+ foot long sites: 20	Doug & Lois Bailard, Owners
Water & elec. sites: 30	Slideout sites: 90	2120 Mary's Lake Rd.
Elec. only sites: 0	Licenses sold: Fishing	PO Box 2514
50 amp sites: 36	LP Gas: weight	Estes Park, Colorado 80517-2514
Hookup sites open in Fall: 90	Credit Cards: VMD	970/586-4411
Winter hookup sites: 0	Elevation: 8000	800/445-MARY (6279)
RV site cost: Not available		

Within 15 minutes:

At RV Park:

National Park Resort Campground & Cabins

Located next to the Fall River entrance to Rocky Mountain National Park, this rustic campground is on a sheltered, tree-filled mountainside. The level sites among the ponderosa pines and aspen trees on the gently sloping hillside are full hookups (15, 20 and 30 amps) with TV hookup, fire pits and barbecue grills. A delightful climate provides warm, sunny days and cool evenings. The pine-scented air, blue skies and grand views all make this a uniquely Colorado vacation.

Across the highway is a grocery store, gift shop, livery stable, laundry and train. Bordering the national park, the campground has hiking trails, fishing, and climbing nearby. Check out the nature walks, films and evening campfires in Rocky Mountain National Park. Estes Park boasts golf courses, sail boats, chuckwagon suppers and other entertainment. And, of course, you'll always have the mountain splendor to sit back and contemplate.

Cabins and motel rooms are also available. Advance reservations are required.

Location: Exit US Highway 34 at milepost 58. Located next to the Fall River entrance to Rocky Mountain National Park,.

Total RV sites: 35
Full hookup sites: 22
Water & elec. sites: 68
Elec. only sites: 0
50 amp sites: 0
Hookup sites open in Fall: 90
Winter hookup sites: 0
RV site cost: $

Pull thru sites: 0
45+ foot long sites: 0
Slideout sites: 35
Licenses sold: None
LP Gas: None
Credit Cards: VMD
Elevation: 8300

Open: 5/1 to 10/1
Dan & Becky Ludlam, Owners
3501 Fall River Rd MR
Estes Park, Colorado 80517-9801
970/586-4563

Within 15 minutes:

At RV Park:

Paradise RV & Travel Park

Paradise RV Park is an adult-oriented RV park close to the YMCA. Camp under huge ponderosa pines along the bubbling Big Thompson River. The shaded, grassy sites are full hookups (20 and 30 amps) with picnic tables. Those camped along the river can fish right from their site. The entrance is a sloping driveway.

Paradise is close to restaurants and shopping. Only one mile away is the entrance to Rocky Mountain National Park which abounds in scenic hikes and drives, mountain ranges, nature talks and a fascinating museum. Two 18-hole golf courses are within 15 minutes of this small campground. Paradise is a quiet, secure, restful base for your mountain vacation.

Ask about the daily, monthly, seasonal and off-season rates.

Location: Two miles West of Estes Park, take US Highway 36 to Highway 66 and go ½ mile South.

Total RV sites: 30	Pull thru sites: 0	Open: 5/1 to 9/30
Full hookup sites: 30	45+ foot long sites: 0	Nedra Pate, Owner
Water & elec. sites: 0	Slideout sites: 4	1836 Moraine Rt
Elec. only sites: 0	Licenses sold: None	Estes Park, Colorado 80517-9801
50 amp sites: 0	LP Gas: None	970/586-5513
Hookup sites open in Fall: 30	Credit Cards: None	
Winter hookup sites: 0	Elevation: 7500	
RV site cost: Not available		

Within 15 minutes:

At RV Park:

Park Place Camping Resort

Welcome to the serenity of the Rocky Mountains. Here you'll find 35 wooded acres of hillside campsites secluded within the confines of Roosevelt National Forest. Many sites are full hookups (20 and 30 amps) with picnic tables, barbecue grills and campfire pits. The secluded sites are shaded by tall ponderosa pines whose scent fills the crisp mountain air. Wild roses, friendly chipmunks, singing birds and loitering wildlife enhance the friendly atmosphere and add to the beauty of the Meadowdale Valley.

Peaceful and convenient, Park Place is near both Rocky Mountain National Park and Estes Park for wilderness and civilized vacation activities. Explore trails in the adjacent Roosevelt National Forest by hiking, biking or horseback riding. Play a game of basketball, have fun in the video arcade or challenge your family to horseshoes, volleyball or badminton. To relax, swim in the heated pool and sunbathe on the large deck.

An outdoor, group meeting area, and rental cabins are also available.

Location: From the junction of US Highways 34 and 36, go 5 ½ miles Southeast on US Highway 36.

Total RV sites: 91
Full hookup sites: 41
Water & elec. sites: 50
Elec. only sites: 0
50 amp sites: 0
Hookup sites open in Fall: 0
Winter hookup sites: 0
RV site cost: $

Pull thru sites: 0
45+ foot long sites:
Slideout sites: 20
Licenses sold: None
LP Gas: None
Credit Cards: VMD
Elevation: 7800

Open: 5/1 to 9/30
Tony & Kathy Palmeri, Owners
5495 N St. Vrain
PO Box 4608
Estes Park, Colorado 80517-4608
970/586-4230
800/722-2928

Within 15 minutes:

At RV Park:

Spruce Lake RV Park

A fine, family campground with great mountain views, Spruce Lake has spacious, full hookup 30 amp sites with picnic tables. The large, level, grassy sites surround a private, deep blue lake. The campground also borders the Big Thompson River so you're surrounded by fresh, rushing, snow-fed water. Cable TV hookup and group RV sites are available.

You'll find everything you need at the fully equipped camp store. On-site activities include a video game room, playground, free miniature golf, horseshoes, and a heated swimming pool. Take a walk along the green areas next to the river at sunset. Your hosts will arrange group activities like horseback riding, hiking trips and local tours. Potlucks, bingo games and ice cream socials bring campers together as well. Anglers will enjoy having both a stocked lake and river fishing right out their back door. A big fire ring and barbecue shelter is ideal for group outings.

Location: Travel 1 ½ miles West of Estes Park on Highway 36, turn at the stoplight on Mary's Lake Road, then 1 block South.

Total RV sites: 110
Full hookup sites: 87
Water & elec. sites: 23
Elec. only sites: 0
50 amp sites: 0
Hookup sites open in Fall: 110
Winter hookup sites: 24

RV site cost: $
Pull thru sites: 1
45+ foot long sites: 6
Slideout sites: 110
Licenses sold: None
LP Gas: metered
Credit Cards: VM
Elevation: 7600

Open: 3/1 to 11/1
Ron & Charlotte Robinson, Owners
1050 Mary's Lake Rd
PO Box 2497
Estes Park, Colorado 80517-2497
970/586-2889

Within 15 minutes:

At RV Park:

Fairplay

Map: F-13.

The Park county seat, tiny Fairplay is nestled on the east side of the Continental Divide and was once a major setting during the gold fever days of the 1860s. That history is kept alive by the South Park City Museum, a careful restoration of life here at the height of the Gold Rush. Discover how the pioneers and prospectors lived, worked and played at this outdoor museum of 32 authentic buildings and wide variety of artifacts. The Old Courthouse, still in use, is one of the oldest in the United States. Prior to gold, the Fairplay area was known for its salt; early French trappers called it "Bayou Salado" ("Salt Creek"). Today adventure abounds, via hiking, mountain climbing, camping, Gold Medal fishing, gold panning, road or mountain biking, cross-country skiing, snowmobiling, horseback riding and hunting. South Park is a broad valley covering over 900 square miles and is surrounded by the Mosquito and Park ranges. July boasts the World Championship Pack Burro Race. This annual event the last weekend of the month honors the contributions of the lowly burro to the area's mining industry. If you love the great outdoors, you'll love Fairplay year round!

Fun Things To Do

- South Park City Museum (719) 836-2387

Bristlecone RV Park & Motel

On the south end of Fairplay, overlooking the Middle Fork South Platte River, Bristlecone has stunning views of snow-capped peaks. The large, full hookups (30 and 50 amps) sites are either shaded or mostly open. Look for the old stagecoach, a remnant of the Wild West, at the entrance.

You are walking distance from shops, restaurants and the town's museum. Outdoor activities abound in this mountainous area: hiking, fishing, cross-country skiing, four-wheel driving, mountain biking, gold panning, snowmobiling and horseback riding. Guest horses are welcomed to camp with you at Bristlecone which adjoins a motel. Whatever you do, bring your camera along to capture the wilderness' beauty.

Location: On Highway 9 at the South end of Fairplay.

Total RV sites: 39
Full hookup sites: 7
Water & elec. sites: 0
Elec. only sites: 4
50 amp sites: 4
Hookup sites open in Fall: 7
Winter hookup sites: 7
RV site cost: Not available

Pull thru sites: 5
45+ foot long sites: 6
Slideout sites: 39
Licenses sold: None
LP Gas: None
Credit Cards: VMD
Elevation: 9950

Open: All Year
Chuck & Dolores Spencer, Owners
PO Box 149
Fairplay, Colorado 80440
719/836-3278

Within 15 minutes:

At RV Park:

Western Inn Motel & RV Park

On the edge of historic South Park, where mountain ranges of incomparable beauty surround you, is the new Western Inn Motel & RV Park. The level, spacious, gravel sites are full hookups (30 and 50 amps) with picnic tables in the open. Some of the sites have extra large pull thrus for big rigs. Enjoy cool nights and sunny days.

This moderately priced RV park is near a restaurant and store. Ice, morning coffee and meals are within walking distance. It is near some of the finest fishing in Colorado. Whether you come to Fairplay for the cool summers with flower strewn meadows or a winter cross-country skiing trip, you'll find all the comforts at the Western Inn.

Ask about the special winter rates and ski packages. Large motel rooms are also available.

Location: Coming from Denver, it's on Highway 285 at the edge of Fairplay.

Total RV sites: 10	Pull thru sites: 7	Open: All Year
Full hookup sites: 10	45+ foot long sites: 10	Harold & Barbara Bland, Managers
Water & elec. sites: 0	Slideout sites: 10	490 Hwy 285
Elec. only sites: 4	Licenses sold: None	PO Box 187
50 amp sites: 3	LP Gas: None	Fairplay, Colorado 80440-0187
Hookup sites open in Fall: 10	Credit Cards: VMA	719/836-2026
Winter hookup sites: 10	Elevation: 9953	800/613-1976
RV site cost: Not available		

Within 15 minutes:

At RV Park:

Fort Collins and Greeley

See also Poudre River Canyon Area. Map: C-16-18

Despite the name, there is no military fort in Fort Collins and hasn't been since the 1860s. The area is just as peaceful today as it was over 100 years ago and is now home to Colorado State University. The Historic Old Town District is centered around a gracious fountain surrounded by wide sidewalks lined with galleries, specialty stores, cafes and brew pubs. West of the city is Horsetooth Reservoir, a 7-mile lake for fishing, water-skiing, boating and swimming. Close by is the Poudre River Canyon — Colorado's only national Wild and Scenic River.

In 1870 Greeley was founded by Nathan C. Meeker who was agricultural editor for Horace Greeley's New York Tribune. The best museum in this part of the state, the Historic Centennial Village, captures the history of the plains through the reconstruction of 24 buildings from 1860 to 1920. James Michener made Greeley his home while writing the novel Centennial. The fourteenth largest rodeo in the country is the 10-day long Greeley Independence Day Stampede ending on July 4 each year. Seventeen miles south is Fort Vasquez, built in 1835, where the State Historical Society runs a visitors center next to the fort with information and exhibits on the once booming fur trade and the Plains Indians. Nearby is the Pawnee National Grasslands where antelope, coyotes and prairie dogs live.

Fun Things To Do

- Anheuser Busch Brewery (970) 490-4691
- Collindale Golf Course (970) 221-6651
- Boomerang Golf Links (970) 351-8934
- Fort Vasquez (970) 785-2832
- Highland Hills Municipal Golf Course (970) 330-7327
- Historic Centennial Village (970) 350-9229
- Pawnee National Grasslands (970) 353-5004

Blue Spruce Mobile Home Park

Canadian Geese fly directly over Blue Spruce Park on their annual migration. With easy access on and off US Highway 287, this campground is clean, quiet and near the scenic Poudre and Rist canyons. The Big Thompson Canyon is not far off either, putting you in some of the most picturesque, roaring river and jagged mountain territory in Colorado. All the grassy sites are full hookups. The sites are cooled by tall shade trees, willows, evergreens and elms.

Prime trout fishing, trophy hunting, stunning hiking trails and out-of-site four-wheel driving are all nearby. A well groomed park with paved streets, Blue Spruce is a clean, quiet, small RV vacation location.

Location: Three miles Northwest of Fort Collins, off US Highway 287.

Total RV sites: 10	Pull thru sites: 2	Open: All Year
Full hookup sites: 10	45+ foot long sites: 8	Harold & Donna Eichman, Owners
Water & elec. sites: 0	Slideout sites: 10	2730 N Shields St.
Elec. only sites: 0	Licenses sold: None	Ft Collins, Colorado 80524-1044
50 amp sites: 2	LP Gas: None	970/221-3723
Hookup sites open in Fall: 10	Credit Cards: None	
Winter hookup sites: 10	Elevation: 4780	
RV site cost: Not available		

Within 15 minutes: *At RV Park:*

Greeley RV Park & Campground

The Greeley RV Park offers long, level pull thrus in a quiet, restful rural setting on 10 acres. The full hookup (20, 30 and 50 amps) sites are in the shade on grass with picnic tables and barbecue grills. Greeley is favored with an average of 315 days of sunshine a year.

At this adult oriented park the camp store has RV parts, gas, groceries and hand-crafted, Colorado souvenirs. Excellent health facilities are in the area. History abounds in Greeley, the fourth largest agricultural area in the United States. Area attractions includes retail outlets, the Greeley Independence Day Stampede Rodeo, the Broncos' football team training camp, the Colorado Farm Show, and the University of Northern Colorado annual Jazz Festival. Drive to Denver for a visit to the zoo, US Mint and IMAX Theater. Estes Park and Rocky Mountain National Park are great for a day trip.

Clubs are welcomed with a special discount and free use of the club room. Winter storage for RVs is available.

Location: In Southeast Greeley, go East on US Highway 34, ½ miles East of US Highway 85 on North Frontage Road. Follow blue camping signs-do not take any business routes!

Total RV sites: 80
Full hookup sites: 80
Water & elec. sites: 0
Elec. only sites: 1
50 amp sites: 46
Hookup sites open in Fall: 80
Winter hookup sites: 40
RV site cost: $–$$

Pull thru sites: 80
45+ foot long sites: 80
Slideout sites: 80
Licenses sold: None
LP Gas: weight
Credit Cards: VM
Elevation: 4648

Open: All Year
Phil & Joan Worthington, Owners
Pam & Gary Kessler, Managers
501 E 27th St.
Greeley, Colorado 80631-9781
970/353-6476

Within 15 minutes:

At RV Park:

Pioneer Mobile Home Park

Near the center of Fort Collins and just south of Colorado State University, well-manicured Pioneer Park has full hookups with TV hookup for monthlies on grassy sites. The level, gravel sites are in the mobile home park and have a few tall shade trees. Pioneer is easily accessible from I-25 or US Highway 285.

All the amenities of Fort Collins, from shops and restaurants to museums and parks are nearby. The campground has its own playground for the kids to romp on.

Daily, weekly, and monthly rates are available.

Location: Exit I-25 at Harmony Road (Exit 265) and go 4 ½ miles West on Harmony Road. On the North side of the road, near the center of Fort Collins.

Total RV sites: 31
Full hookup sites: 31
Water & elec. sites: 0
Elec. only sites: 0
50 amp sites: 0
Hookup sites open in Fall: 31
Winter hookup sites: 31
RV site cost: Not available

Pull thru sites: 0
45+ foot long sites: 0
Slideout sites: 31
Licenses sold: None
LP Gas: None
Credit Cards: None
Elevation: 5000

Open: All Year
Karen & Tim Clark, Managers
300 E Harmony Rd
Ft Collins, Colorado 80525
970/226-3325

Within 15 minutes:

At RV Park:

Georgetown

Includes Empire. Map: F-14

Georgetown's 200 restored Victorian homes and buildings makes it an exceptional National Historic District. Numerous original dwellings survived because the volunteer fire department kept the city from going up in smoke like many others of that era. The town began when two brothers, George and David Griffith, struck gold in 1858. Silver, though, was this mountain town's triumph and downfall. Today, the Hotel de Paris is one of most famous landmarks. Opened in 1875 by Louis Dupuy, a Frenchman with a checkered past, it offered unheard of luxuries in a mining town: hot and cold taps in the rooms, baths, glacial ice water piped in, trout in an Italian fountain, French cuisine and an impressive selection of wines. The hotel is now a museum and if you sniff carefully, you just might catch a hint of roasted goose in red wine. The Georgetown Loop Narrow Gauge Train, an engineering feat, makes a complete spiral as it climbs to Silver Plume. The 22-mile Guanella Pass Scenic and Historic Byway, running south to Grant through Pike and Arapaho National Forests, has a glacial moraine, dense forests of lodgepole pine and spruce trees, beaver ponds and sub alpine meadows past timberline at 11,666 feet.

Empire, at 8,600 feet, was founded in 1860 when gold was discovered. Today numerous hiking trails lead out of town along creeks where columbine flowers and wild strawberries grow to alpine meadows filled with deer and elk.

Fun Things to Do

- City Park (303) 569-2555, (303) 623-6882
- Clear Creek Ranger District, Idaho Springs (303) 893-1474
- Georgetown Loop Historic Mining & Railroad Park (303) 670-1686
- Hamill House (303) 674-2625
- Horse-drawn Historic Tours (303) 569-2675
- Hotel De Paris (303) 569-2311
- Silver Plume School House (303) 569-2145

Mountain Meadow Campground

At the foot of Berthoud Pass which climbs to the ski resort Winter Park, Mountain Meadow Campground is an excellent base camp for Rocky Mountain sight seeing. The shaded, level sites in a pine and spruce forest are pull thrus and full hookups (20 and 30 amps). Group sites are available. Relax under the Ponderosa pine trees in this lush mountain valley and watch the hummingbirds play — countless hummingbirds gather at Mountain Meadow.

Hike right from the campground to alpine meadows awash in brilliant flowers and abandoned mines from yesteryear. From this majestic mountain location, you can fish for rainbow trout in nearby Clear Creek, Clear Lake or Echo Lake. Take an easy day drive to Mt. Evans, Blue River, Lake Dillon, Vail, and old gold mining towns. This campground is centrally located to Denver, Idaho Springs, Georgetown and Central City.

Location: Thirty five miles West of Denver, 5 miles off I-70's Exit 232 on US Highway 40, 1-½ miles West of Empire, ten miles West Idaho Springs, at the foot of Berthoud Pass.

Total RV sites: 30
Full hookup sites: 30
Water & elec. sites: 0
Elec. only sites: 0
50 amp sites: 0
Hookup sites open in Fall: 30
Winter hookup sites: 0
RV site cost: ¢–$

Pull thru sites: 14
45+ foot long sites: 25
Slideout sites: 30
Licenses sold: None
LP Gas: None
Credit Cards: VMD
Elevation: 8700

Open: 5/25 to 9/30
Mac, Edna, John & Dot McPeak, Owners
11961 Hwy 40
PO Box 2
Empire, Colorado 80438
303/569-2424

Within 15 minutes:

At RV Park:

Glenwood Springs Area

Includes Battlement Mesa, New Castle and Silt. Map: G-5-7

Soaking in the large, brick-lined hot springs pool (it's 615 feet by 75 feet), gazing up at pine-covered mountain peaks, you'll understand why first the Ute Indians and then wealthy miners and European aristocrats treasured Glenwood Springs. When the Utes were relocated in 1882, the town sprang up, catering to the rich from around the world. With money came trouble: by 1887 there were 22 bars in a two-block area! Doc Holliday, who was wanted in Arizona for killings at the OK Corral shoot-out, is buried here. The Hotel Colorado that opened in the early 1890s was the summer White House for Teddy Roosevelt. Today, people come for the history and hot springs as much as the rugged and beautiful surroundings. Glenwood Canyon has a 9 mile bike path and rafters enjoy the whitewaters of the Colorado River that flow through it.

Nearby, among the arroyos, bluffs, juniper trees and native grasses, you'll find Battlement Mesa, a carefully planned community, ideal for a comfortable vacation. Activities include hunting in season, bicycling on the trails and paved roads, horseback riding, tennis, golf and sailing. Winter time brings skiing, snowmobiling, ice skating and ice fishing.

Fun Things to Do

- Battlement Mesa Golf Club (970)285-PAR4
- Glenwood Springs Golf Course (970) 945-7086
- Glenwood Springs Hot Springs Pool (970) 945-7131
- Johnson Park Miniature Golf (970) 945-9608
- Rifle Creek Golf Course (Rifle) (970) 625-1093
- Rock Gardens Rafting (970) 945-6737
- Ski Sunlight (800) 445-7931
- Westbank Ranch Golf Course (970) 945-7032
- White River National Forest Headquarters (970) 945-2521
- Yampa Hot Springs Spa & Vapor Cave (970) 945-0667

Ami's Acres Campground

At this scenic, spacious and secluded campground, the level, terraced hillside sites have lovely views of green mountains and the Colorado River. The terracing of the sites provides privacy and gives good, open views. Tall trees of native cedar, piñon pine and oak abound. All sites are full hookups (30 and 50 amps) and many are extra long pull thrus (up to 80 feet) so big rigs can park comfortably. Pick between open or shady sites; all have picnic tables.

Ami's Acres has easy access to the highway and area attractions. The pavilion is great for group meetings. Play horseshoes at the playground, fish on the river or hike along a nature trail. After an active day, soak in the natural Glenwood Springs Hot Springs pool just five minutes down the frontage road. Summertime brings out the golfers. Vacation here and you'll understand why the owners call it a true Rocky Mountain experience.

Camper cabins and reduced monthly and seasonal rates are available.

Location: Exit I-70 at milepost 114 then go West 1 mile on Frontage Road.

Total RV sites: 58	Pull thru sites: 20	Open: 3/15 to 11/15
Full hookup sites: 44	45+ foot long sites: 45	Paul & Jacky Amichaux, Owners
Water & elec. sites: 4	Slideout sites: 15	50235 Hwy 6 & 24
Elec. only sites: 6	Licenses sold: None	PO Box 1239
50 amp sites: 10	LP Gas: None	Glenwood Springs, Colorado 81602-1239
Hookup sites open in Fall: 58	Credit Cards: VM	970/945-5340
Winter hookup sites: 0	Elevation: 5740	
RV site cost: $		

Within 15 minutes:

At RV Park:

Battlement Mesa RV Park

Between Glenwood Springs and Grand Junction, Battlement Mesa is nestled beneath majestic mountain peaks in a sheltered valley where the climate is mild and pleasant. Sites are full hookups with 20, 30 and 50 amps and TV service. Within the Battlement Mesa community, you'll find res-  taurants and shops as well as miles of paved hiking and biking trails winding their way through acres of well-kept parks and green spaces.

The Activity Center has it all, from fishing to tennis. Golf on the 18-hole championship course, swim in the indoor pool, or relax in the Jacuzzi and sauna. Work out in the full-size gym which has racquetball courts, an exercise room, and a video game room. Arts and craft classes on painting, fly typing, wood carving and quilting are available. Hunting, skiing, rafting, and horseback riding are nearby. In the winter, downhill and cross-country skiing, snowmobiling, ice fishing and ice skating are popular activities.

Indoor and outdoor group meeting areas are available.

Location: Take I-70 to Battlement Mesa and take Exit 75.

Total RV sites: 44
Full hookup sites: 44
Water & elec. sites: 0
Elec. only sites: 0
50 amp sites: 0
Hookup sites open in Fall: 12
Winter hookup sites: 12
RV site cost: Not available

Pull thru sites: 4
45+ foot long sites: 0
Slideout sites: 0
Licenses sold: None
LP Gas: None
Credit Cards: VM
Elevation: 5200

Open: All Year
Lyn Hirneisen, Property Manager
PO Box 6006
Battlement Mesa, Colorado 81636
970/285-9740
800/645-5664
970/285-7890 fax

Within 15 minutes:

At RV Park:

Burning Mountain RV Park

Located on the beautiful Colorado River, Burning Mountain's RV sites are full hook-ups with campfire pits. Several ponds dot this New Castle campground.

Fish on-site along the river frontage or at the nearby lake. Play horseshoes, tether ball and volleyball with your family. The county store has groceries, snacks, rental movies, ice, fishing supplies, and hunting licenses.

Minutes away are the Glenwood springs Hot Springs Pool, four wheel drive tours, horseback rides, raft trips, museums, a golf course, mountain bike trails, historic sites and a shopping mall. Hunting enthusiasts will also find this a prime area for their sport. Cross-country and downhill skiing are close during the winter.

Location: Exit I-70 at milepost 105.

Total RV sites: 58
Full hookup sites: 0
Water & elec. sites: 58
Elec. only sites: 0
50 amp sites: 20
Hookup sites open in Fall: 58
Winter hookup sites: 58
RV site cost: $

Pull thru sites: 0
45+ foot long sites: 0
Slideout sites: 58
Licenses sold: Fish & Hunt
LP Gas: M
Credit Cards: VMD
Elevation: 6000

Open: All Year
Kathey Rippy, Manager
7051 Country Rd 335
New Castle, Colorado 81647
970/984-0331

Within 15 minutes:

At RV Park:

Hideout Cabins & Campground

Camp on 9 wooded acres in the shade near Glenwood Springs and the Roaring Fork River. The private, streamside sites are large and level with full hookups (20 and 30 amps) and picnic tables. Group RV sites are available. At night, you'll be lulled to sleep by the gurgling Three Mile Creek — the only

sound in the mountain quiet. The trees of the White River National Forest surround this campground on the bike path to town.

Kids will like the video game room and playground on-site. The outdoor pavilion overlooking the creek is perfect for large family gatherings. Recreation here is endless. Ski nearby slopes such as Sunlight, Snowmass and Aspen. Hike or horseback ride in Hanging Lake and Flat Tops, or fish the Colorado, Roaring Fork and Frying Pan rivers. Raft the wet and wild Colorado River and visit Doc Holliday's grave. Explore the historic towns of Marble, Redstone, the ghost town of Ashcroft and Crystal City Mill — one of the most photographed sites in Colorado. A stop at the world's largest thermal pool is a must. Dine in any of Glenwood Springs fine restaurants after a day of mountain golf.

Rustic, secluded, housekeeping cabins are also available.

Location: Exit I-70 at milepost 116 and follow signs to Aspen for 1 ½ miles. Stay on South Grand Avenue at the fork. Right on bridge, just past Rivers Restaurant. South 1 mile.

Total RV sites: 42	Pull thru sites: 2	Open: All Year
Full hookup sites: 39	45+ foot long sites: 5	Patricia & Richard Tanberg
Water & elec. sites: 2	Slideout sites: 9	Shawna & Jeff Blevins, Owners
Elec. only sites: 1	Licenses sold: None	1293 Rd 117 - 4 mile Road
50 amp sites: 0	LP Gas: None	Glenwood Springs, Colorado 81601
Hookup sites open in Fall: 42	Credit Cards: VM	970/945-5621
Winter hookup sites: 18	Elevation: 5800	800/987-0779
RV site cost: $		

Within 15 minutes:

At RV Park:

New Castle/Glenwood Springs KOA

Located on a trout-stocked mountain creek, encompassed by woods and high mountain peaks, this KOA has shady sites with electricity (20 and 30 amps) and water. Many sites are pull thrus with picnic tables, fire rings and barbecue grills. Relax in the cool shade provided by tall firs, spruce trees and the occasional cottonwood trees bordering East Elk Creek.

Fish right from the campground. Kids young and old will like the horseshoe pits by the creek, the large playground and the video game room. Trails from the campground into the wilderness are great for hikers and mountain bikers. Exercise your pet in the designated dog run. Eat breakfast on the weekends and dinners nightly at the Creekside Cafe from Memorial Day through Labor Day. Each Saturday, chow down on the cowboy steak dinners. This makes an excellent base camp for wind surfing, rafting and horseback riding. Golfers, from the miniature to 18-hole variety, will find courses to challenge them in Glenwood Springs.

Ask about the camper cabins.

Location: Exit I-70 at Elk Creek (105) and go 2 ½ miles North of New Castle, 9 miles West of Glenwood Springs.

Total RV sites: 51
Full hookup sites: 0
Water & elec. sites: 38
Elec. only sites: 0
50 amp sites: 0
Hookup sites open in Fall: 38
Winter hookup sites: 0
RV site cost: $

Pull thru sites: 7
45+ foot long sites: 7
Slideout sites: 7
Licenses sold: Fish & Hunt
LP Gas: metered
Credit Cards: VMD
Elevation: 6000

Open: 5/9 to 9/30
0581 County Rd 241
New Castle, Colorado 81647
970/984-2240

Within 15 minutes:

At RV Park:

Rock Gardens Campground & Rafting

To the tune mild rapids and the spray of foamy whitewater, camp along the mighty Colorado River at Rock Gardens. The scenic, grassy sites on 17 acres have electricity (15, 20 and 30 amps), water, picnic tables and fire rings. Chose between a tree-lined riverside site or a shaded, mountainside site.

Your hosts operate daily, guided whitewater raft trips and leisure float trips through beautiful Glenwood Canyon. Experience an exciting ride through Tuttle's Tumble, the Wall, Tombstone and Man Eater on a short trip or go for the full day river adventure that includes a picnic lunch riverside midway through the six hour ride. Inflatable, rental kayaks are available for those who want to play in the river on their own. The trout fishing in the river is excellent. Rent a bike and coast through the picturesque canyon on the paved bike path. Walk along the foot trail to Glenwood Springs Hot Springs Pool where you can soothe yourself after a day of outdoor adventures.

Location: Two miles East of Glenwood Springs, Exit I-70 at milepost 119.

Total RV sites: 35	Pull thru sites: 0	Open: 4/15 to 11/15
Full hookup sites: 0	45+ foot long sites: 12	Kim Mechling, Owner
Water & elec. sites: 19	Slideout sites: 12	1308 County Rd 129
Elec. only sites: 16	Licenses sold: None	Glenwood Springs, Colorado 81601-9717
50 amp sites: 0	LP Gas: None	970/945-6737
Hookup sites open in Fall: 35	Credit Cards: VM	
Winter hookup sites: 0	Elevation: 5746	
RV site cost: $		

Within 15 minutes:

At RV Park:

Viking RV Park & Campground

Between Grand Junction and Glenwood Springs on a river frontage road, the Viking Campground has grassy sites along the mighty Colorado River. Sites are full hookups (20, 30 and 50 amps) and pull thru. Phone hookups are available for those staying by the month. Large, group camping sites for family reunions are available. The state-stocked river is brimming with trout — perfect for a fresh cooked breakfast.

Fishing in the Colorado River, which borders one side of the campground, is practically required here. Kids can romp on the playground while the teenagers play basketball and horseshoes. Golfers will find the nearby courses excellent while those who favor whitewater rafting will not be disappointed. Bird watchers will want to check out the great blue heron rookery and Canadian geese here. Guest horses are permitted at Viking and horseback riding is a short drive away. You're only a 20 minute drive from the world's largest hot springs pool. Viking RV Park offers low rates and friendly smiles.

Ask about the RV and boat storage.

Location: Nineteen miles West of Glenwood Springs and 70 miles East of Grand Junction. Exit I-70 at milepost 97.

Total RV sites: 40	Pull thru sites: 11	Open: All Year
Full hookup sites: 40	45+ foot long sites: 20	Tom & Sue Scott, Owners
Water & elec. sites: 0	Slideout sites: 30	32956 River Frontage Road
Elec. only sites: 10	Licenses sold: None	PO Box 190
50 amp sites: 4	LP Gas: metered	Silt, Colorado 81652-0190
Hookup sites open in Fall: 0	Credit Cards: None	970/876-2443
Winter hookup sites: 0	Elevation: 5410	
RV site cost: ¢–$		

Within 15 minutes:

At RV Park:

Granby & Grand Lake

Map: D-13

These mountain towns, at the western entrance to Rocky Mountain National Park, sit on great fishing lakes with beautiful, unspoiled views. Anglers will find rainbow, brook, mackinaw and cutthroat trout in abundance and large kokanee salmon as well. Grand Lake, Granby, Lake Granby, Shadow Mountain Reservoir and Willow Creek Reservoir are all close at hand. Resting on the shores of the largest natural lake in Colorado, Grand Lake is an alpine village with board sidewalks, log-front stores and the modern amenities of dining and shopping. At 8,369 feet, this rustic town is enveloped by peaks, especially the impressive, bald Mt. Craig. Grand Lake has access to two reservoirs, two national forests, the national park and the Never Summer Wilderness Area which is accessible only by hiking trails. You can horseback ride, boat, hike, golf and river raft. When the snow starts, this becomes a winter playground, with groomed trails for snowmobiling, cross-country skiing, snowshoeing and close by slopes for downhill skiing. Ute, Arapaho and Cheyenne tribes used to hunt and fish in this Middle Park area and when you visit you'll see why this was land worth fighting over.

Fun Things to Do

- Arapaho National Forest (970) 887-3331
- Granby County Museum (970) 725-3939
- Grand Lake Golf Course (970) 627-8008
- Grand Lake Theatre Association (970) 627-3380
- Hot Sulphur Springs Mineral Baths and Pool (970) 725-3306
- Kaufman House (970) 627-3351
- Klein's Fishing Lodge, Granby (970) 887-3507, (970) 887-3209
- Lake Shore Marina, Granby (970) 887-2295, (303) 421-0060 off season
- Never Summer Wilderness Area (970) 887-3331
- Rocky Mountain National Park (970) 627-3471

Elk Creek Campground

Camp along a snow-fed creek at the closest wooded campground to Grand Lake Village. At the western entrance to Rocky Mountain National Park, all the sites at Elk Creek have electricity (20 and 30 amps) and water; half are full hookups. Choose between open sites with views or wooded sites in the shade. Each site has a picnic table, fire ring and barbecue grill.

Wood, RV supplies, ice and snacks can be purchased at the camp store. On-site activities includes badminton, volleyball, horseshoes and fishing. Hike or mountain bike along the many trails leading out of the campground. During the snowy months, the trails are groomed for cross-country skiing and snowmobiling. Guest horses are permitted or rent one at nearby stables. The recreation room with a fireplace, playground and movies will keep the kids busy. And, of course, the ice cream socials will be popular too. The Grand Lake marina and boat launch are just down the road. Anglers will find the lake fishing fantastic and the stocked trout pond filled with fish just aching to be caught. Elk Creek welcomes snowmobilers in the winter and golfers who play the nearby 18-hole course in the summer. The campground boasts wheelchair accessible facilities.

Camper cabins are also available. Ask about the off-season rates and winter storage.

Location: North of Grand Lake on US Highway 34 at the West entrance to Rocky Mountain National Park.

Total RV sites: 33	Pull thru sites: 1	Open: All Year
Full hookup sites: 16	45+ foot long sites: 27	Tom Stanley, Owner
Water & elec. sites: 17	Slideout sites: 33	143 CR 48
Elec. only sites: 0	Licenses sold: None	PO Box 549
50 amp sites: 0	LP Gas: None	Grand Lake, Colorado 80447-0549
Hookup sites open in Fall: 33	Credit Cards: VM	970/627-8502
Winter hookup sites: 10	Elevation: 8500	800/ELK-CREEK
RV site cost: Not available		

Within 15 minutes:

At RV Park:

Lake Shore Marina & RV Park

On the shores of beautiful Lake Granby under tall pine trees which sway gently in the breeze, Lake Shore RV Park has full hookup RV sites in the shade. At the marina, you'll find picture perfect views.

Lake Granby, the second largest lake in Colorado with 65 miles of shoreline, has excellent trout and salmon fishing. Its size also makes for some great mountain sailing! The campground has its own boat ramp as well as pontoon boat rentals, slips and moorings for your convenience. The small store has fishing tackle and snacks. When water sports get to be too much, head into the hills for four-wheel driving, mountain biking and horseback riding.

Daily, weekly and monthly reservations are available. Ask about the indoor, group meeting area.

Location: South of Grand Lake off Highway 34 near milepost 8.

Total RV sites: 10	Pull thru sites: 0	Open: 5/1 to 11/1
Full hookup sites: 10	45+ foot long sites: 10	Jim & Jackie & Mike Phillips, Owners
Water & elec. sites: 0	Slideout sites: 10	250 CO Rd 640
Elec. only sites: 0	Licenses sold: None	Granby, Colorado 80446-8710
50 amp sites: 0	LP Gas: None	970/887-2295
Hookup sites open in Fall: 10	Credit Cards: VM	
Winter hookup sites: 0	Elevation: 8280	
RV site cost: Not available		

Within 15 minutes:

At RV Park:

Western Hills Cottages & RV Park

A beautiful setting with towering, lodgepole pines along the boulder-strewn, north fork of the Colorado River is yours for the taking at Western Hills. Bordered by national forest with lovely Shadow Mountain Lake a short walk away, the RV park has sites with electricity and water. You can't get much more scenic and serene than a vacation in the mountains at Western Hills.

Hiking, biking and snowmobile trails begin at your site. It goes without saying that the fishing here is fantastic. A soothing soak in the hot tub under the stars is a must after reeling in that huge trout! Near the play area are picnic tables and barbecue grills for your convenience. Let your hosts arrange horseback rides, hayrides, breakfast rides, steak-fry rides and pack trips through well managed, local stables. Just to the north of the campground is Rocky Mountain National Park where scheduled programs include nature hikes, lectures and tours conducted by the Park Service Rangers. Daily, sight-seeing boat cruises on the two lakes are available as are charter boats for the serious anglers.

Cabins with fireplaces are also available.

Location: Between Granby and Grand Lake off Highway 34.

Total RV sites: 8
Full hookup sites: 0
Water & elec. sites: 8
Elec. only sites: 0
50 amp sites: 0
Hookup sites open in Fall: 8
Winter hookup sites: 0
RV site cost: Not available

Pull thru sites: 0
45+ foot long sites: 4
Slideout sites: 6
Licenses sold: None
LP Gas: None
Credit Cards: VM
Elevation: 8350

Open: 5/25 to 10/15
Doug & Norma Stroemel, Owners
12082 Hwy 34
Grand Lake, Colorado 80447
970/627-3632

Within 15 minutes:

At RV Park:

Winding River Resort Village

You'll have plenty of room to romp on this 160-acre wooded, family-run ranch resort bordering Rocky Mountain National Park. The spacious sites have electricity (20 and 30 amps) and water; many are full hookups with pull thrus. The shaded sites, some are open, are hidden among the pine trees in this mountainous region. Adjacent to Rocky Mountain National Park, Arapaho Forest and the North Fork of the Colorado River, Winding River is a family-oriented, great-for-kids resort.

Winding River Resort sponsors numerous activities, such as horseback rides, pony rides, hayride steak dinners, sleigh rides, a Frisbee golf course, chuckwagon breakfasts, ice cream socials and an animal farm for the kids. Bring along your horse for high country riding and spend the evening around your campfire. Nearby sports includes mountain biking, hiking, fishing, cross-country skiing and snowmobiling. Rent a mountain bike here or play baseball, basketball, horseshoes and volleyball. The hayride and "steak frys" are great for family reunions. You'll be hard put to not find something you like to do at Winding River Resort.

Quaint cabins and lodge rooms (all non-smoking) are available. Ask about the indoor and outdoor group meeting areas. Winding River has two seasons: from May 15 to Oct 15 and December 10 to January 2.

Location: Take US Highway 34 to the Kawuneeche Visitor Center and turn West on 491. Proceed 1 ½ miles North.

Total RV sites: 130	Pull thru sites: 46	Open: 5/15 to 10/15 & 12/10 to ½
Full hookup sites: 22	45+ foot long sites: 68	Wes House, Owner
Water & elec. sites: 65	Slideout sites: 50	1447 Road 491
Elec. only sites: 0	Licenses sold: Fish & Hunt	PO Box 629
50 amp sites: 0	LP Gas: None	Grand Lake, Colorado 80447-0629
Hookup sites open in Fall: 87	Credit Cards: VMD	303/623-1121 Denver Metro
Winter hookup sites: 10	Elevation: 8700	970/627-3215
RV site cost: $		800/282-5121

Within 15 minutes:

At RV Park:

Grand Junction

Includes Clifton and Fruita. Also see Grand Mesa Area. Map: H-2

Layers of shale, sedimentary rock and red slickrock sandstone, holding countless dinosaur bones, dominate Grand Junction. From rusty oranges to brilliant reds, colors light up the terrain. At the Colorado National Monument, drive Rim Rock Drive for haunting views of sandstone monoliths and red rock canyons. Along the Colorado River are bike paths, places to bird watch or fish. Try boating or canoeing on the river. For mountain bikers, the Kokopelli's Trail is a 136-mile trek to Moab, Utah. Or try four-wheel driving at the Little Book Cliffs Wild Horse Range, 8 miles north of town. The Unaweep/Tabeguache Scenic and Historic Byway, a 138-mile route, begins just outside of Grand Junction. It follows the course of Unaweep Canyon, through the vivid red desert of the Dolores River Canyon, opening up on the high plains. Opportunities to discover nature in Grand Junction are endless. Today, the mainstay of the community can be found in the acres of apricots, cherries, grapes and peaches sold around the country. Discover one of Colorado's best kept secrets: wineries. In nearby Palisade are five vineyards with tasting rooms and winery tours. Be sure and visit the newly opened Devils Canyon Science and Learning Center in Fruita where you can go back in time to when dinosaurs roamed.

Fun Things To Do

- Adobe Creek National Golf Course, Fruita (970) 858-0521
- Colorado National Monument (970) 858-3617
- Cross Orchards Historic Site (970) 434-9814
- Deer Creek Village Golf Course, Grand Junction (970) 856-7781
- Devil's Canyon Science and Learning Center (970) 858-7282
- Dinosaur Valley Museum (970) 243-9210
- Doo Zoo Children's Museum (970) 241-5225
- Fruita Welcome Center (970) 858-9335
- Lincoln Park Golf Club (970) 242-6394
- Museum of Western Colorado (970) 242-0971
- Tiara Rado Golf Course (970) 245-8085
- Wineries (970) 464-7458

Fruita Junction RV Park

Next to the Colorado Welcome Center in Fruita, this campground on 5 ½ acres has grassy, level sites under lush, over-hanging shade trees. The pull thru, full hookup sites (20, 30 and 50 amps) have picnic tables and barbecue grills. Fruita Junction RV Park is a good stopping point between the

Front Range, Lake Powell and Las Vegas. You'll find the service friendly and helpful and the campground clean, quiet and convenient.

The park store has limited groceries, RV supplies and ice. The arcade, playground and volleyball court will keep the kids busy while the three dog runs will make your pet happy. The park is right across from the new Devils Canyon Science and Learning Center, an international center for dinosaur study. The spectacular Colorado National Monument with its sandstone monoliths and red rock canyons is nearby.

Ask about the large group accommodations and special rates.

Location: Exit I-70 at milepost 19 and go South ¼ mile. Next to the Colorado Welcome Center in Fruita.

Total RV sites: 60	Pull thru sites: 24	Open: All Year
Full hookup sites: 60	45+ foot long sites: 60	Chuck & Jeannie Lutz, Owners
Water & elec. sites: 28	Slideout sites: 60	607 Hwy 340
Elec. only sites: 0	Licenses sold: None	Fruita, Colorado 81521-9520
50 amp sites: 8	LP Gas: metered	970/858-3155
Hookup sites open in Fall: 60	Credit Cards: VM	
Winter hookup sites: 60	Elevation: 4495	
RV site cost: ¢–$		

Within 15 minutes:

At RV Park:

Grand Junction/Clifton KOA

The lovely, oversized grassy sites are surrounded by trees at this KOA. Most sites are full hookups (20 and 30 amps) with barbecue grills. From your level, gravel site in the shade or out in the open, you'll have great mountain views. The campground is at the foot of the Grand Mesa National Forest where the lakes and streams are teaming with trout and the lush meadows among the timberland are perfect for a high country picnic.

Volleyball, horseshoes, badminton, nightly movies, the arcade and playground will keep the kids busy while you soak in the heated swimming pool. As dusk falls, gather the family together for a sumptuous dinner in the patio cafe on-site. Or start your day with one of their delicious breakfasts. A dog walking area borders the campground. Area activities include visiting the Colorado National Monument at sunset and exploring the Dinosaur Valley Museum. Fish in the 200 lakes of the Grand Mesa territory for rainbow, native and brook trout. Golfing, hunting, hiking and mountain biking are also nearby.

Ask about the outdoor, group meeting area. Camper cabins are also available for rent.

Location: Northeast of Grand Junction on the E I-70 Business Loop in Clifton.

Total RV sites: 102	RV site cost: $	Open: All Year
Full hookup sites: 80	Pull thru sites: 80	Paul & Agnes Evans, Owners
Water & elec. sites: 22	45+ foot long sites: 80	3238 E I-70 Business Loop
Elec. only sites: 0	Slideout sites: 80	Clifton, Colorado 81520
50 amp sites: 4	Licenses sold: None	970/434-6644
Hookup sites open in Fall: 102	LP Gas: metered	
Winter hookup sites: 60	Credit Cards: VMD	
	Elevation: 4600	

Within 15 minutes:

At RV Park:

Junction West RV Park

In a quiet country setting on 14 acres convenient to the Colorado National Monument and Grand Mesa, Junction West is also close to all the amenities in town, from shopping malls and restaurants to golf courses. The open, level, full hookup (20, 30 and 50 amps) sites are pull thrus with picnic tables and barbecue grills. Some sites are shaded, all are ultra-level, gravel sites. There's split rail fences between the wider, longer sites for privacy. The entire park is fully fenced for added security and group camping sites are available.

The on-site general store, TV, pool table and playground will make you feel right at home. Sports includes basketball, badminton, horseshoes, tetherball and volleyball. Pets are okay for non-canvas campers. Junction West also has a unique service — a free paperback book exchange. Turn in the novel you've just finished for a new one to read before falling asleep under the stars. With fishing, four-wheel driving, mountain biking, horseback riding and rafting all nearby, you'll find plenty to do in the sunshine of western Colorado.

Fenced boat and RV storage is available. Ask about the group rates.

Location: Exit I-70 at milepost 26 and proceed West 4 blocks to 22 Road then North 4 blocks.

Total RV sites: 51	Pull thru sites: 54	Open: All Year
Full hookup sites: 42	45+ foot long sites: 54	Paul & Penny Patterson, Owners
Water & elec. sites: 9	Slideout sites: 54	793 - 22 Rd
Elec. only sites: 0	Licenses sold: None	Grand Junction, Colorado 81505
50 amp sites: 16	LP Gas: metered	970/245-8531
Hookup sites open in Fall: 51	Credit Cards: VMD	
Winter hookup sites: 51	Elevation: 4500	
RV site cost: ¢–$		

Within 15 minutes:

At RV Park:

Mobile City RV Park

The closest RV park to Mesa Mall, the largest mall in western Colorado, and a minute away from good restaurants, Mobile City RV Park has open, level sites. The pull thru sites are full hook-ups (20, 30 and 50 amps) and some sites are shady. Many new trees have been planted at this easily accessible RV park. Clean restrooms and a laundromat are provided.

The unusual formations of the Colorado National Monument and the breathtaking beauty of Grand Mesa are an easy drive from here. Kids will enjoy the on-site, new playground. Area activities include four-wheel driving, horseback riding, fishing, river rafting, mountain biking and winery touring. In the winter, try snowmobiling, downhill and cross-country skiing close by. A public swimming pool is just down the road, perfect for a relaxing float after a day of playing on your vacation.

Location: Three miles West of Grand Junction. East bound: Exit I-70 at milepost 26, then East 1 ½ mile, West bound: Exit I-70 at milepost 28, then 1+ miles South on 24 Road and West 1 mile on US Highway 6 and the I-70 Business Loop.

Total RV sites: 30	Pull thru sites: 20	Open: All Year
Full hookup sites: 30	45+ foot long sites: 30	Penny Merriett & Dick Powell, Owners
Water & elec. sites: 0	Slideout sites: 30	2322 Hwy 6 & 50 (I-70 Bus Loop W)
Elec. only sites: 0	Licenses sold: None	Grand Junction, Colorado 81505
50 amp sites: 30	LP Gas: None	970/242-9291
Hookup sites open in Fall: 30	Credit Cards: VM	
Winter hookup sites: 30	Elevation: 4586	
RV site cost: ¢–$		

Within 15 minutes:

At RV Park:

Rose Park RV Campground

Camp in the city of Grand Junction at Rose Park. The separate RV area in this mobile home park has full hookup (20, 30 and 50 amps) sites with phone hookup available for monthlies. The park's streets are newly paved and a laundromat is available. Rose Park is a "plain Jane" campground with the lowest rates in Grand Junction.

Both the natural wonder of the Colorado National Monument and the vistas of Grand Mesa are nearby. For those who prefer the civilized pursuits, a large shopping mall is minutes away. Restaurants, shopping and an amusement park are within walking distance. Of course, good fishing and bountiful hunting are popular activities as well. Come to the banana belt of Colorado and play in the sunshine.

Location: Going West, Exit I-70 at milepost 37, proceed Southwest on I-70 Business Loop to North Avenue (US Highway 6) and turn right (West) on North Avenue. Going East, Exit I-70 at milepost 26, proceed Southeast on I-70 Business Loop (US Highways 6 & 50) and turn left (East) on North Avenue (US Highway 6).

Total RV sites: 25	Pull thru sites: 11	Open: All Year
Full hookup sites: 25	45+ foot long sites: 0	Bud & Gail Day, Owners
Water & elec. sites: 0	Slideout sites: 24	644-29 ½ Road
Elec. only sites: 0	Licenses sold: None	Grand Junction, Colorado 81504-5279
50 amp sites: 25	LP Gas: None	970/243-1292
Hookup sites open in Fall: 25	Credit Cards: None	
Winter hookup sites: 25	Elevation: 4600	
RV site cost: ¢		

Within 15 minutes:

At RV Park:

Grand Mesa Area

Includes Cedaredge. Also see Delta and Grand Junction. Map: I-5

At 10,000 feet, Grand Mesa, the largest flat-top mountain in the world, rises more than a mile above the valley floor. Traveling across Grand Mesa, you'll see aspen and spruce groves, flowered meadows and over 200 cool clear lakes offering fantastic fishing for rainbow, brook, and brown trout. Some lakes have boat launches and you can reach many of them from the highway, but for the more adventurous, visit the lakes only accessible by four-wheel drive, foot or horseback. Utes called this the "Home of the Departed Spirits" and they brought hostages here after the 1879 Meeker Massacre. Almost entirely within the Grand Mesa National Forest, Grand Mesa's abundant wildlife makes this a popular area for fall hunting. Elk, deer and many smaller mammals roam the alpine forest. Take a fall tour of the changing aspen when you drive the Grand Mesa Scenic and Historic Byway. Visit Surface Creek Valley Historical Society's Pioneer Town in Cedaredge where you can explore the American West at the turn of the century. Hikers will want to trek along the Crag Crest National Recreation Trail, a 10-mile circular trail rising from east and west trailheads. The 6 ½ mile long path stretching across the top of Crag Crest is open to foot traffic only. Escape the summer heat and relax in Grand Mesa's cool mountain air.

Fun Things to Do

- Adobe Creek Village Golf Course, Cedaredge (970) 856-7781
- Aspen Trails Ice Cream & Gift Shop (970) 856-6321
- Grand Mesa Lodge Store & Gift Shop (800) 551-MESA
- Mesa Lakes Restaurant & Boat Rentals (970) 268-5467
- Surface Creek Historical Society Pioneer Town, Cedaredge (970) 856-3006

Alexander Lake Lodge, Cabins & Campground

Vacation on top of the world at over 10,000 feet in the landmark of Grand Mesa where pine and aspen forests are criss-crossed by streams and bordered by lush, alpine meadows. The lodge was built at the turn of the century from local materials and has an enormous fireplace said to contain 200 tons of rock. The historic lodge and campground overlook Alexander Lake and Twin Lakes. The RV sites are full hookups. Your hosts are fond of saying Mother Nature makes Alexander Lake Lodge her summer retreat.

Fish right on the premises or rent paddle boats and motor boats here for the Grand Mesa lakes. Enjoy the lodge dinning room when you eat one of the memorable meals served here daily. The lodge store sells groceries and all the supplies you'll need for your nearby fishing or big-game hunting expeditions. Hiking and sight-seeing are a must in this area of natural wonders. Ride gentle horses or hike to the nearly 280 lakes of Grand Mesa. Or hunt the abundant deer and elk that roam the large, flat top mountain's wild flower filled meadows. If you stop along the way for a picnic or to snap a photo, pause a moment and listen carefully — the chances are good you won't hear a sound.

Cabins are also available. Ask about the executive retreat packages.

Location: On Grand Mesa, 2 miles East of Highway 65 (Ward Lake Recreation Area turnoff).

Total RV sites: 11	Pull thru sites: 9	Open: 6/1 to 9/30
Full hookup sites: 11	45+ foot long sites: 0	Gordon & Grace Nelson, Owners
Water & elec. sites: 0	Slideout sites: 5	2121 AA 50 Rd
Elec. only sites: 0	Licenses sold: Fish & Hunt	PO Box 900
50 amp sites: 0	LP Gas: metered	Cedaredge, Colorado 81413-0900
Hookup sites open in Fall: 11	Credit Cards: VM	970/856-6700
Winter hookup sites: 0	Elevation: 10200	
RV site cost: ¢–$		

Within 15 minutes:

At RV Park:

Aspen Trails Campground & Store

Just off the Grand Mesa Scenic Byway, Aspen Trails Campground has cool, mosquito-free camping. Many of the open and grassy sites are full hookup (30 amps) and pull thru. Each site has a picnic table, fire ring, and barbecue grill.

On-site amenities include a heated swimming pool, pavilion, and an old time ice cream and soda fountain with sandwiches and treats. Anglers will appreciate the free fishing information, the fish cleaning sink and camp store with a variety of tackle. The Gnomad Gift Gallery features local artists' crafts and gifts. Bring along your horse or rent one from the nearby stables to explore the countless trails to beaver ponds and cool mountain streams. Hike the beautiful Crag Crest Trail or canoe the Mesa lakes. Summer festivities include the Lands End Hill Climb for thrills and the Forks to Muddy Flats raft race on the Gunnison River. In the winter, ski, snowmobile, ice fish, inter-tube and watch a dog sled race. Experience the ultimate in outdoor vacations at Aspen Trails.

Ask about the group, weekly and monthly rates.

Location: On the Grand Mesa Scenic Byway Highway 65, 3 miles North of Cedaredge.

Total RV sites: 30	Pull thru sites: 12	Open: All Year
Full hookup sites: 12	45+ foot long sites: 12	Tony & Pat & Dolly Mercep, Owners
Water & elec. sites: 0	Slideout sites: 8	1997 Hwy 65
Elec. only sites: 0	Licenses sold: None	Cedaredge, Colorado 81413-9406
50 amp sites: 0	LP Gas: metered	970/856-6321
Hookup sites open in Fall: 12	Credit Cards: VMD	
Winter hookup sites: 12	Elevation: 6800	
RV site cost: Not available		

Within 15 minutes:

At RV Park:

Gunnison Area

Includes Almont, Ohio City and Parlin. Map: K-9 and J - 10

Named for a topographer who was mapping a railroad route to the Pacific in 1853, Gunnison is surrounded by over 1.7 million acres of public land. The Gunnison River Territory stretches from one spectacular naturescape to another with plunging canyon walls, emerald lakes, imposing peaks and wildflower meadows. Ute Indians, miners, ranchers and the railroads all contributed to the Western character of this area. Today, Gunnison prides itself on having some of the best outdoor recreation in the state. Blue Mesa Reservoir in the Curecanti National Recreation Area, 9 miles west, is the largest man-made lake in Colorado with 96 miles of shoreline — an angler's paradise. Gunnison National Forest has more than 750 miles of teeming trout streams and reservoirs.

Ohio City, once a silver and gold mining town, is 24 miles east of Gunnison. Take a scenic drive to the Alpine Tunnel beyond Pitkin. The tunnel was constructed by the Denver South Park & Pacific Railroad in 1881 and is 1,800 feet long, drilled right through the Continental Divide. Crested Butte, 30 miles north via a scenic byway passing through Almont, offers a host of summertime activities, especially mountain biking, rafting and fishing.

Fun Things to Do

- Almont Resort Restaurant (970) 641-4009
- Curecanti National Recreational Area (970) 641-2337
- Dos Rios Golf Course (970) 641-1482
- Gunnison National Forest (970) 641-0471
- Morrow Point Boat Tour (970) 641-0402
- Skyland Resort Golf Course, Crested Butte (970) 349-6129
- Taylor Reservoir (970) 641-0471
- Three Rivers Rafting & Fly Fishing Shop (970) 641-1303

7-11 Ranch

In picturesque Parlin, 7-11 Ranch adjoins Bureau of Land Management property in the heart of the mountains. You'll find peace and quiet at this working ranch where most of the RV sites are full hookups with campfire pits. All the RV sites have room for slideouts and several are pull thrus. Tent sites and hot showers are available.

On the sparkling Quartz Creek, 7-11 Ranch has fly fishing and a privately stocked trout lake. With national forest land only 3 miles away, you can hike, mountain bike or take a wilderness trail ride. Guest horses are welcomed. The Fossil Ridge Guide Service and Alpine Guide School are located here. The ranch is a great place for the whole family to experience the old West. Breakfast can be served to those who request it when making advanced reservations. If you tire of cooking, try a nearby restaurant. In season, hunt for big horn sheep, mule deer and elk. Winter time brings skiing and snowmobiling.

A bunk house, and modern and rustic cabins (cold water) with stoves and baths are also available.

Location: North of Highway 50, between Parlin and Ohio City.

Total RV sites: 6
Full hookup sites: 4
Water & elec. sites: 0
Elec. only sites: 2
50 amp sites: 0
Hookup sites open in Fall: 4
Winter hookup sites: 4
RV site cost: Not available

Pull thru sites: 4
45+ foot long sites: 2
Slideout sites: 7
Licenses sold: None
LP Gas: None
Credit Cards: None
Elevation: 8500

Open: 5/15 to 11/30
Rudy & Deborah Rudibaugh, Owners
5291 CR 76
Parlin, Colorado 81239
970/641-0666

Within 15 minutes:

At RV Park:

Mesa Campground

Within walking distance of the roaring Gunnison River and 3 miles to downtown, Mesa Campground has clean, grassy, well landscaped and very well cared for sites, shaded by hundreds of cottonwood trees. All sites are full hookups (20 and 30 amps) with phone hookups, picnic tables and barbecue grills. Some sites have cement patios. TV reception is good at Mesa Campground. Summer high temperatures average a comfortable 80 degrees while the evening lows average a cool 40 degrees. Many seniors stay here seasonally.

The camp store is stocked with RV parts, ice, tackle, beer and groceries. Exercise your pet on the dog walk. Join in the occasional barbecue suppers and Friday night worship services. Life in Gunnison centers around mountain-fed waters, and a whitewater rafting trip or a leisure float trip are a must down the spectacular Gunnison river. For those who prefer the sidelines, the fishing is bountiful with the large Blue Mesa Lake in the Curecanti National Recreation Area only minutes away. Trout and kokanee salmon fill some 2,000 miles of trout streams and rivers feeding the local lakes.

Ask about the daily, weekly, monthly and seasonal rates. On-site rental park models and RV and boat storage are available.

Location: Three miles West of Gunnison on Highway 50.

Total RV sites: 100	RV site cost: ¢–$	Open: 5/1 to 11/1
Full hookup sites: 100	Pull thru sites: 40	Kenny & Mary Bergan, Owners
Water & elec. sites: 0	45+ foot long sites: 20	36128 W Hwy 50
Elec. only sites: 0	Slideout sites: 80	Gunnison, Colorado 81230-9310
50 amp sites: 0	Licenses sold: Fish & Hunt	970/641-3186
Hookup sites open in Fall: 100	LP Gas: metered	
Winter hookup sites: 0	Credit Cards: VMD	
	Elevation: 7700	

Within 15 minutes:

At RV Park:

Monarch Valley Ranch, Horses & RV Park

Surrounded by snow-capped peaks of the Rocky Mountains, Monarch Valley Ranch is a real working ranch. The Tomichi River roars through the campground, feeding private trout lakes. All the roomy sites are full hookups (20, 30 and 50 amps) and many are pull thrus. The level, open and shaded sites are in a forest meadow with spectacular views. Group camping sites are available.

The Tin Cup Lodge has a redwood deck where you can enjoy that first cup of coffee. Your family will never leave hungry from the Grub House restaurant, serving meals daily. Load up at the sporting goods and grocery stores. Ride one of the ranch horses to the Continental Divide where natural lakes offer fishing and dramatic scenery. Your horse is welcomed to join you on the ranch. Fish for trout in the river or on one of Monarch Valley's private lakes. Participate in world-record elk hunting among the 3.7 million acres of the Gunnison and Rio Grande National Forests adjacent to the ranch. For downhill skiers, Monarch Pass Ski Area is known for its deep powder and short lift lines, while Crested Butte is ranked one of the best in the country. Cross-country skiers will find numerous forest trails to explore. After a day of hiking, take a refreshing dip in a lake. After a day of skiing, relax your sore muscles in soothing, private hot tubs.

Cabins and lodge rooms are also available.

Location: 25 miles East of Gunnison, off Highway 50, between Parlin and Sargents.

Total RV sites: 70	Pull thru sites: 60	Open: All Year
Full hookup sites: 70	45+ foot long sites: 70	Gerald & Nancy Brown, Owners
Water & elec. sites: 0	Slideout sites: 70	67366 Hwy 50 E
Elec. only sites: 0	Licenses sold: None	Gunnison, Colorado 81230-9401
50 amp sites: 10	LP Gas: M	970/641-0626
Hookup sites open in Fall: 35	Credit Cards: VM	
Winter hookup sites: 5	Elevation: 8300	
RV site cost: Not available		

Within 15 minutes:

At RV Park:

Rockey River Resort

Homesteaded in 1892, Rockey River Resort has full hookup (30 amps), grassy sites near the cottonwood trees along the steady flow of the Gunnison River. Most sites have barbecue grills and some have picnic tables. Here you'll find modern comfort in a rustic atmosphere.

The abundant beauty of this country is unmatched. All of nature's colors in rocks and mountain flowers are displayed throughout the many scenic circle trips designed for your enjoyment. Check out a bit of history in the numerous ghost towns, old mines and relics of a by-gone era. If you're more interested in sports, the resort is within easy access to hunting, lake fishing, skiing, whitewater rafting and horseback riding. Fish along almost a half-mile of privately owned river frontage of the churning Gunnison or try lake fishing at nearby Taylor, Spring Creek and Blue Mesa Reservoirs. The playground, with volleyball, basketball, horseshoes, and badminton will keep the kids entertained while you prepare a meal of freshly caught rainbow trout. The library has books for all ages.

Log cabins along the Gunnison River are also available.

Location: ¼ mile East of Highway 135, 6 miles North of Gunnison on County Road 10.

Total RV sites: 27
Full hookup sites: 27
Water & elec. sites: 0
Elec. only sites: 0
50 amp sites: 0
Hookup sites open in Fall: 27
Winter hookup sites: 0
RV site cost: $

Pull thru sites: 10
45+ foot long sites: 27
Slideout sites: 27
Licenses sold: None
LP Gas: None
Credit Cards: VMA
Elevation: 7860

Open: 5/1 to 10/31
Joe Marvel & Rob & Dani Wattles, Owners
4359 County Rd 10
Gunnison, Colorado 81230-9606
970/641-0174

Within 15 minutes:

At RV Park:

Rowe's RV Park & Gun Shop

Off the beaten path, high up in the mountains, Rowe's has full hookup (20 and 50 amps) sites with pull thrus and campfire pits. Camp among beautiful scenery and high country solitude.

Visit the old time general camp store founded in 1886! Rowe's also boasts one of the best gun shops in western Colorado. Get your fish tackle here before casting in the numerous, fast flowing streams and clear blue mountain lakes. Other activities include hunting, four-wheel driving, mountain biking and exploring ghost towns and historical mining towns. A visit to the gourmet Gold Creek Inn next door is a must!

Location: Exit US Highway 50 at milepost 169 and go North 9 miles, turn at Parlin.

Total RV sites: 8	Pull thru sites: 8	Open: 5/1 to 11/15
Full hookup sites: 8	45+ foot long sites: 8	James & Willamina Rowe, Owners
Water & elec. sites: 0	Slideout sites: 8	1 Main Street
Elec. only sites: 0	Licenses sold: Fish & Hunt	PO Box 61
50 amp sites: 5	LP Gas: None	Ohio City, Colorado 81237-0061
Hookup sites open in Fall: 8	Credit Cards: None	970/641-4272
Winter hookup sites: 0	Elevation: 8560	
RV site cost: Not available		

Within 15 minutes:

At RV Park:

Shady Island Resort, Cabins & RV Park

Camp 10 feet from the banks of the Gunnison River at Shady Island Resort. The level, cottonwood-shaded sites are full hookups (30 amps) with cable TV hookup. Some sites are pull thru and all have picnic tables and fire rings with wood available. At night, the only sounds you'll hear are the steady gurgle of the river and the crackling of your campfire. In the morning watch the trout jump for breakfast on the river.

Send the kids off to the playground to play miniature golf, badminton, horseshoes and volleyball while you relax in the shade. Ask your hosts about organized raft trips leaving from the campground and tubing on the Gunnison River. Shady Island Resort is conveniently close to Gunnison, within 2 miles of a shopping center, service station and laundromat. Enjoy fishing the Gunnison River or on many of the other nearby lakes and streams. Guest horses are permitted or rent one at local stables. Area activities include four-wheel driving, hiking and mountain biking.

Cabins are also available.

Location: Two ½ miles North of Gunnison on Highway 135.

Total RV sites: 40
Full hookup sites: 40
Water & elec. sites: 0
Elec. only sites: 0
50 amp sites: 0
Hookup sites open in Fall: 40
Winter hookup sites: 0
RV site cost: $

Pull thru sites: 5
45+ foot long sites: 4
Slideout sites: 10
Licenses sold: None
LP Gas: None
Credit Cards: VMD
Elevation: 7700

Open: 5/1 to 11/15
Arlie & Odessa Griffith, Owner
2776 North Hwy 135
Gunnison, Colorado 81230-9705
970/641-0416

Within 15 minutes:

At RV Park:

Sunnyside Campground & RV Park

Sunnyside Campground is on a green hillside overlooking the picturesque Blue Mesa Reservoir, Colorado's largest body of water. The open sites are full hookups (20, 30 and 50 amps) with cable TV hookup available. From your quiet site, you have a view of the vast expanse of Blue Mesa backed by snow-kissed mountain peaks in the distance.

The camp store has fishing tackle, RV supplies, Indian jewelry and video tape rentals. The large picnic shelter is great for group dinners. A boat launch is nearby for those who like to troll for the large rainbow trout, brown trout and kokanee salmon swimming in the Blue Mesa. Or hike and fish the miles of shoreline. Other nearby activities include hunting, sight seeing, mountain biking, horseback riding and whitewater rafting.

Ask about the daily, weekly, monthly and yearly rates. Covered and open RV and boat storage is available. An outdoor, group meeting area is available.

Location: Twelve miles West of Gunnison on US Highway 50 between mileposts 145 and 146.

Total RV sites: 24	Pull thru sites: 5	Open: 4/1 to 10/30
Full hookup sites: 24	45+ foot long sites: 7	Richard & Barbara Oswald, Owners
Water & elec. sites: 0	Slideout sites: 7	28357 W Hwy 50
Elec. only sites: 0	Licenses sold: Fish & Hunt	Gunnison, Colorado 81230
50 amp sites: 3	LP Gas: metered	970/641-0477
Hookup sites open in Fall: 24	Credit Cards: VMD	
Winter hookup sites: 0	Elevation: 7650	
RV site cost: ¢–$		

Within 15 minutes:

At RV Park:

Tall Texan Campground

High in the Rockies at Tall Texan Campground you'll find pull thru, shaded sites with full hookup (20 and 30 amps) and TV hookup available. All sites have a picnic table and barbecue grill. Some sites have a cement patio. Here in the high country, the weather is cool and refreshing and, at night, the campfire will keep you warm and your marshmallows toasty.

Families will enjoy playing horseshoes on-site. The large club house's recreation room with a huge fireplace is great for the adults while the kids carouse in the game room or on the playground. The large, community type pavilion is ideal for family reunions or group gatherings. Young and old anglers alike will want to practice at the campground's fishing pond before walking to the bigger waters of the Gunnison River. Tall Texan has an annual 4th of July barbecue and picnic that is not to be missed. The nearby mountain trails are a paradise to photographers, hikers and horseback riders. Ask your hosts to make trail ride arrangements for you.

Location: Two miles North of Gunnison on Highway 135 (200 yards East of the Highway) on County Road 11.

Total RV sites: 70
Full hookup sites: 60
Water & elec. sites: 15
Elec. only sites: 0
50 amp sites: 0
Hookup sites open in Fall: 75
Winter hookup sites: 0
RV site cost: Not available

Pull thru sites: 70
45+ foot long sites: 25
Slideout sites: 30
Licenses sold: None
LP Gas: metered
Credit Cards: VM
Elevation: 7703

Open: 4/15 to 10/15
Mike & Linda Huber, Owners
2460 Hwy 135
Gunnison, Colorado 81230-9704
970/641-2927

Within 15 minutes:

At RV Park:

Three Rivers Resort & Outfitting

Named for the Taylor, East and Gunnison rivers in the heart of Gunnison National Forest, Three Rivers Resort features full hookups (20 and 30 amps) with campfire pits, concrete patios, and picnic tables in landscaped sites. Sit next to the Taylor River and exchange tales about the one that *didn't* get away!

The indoor pavilion can accommodate up to 80 people and has a pool table, foosball and many other table games. It's perfect for large family reunions. Other on-site facilities include a general store and a professional fly and tackle shop with everything from to beginner's bait to the best fly fishing rods around. In the summer, participate in resort-sponsored activities such as square dances, bingo and potlucks. The resort also offers mild or wild raft trips and inflatable kayak trips. Raft down scenic Taylor Canyon to areas only accessible by boat. Or combine a rafting trip with fishing in those deep pools hard to reach from the shore. Hike in the national forest where you'll discover bubbling streams, clear lakes, delicate wildflowers, colorful rocks, dense forests and a variety of wildlife in abundance.

Rustic and modern, river front cabins are also available.

Location: Ten miles North of Gunnison in Almont off Highway 135.

Total RV sites: 43	Pull thru sites: 6	Open: All Year
Full hookup sites: 26	45+ foot long sites: 0	Mark & Mary Jo Schumacher, Owners
Water & elec. sites: 17	Slideout sites: 26	130 County Road 742
Elec. only sites: 0	Licenses sold: Fish & Hunt	PO Box 339
50 amp sites: 0	LP Gas: metered	Almont, Colorado 81210-0339
Hookup sites open in Fall: 43	Credit Cards: VMAD	970/641-1303
Winter hookup sites: 12	Elevation: 8000	970/641-1317 fax
RV site cost: $		

Within 15 minutes:

At RV Park:

Idaho Springs

Map: F-14

The first major gold strike in Colorado on January 7, 1859, in Idaho Springs by George Jackson changed the state forever. Today would-be miners should check out the Argo Mine & Mill where they can pan for gold and gemstones or tour the still operating Phoenix Gold Mine. South of town, on Flirtation Peak is the Bridal Veil Falls where the largest water wheel in the state was built in 1893. Idaho Springs was named for the geothermal pool and baths fed by waters considered scared to the Utes who once relaxed here. Drive the Mt. Evans Scenic and Historic Byway 14 miles to the summit of the 14, 264 foot peak. Along the highest paved highway in America you'll see big-horn sheep, elk and goats among alpine tundra and bristlecone pines. There's always the "Oh My God Road" which links Central City to Idaho Springs, passing by hundreds of abandoned mines and mills. Encompassing the town, Arapaho National Forest offers endless alpine hikes.

Fun Things To Do

- Arapaho National Forest (303) 567-2901, (303) 460-0325
- Argo Mine & Mill (303) 567-2421, (303) 567-2191
- Clear Creek Ranger District Office (303) 567-2901, (303) 893-1474
- Echo Lake Lodge (303) 567-2138
- Edgar Mines (303) 567-2911
- Historic District Walking Tours (303) 567-4709
- Phoenix Gold Mine (303) 567-0422
- Underhill Museum (303) 567-4709

Cottonwood RV Campground

At Cottonwood RV Campground, the well landscaped, grassy sites are in the shade of tall cottonwood trees along a refreshing mountain creek. The sites, half are full hook-ups (30 amps), are for self-contained units only and cable TV hookup is available. The campground has groomed lawns and beautiful flower beds overflowing with colorful, gorgeous blossoms.

The mountain-fed Chicago Creek runs right through the campground — you can fish walking distance from your site. Or take the car on the highest paved highway in the United States to Mt. Evans. Along the road to Echo Lake, you'll see beautiful, 2,000 year old living bristle cone pine trees. Raft trips, horseback rides and mountain bike trails are nearby. Enjoy dinner at nearby Beau Jo's, said to be the best pizza in Colorado.

Ask about the weekly and monthly rates.

Location: One ½ miles South of I-70 on Highway 103 at milepost 240.

Total RV sites: 20	Pull thru sites: 0	Open: All Year
Full hookup sites: 10	45+ foot long sites: 10	Glen & Winnie Straub, Owners
Water & elec. sites: 10	Slideout sites: 15	1485 Hwy 103
Elec. only sites: 0	Licenses sold: None	Idaho Springs, Colorado 80452
50 amp sites: 0	LP Gas: None	303/567-2617
Hookup sites open in Fall: 20	Credit Cards: None	
Winter hookup sites: 20	Elevation: 7500	
RV site cost: ¢–$		

Within 15 minutes:

At RV Park:

I-25 South Area

Includes Trinidad, Walsenburg and Weston
Also see Pueblo and San Luis Valley Area.
Map: P-19 and N-18.

Trinidad, just 13 miles from the New Mexico border, is awash in Victorian and Hispanic influences from its native brick streets to the Corazon de Trinidad National Historic District where you'll find eclectic architecture with an adobe twist. In the early years, Trinidad was a sheep and cattle center until coal was discovered in the nearby hills. The Cokedale National Historic District, 8 miles west, is the best example of an intact Colorado coal camp and once housed 1,500 miners. Currently it is home to the area's artistic community. Explore the local flora and fauna to the east along the Santa Fe Trail in the Comanche National Grasslands where the longest dinosaur track site in the world lies almost untouched by civilization. To the west, up the Scenic Highway of Legends, Monument and North lakes offer fishing and other outdoor activities. Continue along this byway to the town of Walsenburg, settled originally by New Mexico natives and later attracted many Anglo-Americans, especially those of German ancestry. Easily visited from here are Mosca Pass, an historic route, which was once a toll road and the Great Sand Dunes National Monument. On the way to Mosca Pass, stop at the deserted historic landmark of Sharp's Trading Post, a two-story adobe which once served as a hotel and trading post.

Fun Things To Do

- A.R. Mitchell Memorial Museum of Western Art (719) 846-4224
- Children's Museum/Old Firehouse #1 (719) 846-8220/(719) 846-7721
- Colorado Welcome Center at Trinidad (719) 846-9512
- Comanche National Grasslands (719) 523-6591
- Monument Lake Resort Marina & Horseback Riding (800) 845-8006
- Trinidad Country Club & Golf Course (719) 846-4015

Cawthon Motel & Campground

The sunsets are gorgeous over the towering Sangre de Cristo Mountains at Cawthon Campground's shady and open sites. Quiet, off the road, with clean air and low humidity, the campground has level, pull thru, full hookup (20, 30 and 50 amps) sites with free cable TV. Gather your family around the picnic area for an evening cookout. Along the Santa Fe Trail, the campground is adjacent to and overlooks the Trinidad Municipal Country Club golf course. Enjoy a great view of Fisher's Peak from your site.

From Cawthon, you'll have cart access to this 9-hole city golf course. The campground also sports shuffleboard courts, sports fields, horseshoes and hiking trails. Close to town, you'll be able to walk to restaurants, grocery and liquor stores. Plentiful fishing areas filled with fast moving trout tempt even those who can't bait their own hook. Area streams actually offer more fish than you could possibly catch! Take a refreshing dip in the heated swimming pool after a day of fun in southern Colorado's sun.

Air-conditioned motel rooms, some with kitchenettes, are also available.

Location: Exit I-25 at milepost 13A to Santa Fe Trail, right ¼ miles. Follow blue camp signs.

Total RV sites: 38	Pull thru sites: 38	Open: All Year
Full hookup sites: 38	45+ foot long sites: 38	Margaret & Paul Koreny, Owners
Water & elec. sites: 0	Slideout sites: 38	1701 Santa Fe Trail
Elec. only sites: 0	Licenses sold: None	Trinidad, Colorado 81082
50 amp sites: 4	LP Gas: None	719/846-3303
Hookup sites open in Fall: 38	Credit Cards: VM	
Winter hookup sites: 38	Elevation: 6400	
RV site cost: Not available		

Within 15 minutes:

At RV Park:

Country Host Motel & Campground

Next to a motel, Country Host has mostly open and some shaded, full hookup sites of grass and gravel. The pull thru sites have cement patios for your convenience. Stay here in-route to the Great Sand Dunes National Monument or Cuchara Ski Area. A few Russian Olive, elm, piñon pine and juniper trees are scattered throughout the campground. Camp on the open plains with views of the nearby Spanish Peaks. Easily accessible, Country Host is a "plain Jane" campground.

If you get tired of cooking, try someone else's at the restaurant across the street. Let the kids carouse on the playground or take them fishing and mountain biking nearby. Bring your own horse, or rent one from local stables, for exploring the countryside.

Motel rooms are also available.

Location: ¼ mile South of I-25 at Exit 52 on the I-25 bus loop.

Total RV sites: 18
Full hookup sites: 18
Water & elec. sites: 0
Elec. only sites: 0
50 amp sites: 0
Hookup sites open in Fall: 18
Winter hookup sites: 18
RV site cost: $

Pull thru sites: 9
45+ foot long sites: 9
Slideout sites: 18
Licenses sold: None
LP Gas: None
Credit Cards: VMAD
Elevation: 6200

Open: All Year
Gerald & Shirley Eisenzimmer, Managers
PO Box 190
Walsenburg, Colorado 81089-0190
719/738-3800

Within 15 minutes:

At RV Park:

Dakota Campground

Camp in open and level sites with views of the majestic Rocky Mountains. The long pull thrus are full hookups with 30 and 50 amps. Most sites have a picnic table, barbecue grill, fire ring and free wood.

The recreation room with a pool table and coin video games is for kids of all ages. The playground and horseshoes will keep you entertained. The camp store is stocked with pop, beer, ice, ice cream, RV toiletries, soap, eggs, candy and local newspapers. The complete Birco RV Parts, Services & Auto Repair with an auto mechanic on duty seven days a weeks makes for a worry-free vacation. Swimming, boating, fishing, and golfing are nearby.

Location: ½ mile South of Exit 52 on the I-25 business loop.

Total RV sites: 60	Pull thru sites: 60	Open: All Year
Full hookup sites: 52	45+ foot long sites: 60	George & Mikell Birrer, Owners
Water & elec. sites: 6	Slideout sites: 60	1079 Hwy 85/87
Elec. only sites: 2	Licenses sold: None	PO Box 206
50 amp sites: 4	LP Gas: metered	Walsenburg, Colorado 81089-0206
Hookup sites open in Fall: 52	Credit Cards: None	719/738-9912
Winter hookup sites: 52	Elevation: 6300	
RV site cost: ¢–$		

Within 15 minutes:

At RV Park:

Monument Lake Resort

On the banks of beautiful Monument Lake, the resort has 2 miles of shoreline and close to thousands of acres in San Isabel National Forest. The full hookup sites have campfire pits. The lake is an angler's paradise with Kokanee salmon, rainbow and brown trout waiting to be caught! Breathe the fresh mountain air while walking around the lake or horseback riding in the surrounding forest where wildlife abounds.

Resort amenities include the Southwestern flair of Oza Lee's restaurant, the Miramonte Lodge, game room and lake marina. Summer and fall activities include fishing, boating, horseback riding, mountain biking, hunting and playing volleyball and horseshoes. Take a hay ride and a fall color tour to appreciate the kaleidoscope of changing aspen leaves. In the winter, you can downhill ski at Cuchara Resort, cross-country ski, ice skate, ice fish, snowmobile, take a sleigh ride and wildlife tour.

Family reunions and other groups are welcomed. Adobe cottages and lodge rooms are also available.

Location: Thirty six miles West of Trinidad (I-25, Exit 14A) on scenic Highway 12 or from the junction of US Highways 160 and 12, at milepost 33, go 33 miles South to Monument Lake.

Total RV sites: 61
Full hookup sites: 19
Water & elec. sites: 30
Elec. only sites: 0
50 amp sites: 0
Hookup sites open in Fall: 49
Winter hookup sites: 0
RV site cost: Not available

Pull thru sites: 4
45+ foot long sites: 5
Slideout sites: 49
Licenses sold: Fishing
LP Gas: metered
Credit Cards: VM
Elevation: 8523

Open: All Year
Andy & Connie Popejoy, Hosts
4789 Hwy 12
Weston, Colorado 81091
719/868-2226
800/845-8006

Within 15 minutes:

At RV Park:

I-70 East Area

**Includes Limon, Genoa, Flagler, Seibert, Stratton, and Burlington.
Map: H-22; H-23; G-24; G-25; G-26; G-28.**

From Limon east on I-70, there's a myriad of things to see and do. Located on Colorado's high plains, Limon is a convenient stopping point while traveling. Limon has a municipal swimming pool, nine-hole golf course and numerous picnic areas. Watch for the abundant wildlife on the plains surrounding Limon. The town's Schoolhouse Museum was build in 1895 and is an excellent example of early school houses in Lincoln County. Nearby, in the town of Genoa, is the Genoa Tower Museum where you can see six states from the tower on a clear day. The museum also has a large collection of fossil skulls, guns, bottles, Indian artifacts and oddities like two-headed calves and jackalopes! Northeast from Flagler is the Flagler Reservoir and State Wildlife Area where you can fish and picnic while protected wildlife wander in the reserve. The Kit Carson County Carousel in Burlington is a fully restored and operating, hand-carved 1905 wooden merry-go-round. One of fewer than 170 such carousels left in the country, this gaily painted, charming antique was a toy of the American Victorian middle class and is a National Landmark. As you travel I-70 west, you can watch the beautiful Rocky Mountains rise majestically up out of the plains.

Fun Things to Do

- Burlington Old Town Museum (800) 288-1334, (719) 346-7382
- Flagler Reservoir & State Wildlife Area (719) 765-4422
- Genoa Tower Museum (719) 763-2309
- Pioneer Schoolhouse Museum (719) 775-2350
- Tamarack Golf Course (719) 775-9998
- Welcome Center at Burlington (719) 346-5554

Limon KOA

Convenient to the Interstate, Limon KOA has level, gravel parking pads. The long pull thrus are open and surrounded by grass. Shade trees dot the campground providing cool spots to relax in. Most sites are full hookups (20, 30 and some 50 amps) and all have picnic tables, fire pits and barbecue

grills. Cable TV hookups are available. Sit back and watch the colorful sunrises and sunsets flood the endless sky with color.

The heated swimming pool, playground and game room are among the on-site amenities. The sports fields have basketball, volleyball, badminton and tournament quality horseshoes. The camp store has RV supplies, snacks, souvenirs and limited groceries. Limon KOA is a great stopover before entering Denver, Colorado Springs or the Rocky Mountains. Restaurants, shops, service stations, and golf are within walking distance.

Camper Cabins are also available.

Location: At the junction of I-70 (Exit 361) and US Highways 24/40/287, go to the Pizza Hut then North 2 blocks.

Total RV sites: 64	Pull thru sites: 30	Open: 4/1 to 10/31
Full hookup sites: 22	45+ foot long sites: 30	Jim & Kay McCormick, Owners
Water & elec. sites: 30	Slideout sites: 30	575 Colorado Ave
Elec. only sites: 0	Licenses sold: None	Limon, Colorado 80828
50 amp sites: 10	LP Gas: metered	719/775-2151
Hookup sites open in Fall: 52	Credit Cards: VMD	800/775-2151 RESERV. ONLY
Winter hookup sites: 0	Elevation: 5366	
RV site cost: ¢–$		

Within 15 minutes:

At RV Park:

Little England Motel & RV Park

The level, pull thru sites at this RV park in Flagler are adjacent to the motel with easy access to the Interstate. Many sites are full hookups (30 amps) with cable TV hookup.

Get your swing down at the practice putting green before playing at the public 9-hole golf course close by. Or challenge a friend to a game of horseshoes. A 24-hour convenience store and coin laundry are next door. The Flagler State Wildlife area is nearby.

Modern motel rooms with air conditioning are also available.

Location: Exit North off I-70 at milepost 395, then left on 1st Street.

Total RV sites: 22	Pull thru sites: 22	Open: All Year
Full hookup sites: 10	45+ foot long sites: 16	Edward & Donna Ward, Owners
Water & elec. sites: 12	Slideout sites: 2	Box 248
Elec. only sites: 0	Licenses sold: None	Flagler, Colorado 80815-0248
50 amp sites: 3	LP Gas: None	719/765-4875
Hookup sites open in Fall: 22	Credit Cards: VMAD	
Winter hookup sites: 22	Elevation: 4959	
RV site cost: Not available		

Within 15 minutes:

At RV Park:

Trail's End Campground

Out on the eastern plains, Colorado's outback, is Trail's End Campground in Stratton where the well-maintained sites are surrounded by lush trees and green grass. The long, level pull thrus are full hookups (20, 30 and 50 amps) with TV and phone hookups. A countryside campground, the sites here are open and shaded with picnic tables and barbecue grills.

Camp amenities include a heated swimming pool, miniature golf, a video game room, a playground and a convenience store on-site. This quiet campground with its friendly service is a short drive from Burlington's Old Town and historic carousel. Fine dining, a golf course, a movie theater and bowling are all within walking distance in Stratton. After a day on the road, put up your feet and watch the sun set in a blaze of rusty oranges, brilliant reds and mellow yellows — it's a site you won't soon forget.

Location: Exit I-70 at milepost 419, go North to 7th Street and take the first right turn.

Total RV sites: 30
Full hookup sites: 30
Water & elec. sites: 4
Elec. only sites: 0
50 amp sites: 4
Hookup sites open in Fall: 30
Winter hookup sites: 30
RV site cost: Not available

Pull thru sites: 30
45+ foot long sites: 26
Slideout sites: 26
Licenses sold: None
LP Gas: metered
Credit Cards: VMD
Elevation: 4400

Open: All Year
TC & Tracy Travis, Owners
700 New York Ave
PO Box 419
Stratton, Colorado 80836-0419
719/348-5529
800/777-6042

Within 15 minutes:

At RV Park:

I-76 Northeast Area

Includes Fort Morgan and Sterling. Map: D-21 and B- 24

Fort Morgan is a quiet, small town with beautiful, historic houses. The town's Riverside Park is 240 acres of nature along the South Platte River. To the northeast is Jackson Lake where the warm water fishing is excellent in the spring and early summer. Six other state wildlife areas are located near here: Boyd Ponds, Brush, Brush Prairie Ponds, Cottonwoods State Park, Dodd Bridge and Elliott Lake. The Pawnee Pioneer Scenic and Historic Byway passes through Fort Morgan on the way to Pawnee National Grasslands and the Pawnee Buttes — 300-foot sandstone towers which have survived erosion in the prairie.

Sterling, called the builder and civilizer of the Overland Trail, was founded in 1873. The Overland Trail Museum is a tribute to the greatest migration of people this country has ever experienced. The trail, leading to gold fields and the West, was used by Indians, fur trappers, explorers and early government expeditions. Check out the Living Trees scattered throughout Sterling — sculptures created by artist Bradford Rhea who turns trees into giraffes, clowns, mermaids and golfers. The North Sterling Reservoir Colorado State Park, 8 miles north, offers warm water fishing and water sports along with rabbit, dove and waterfowl hunting. The Pawnee Pioneer Trail Scenic & Historic Byway begins just west of Sterling on Highway 14.

Fun Things To Do

- Fort Morgan Golf Course (970) 867-5990
- Overland Trail Museum(970) 522-3895
- Riverview Golf Course (970) 522-3035

Buffalo Hills Camper Park

Make Buffalo Hills Camper Park your first and last stop in Colorado. With easy access on and off the highway, the park has lots of shady elm and cottonwood trees and cool, quiet nights. The level, full hookup (20 and 30 amps), pull thru sites are mostly shaded with TV and phone hookups available. Group camping is available. Gather the family around the picnic tables and barbecue grills. Some of the most beautiful sunsets you have ever seen will welcome you to Buffalo Hills.

The store has camping supplies, groceries, gifts, snacks and ice for your convenience. There is also an extensive RV supply and parts center on-site. You and yours will keep busy with the arcade, heated swimming pool, wading pool, miniature golf, playground and horseshoes. Ask your hosts for information about Sterling's unique sculptured trees, Pioneer Museum, golf course and many restaurants.

Teepees are also available for rent.

Location: Easy on/off access I-76 at Exit 125, ¼ mile East on US Highway 6.

Total RV sites: 60	Pull thru sites: 47	Open: All Year
Full hookup sites: 47	45+ foot long sites: 40	Ken & Jennie Claybaugh & Bill, Mary Lee, &
Water & elec. sites: 0	Slideout sites: 40	Marguerite Stoughton, Owners
Elec. only sites: 14	Licenses sold: None	22018 Hwy 6 East
50 amp sites: 0	LP Gas: weight	Sterling, Colorado 80751-8418
Hookup sites open in Fall: 47	Credit Cards: VM	970/522-2233
Winter hookup sites: 4	Elevation: 3950	800/569-1824
RV site cost: $		

Within 15 minutes:

At RV Park:

Wayward Wind Campground

Relax under starry skies in this cowboy campground with plenty of stomping room for all! The level sites are full hookups and pull thrus. Some sites are shady, others are open. Wayward Wind Campground has easy access from the interstate.

Wayward Wind is a full-service camp-ground with a game room and fenced corral (playground) to entertain the little cowpokes. Play horseshoes or volleyball with other campers. A wading pool and swimming pool will soothe your saddle sores after a day of fun in the sun. Both Jackson and Pruett lakes are nearby and offer great fishing and boating. Estes Park and Rocky Mountain National Park are an easy day trip from here. In Fort Morgan you'll find restaurants, golf courses and tennis courts.

Weekly and monthly rates are available.

Location: Near I-76 Exit 75A, West of Fort Morgan.

Total RV sites: 48	Pull thru sites: 42	Open: All Year
Full hookup sites: 48	45+ foot long sites: 48	Laurie Ryan, Manager
Water & elec. sites: 3	Slideout sites: 48	14390 Hwy 34 #51
Elec. only sites: 0	Licenses sold: None	Ft Morgan, Colorado 80701
50 amp sites:	LP Gas: metered	970/867-8948
Hookup sites open in Fall: 0	Credit Cards: None	
Winter hookup sites: 0	Elevation: 4330	
RV site cost: ¢–$		

Within 15 minutes:

At RV Park:

Kremmling

Map: E-11

Rugged mountains, gentle river valleys and vast national forests offering an uncrowded playground, shared only with wildlife and wildflowers, are the backdrop to Kremmling. Hikers, photographers, hunters, artists, archeologists and anglers revel in the area's beauty. The fishing along the Colorado River between Kremmling and Hot Sulphur Springs is said to be golden, a gold-medal trout stream that is. Gold-medal designation refers to rivers where anglers must test their mettle against trout using only flies or lures. Some parts of gold-medal rivers are catch-and-release only, where fighting the fish is more appealing than frying it. The 9 miles between Kremmling and Hot Sulphur Springs is one of those unique, wild rivers. If fishing isn't your thing, try a scenic float trip on the Little Gore and Red Gorge canyons on the Colorado River. Or windsurf and waterski on Green Mountain Reservoir. Williams Fork Reservoir, nearby in the Arapaho National Forest, has fishing, boating and picnicking. The Wolford Dam Reservoir also offers fishing and swimming. Hike to the remote lakes in the Eagle's Nest Wilderness area and Routt National Forest.

Fun Things To Do

- Kremmling Museum (970) 724-3472
- Little Gore/Red Gorge Canyons (970) 724-3472
- Routt & Arapaho National Forests (970) 724-3472

Alpine RV Park

With a view toward the magnificent Kremmling Cliffs and Gore Canyon Alpine RV Park offers full hook up spacious grassy sites with the convenience of an easy two block walk to shopping and restaurants. Enjoy the serenity of rural Colorado while camping at the base of the bluffs.

This bare bones RV Park has grassy sites and is convenient to hiking, fishing and golf. Mountain bike and motor bike trails leave right from the property. Horseback riding is in the area and guest horses are welcome. In the fall it is an excellent basecamp for some of the best hunting in Colorado. In the winter you can snowmobile from your site.

Location: NW corner of Kremmling at the junction of Highway 40 and Colorado 9.

Total RV sites: 19	Pull thru sites: 1	Open: 4/1 to 11/31
Full hookup sites: 19	45+ foot long sites: 1	Eric C. Woog, Owner
Water & elec. sites: 0	Slideout sites: 19	115 W Central Ave
Elec. only sites: 0	Licenses sold: None	PO Box 992
50 amp sites: 0	LP Gas: None	Kremmling, Colorado 80459
Hookup sites open in Fall: 19	Credit Cards: VMAD	970/724-9655
Winter hookup sites: 6	Elevation: 7400	
RV site cost: ¢		

Within 15 minutes:

At RV Park:

Kremmling RV Park & Campground

Smack dab in the middle of Sportsman's Paradise, Kremmling RV Park is near a Gold Medal section of the Colorado River. The large, level, full hookup (30 and 50 amps) sites are open with pull thrus. Trees and native shrubs surround the sites which have picnic tables.

The playground will make the kids happy. Centered in the Rocky Mountains, Kremmling boasts a wide range of recreation possibilities. The fishing on the Colorado and Blue rivers is, of course, excellent. For those who prefer lake fishing, Green Mountain and Williams Fork Reservoir are close. The hunting is some of the best big game sport in the state. There's also plenty of water sports, hiking trails in Arapaho and Routt National Forests, scenic drives and summer entertainment to keep you entertained.

Location: One ½ miles East of the junction of Highways 9 and 40, then 1 block North on County Road 22.

Total RV sites: 20	Pull thru sites: 20	Open: 5/1 to 11/15
Full hookup sites: 20	45+ foot long sites:	Jo Milner, Owner
Water & elec. sites: 0	Slideout sites: 19	US Highway 40
Elec. only sites: 0	Licenses sold: None	Box 532
50 amp sites: 0	LP Gas: None	Kremmling, Colorado 80459-0532
Hookup sites open in Fall: 20	Credit Cards: VM	970/724-9593
Winter hookup sites: 20	Elevation: 7411	
RV site cost: $–$$		

Within 15 minutes:

At RV Park:

Lake City

Also see Silverton. Map: M-7

Lake City is home to several 14,000-foot mountain peaks: Uncompahgre, Sunshine, Handies, Red Cloud and Wetterhorn. Tucked into the grassy canyon where Henson Creek and the Lake Fork of the Gunnison River meet, Lake City is a state secret. Hike in any of the four national forests that surround this small town. The Alpine Scenic Loop Backcountry Byway which begins in town, runs to Silverton and has some of the most stunning Jeeping in the world. Try boating on spectacular Lake San Cristobal, one of Colorado's largest natural lakes. Fish for rainbow trout in the swirling Lake Fork River or explore the Victorian charm of downtown with over 75 buildings from the late 1800s. Lake City's history is pretty mild compared to the more notorious mining towns. But one story just won't die: Alfred Packer. In 1874, Packer convinced some prospectors to let him guide them through the snow-covered mountains. Six weeks later, he appeared 76 miles to the northeast alone with a beard and long hair. He claimed to have survived on roots and berries but the truth soon came out and Packer was accused of murder and cannibalism. He was sentenced to hang in 1883 at Lake City's courthouse but Packer got off on a technicality and ended up only serving 14 years. Every September, Lake City remembers its famous cannibal with the Alfred Packer Jeep Tour and Barbecue!

Fun Things to Do

- Castle Lakes Jeep Rentals (970) 944-2622
- Hinsdale County Historical Museum (970) 944-2515
- National Historic District (970) 944-2527
- Rocky Mountain Jeep Rental (970) 944-2262, (303) 526-0364

Castle Lakes Campground Resort & Cabins

Situated in a remote, quiet 45-acre aspen and spruce forest, this campground is on the Alpine Scenic Loop Backcountry Byway which takes you through the pictur-esque back country of Colorado. Camp right in the forest at large, level, full hookup (20, 30 and 50 amps) sites under starry skies. In the early morning, watch the bugs dance over the deep green lake waters before casting your line.

The on-site recreation room has a fireplace, pool table and a play area for children. Breakfast, lunch and dinner are served on request. The high-altitude valley, surrounded by snow-capped mountains, has two private, fee-fishing lakes with no state license required. You can also fish the area's many lakes and streams, climb to the tops of nearby 14,000-foot peaks or rent four-wheel drive vehicles and horses to traverse the remote areas. Your horse is welcome to vacation with you at Castle Lakes. Drive the nationally designated Alpine Scenic Loop at the campground's entrance over Cinnamon Pass, returning over Engineer Pass. Or explore the famous ghost towns in nearby Carson. At Castle Lakes, the spring is green, the summer cool and the fall colorful.

Fully furnished cabins and on-site trailers are also available.

Location: On the Alpine Scenic Loop Backcountry Byway, 2 ½ miles South of Lake City, 7 ½ miles above Lake San Cristobal on Cinnamon Pass Road, keep to the right.

Total RV sites: 36	Pull thru sites: 0	Open: 5/15 to 10/1
Full hookup sites: 29	45+ foot long sites: 20	Dick & Mary-Lee Cooper, Owners
Water & elec. sites: 7	Slideout sites: 20	PO Box 909
Elec. only sites: 0	Licenses sold: Fish & Hunt	Lake City, Colorado 81235-0909
50 amp sites: 5	LP Gas: None	970/944-2622
Hookup sites open in Fall: 36	Credit Cards: VM	
Winter hookup sites: 0	Elevation: 9200	
RV site cost: Not available		

Within 15 minutes:

At RV Park:

Henson Creek RV Park

In the center of historic Lake City, Henson Creek RV Park has a friendly, family atmosphere. Residing on the scenic banks of Henson Creek, the campground has open and shaded, level sites with pull thrus and full hookups (20 and 30 amps). TV hookup is available. Each site has a picnic table to complete the camping experience.

Lake City's shops, town park, restaurants and Hinsdale County Museum are within walking distance. Take the kids to the nearby miniature golf course and then treat them at the ice cream parlor afterwards. The on-site store has ice, snacks, RV supplies, fishing licenses, tackle and bait. Fish from the campground or take a stroll on one of the many hiking trails that begin here. Five peaks over 14,000 feet are in Hinsdale County, so bring along your hiking boots! The Alpine Scenic Loop Backcountry Byway begins right behind the campground. Lake San Cristobal, the second largest natural lake in the state, is only 4 miles from Henson Creek. Participate in the pot luck suppers scheduled throughout the summer while you kick-back and relax in the crisp mountain air and cool sunshine.

An outdoor pavilion for group meetings is available.

Location: In the center of Lake City, on Henson Creek, at Highway 149.

Total RV sites: 33	Pull thru sites: 5	Open: 5/15 to 10/10
Full hookup sites: 29	45+ foot long sites: 17	Terry Morrow, Owner
Water & elec. sites: 4	Slideout sites: 17	110 S Hwy 149
Elec. only sites: 0	Licenses sold: Fish & Hunt	PO Box 621
50 amp sites: 0	LP Gas: metered	Lake City, Colorado 81235
Hookup sites open in Fall: 33	Credit Cards: None	970/944-2394
Winter hookup sites: 0	Elevation: 8671	
RV site cost: ¢–$		

Within 15 minutes:

At RV Park:

Highlander RV Park

Highlander is a new RV park, scheduled to open in June 1995. Call before planning your vacation to make sure their opening is on schedule. Be one of the first to camp at Highlander RV Park.

Just north of Lake San Cristobal, the Highlander RV Park has large, level sites with full hookups. Cable TV and phone hookups are available at each site. The facilities are ADA handicapped accessible. Relax in the shade of your site with views of the Continental Divide and aspen-covered peaks.

Enjoy fishing at un-crowded trout streams. Area activities include boating, mountain biking, hiking, four-wheel driving, hunting and ghost-town exploring.

Location: On County Road 30, 3 miles South of Lake City.

Total RV sites: 25	Pull thru sites: 2	Open: 5/1 to 11/30
Full hookup sites: 21	45+ foot long sites: 25	Don & Diane Campbell, Owners
Water & elec. sites: 4	Slideout sites: 21	CR 30
Elec. only sites: 0	Licenses sold: Fish & Hunt	PO Box 880
50 amp sites: 21	LP Gas: None	Lake City, Colorado 81235-0880
Hookup sites open in Fall: 16	Credit Cards: None	970/944-2878
Winter hookup sites: 16	Elevation: 9000	
RV site cost: ¢–$$		

Within 15 minutes:

At RV Park:

Lake City Campground

Within walking distance of quaint Lake City, this campground has full hookup 20/30/50 amps sites with picnic tables and barbecue grills. Some of the sites are shady and some grassy. All sites have room for slide outs. Hot showers and a laundry are also available. This "plain Jane" park is close enough to Lake City to enjoy city camping and close enough to the great outdoors to enjoy many activities.

Drive the Alpine Scenic Loop Backcountry Byway in the heart of the majestic San Juan Mountains where 96 percent of the land is public. With Lake San Cristobal just 2 miles away, fishing and boating are nearby. Other area activities include hunting, four-wheel driving, hiking and horseback riding. The restaurants, museum and shops of Lake City are a pleasant stroll away.

Location: From Highway 149 in Lake City take North Bluff Street.

Total RV sites: 8
Full hookup sites: 8
Water & elec. sites: 0
Elec. only sites: 6
50 amp sites: 0
Hookup sites open in Fall: 8
Winter hookup sites: 0
RV site cost: Not available

Pull thru sites: 0
45+ foot long sites: 0
Slideout sites: 8
Licenses sold: None
LP Gas: None
Credit Cards: None
Elevation: 8700

Open: 5/15 to 11/1
Bob Carey, Owner
713 North Bluff Street
PO Box 627
Lake City, Colorado 81235
970/944-2287

Within 15 minutes:

At RV Park:

Lakeview Resort Cabins & RV Park

Lakeview Resort offers what Colorado used to be — few people, a deep blue lake, bubbling streams, mountain peaks, dusty ghost towns and high mountain passes. A family resort on the shores of one of Colorado's most beautiful natural lake, the park has spacious RV sites with full hookups (20 amps) and campfire pits in the pine trees adjacent to a lodge, restaurant and marina on Lake San Cristobal.

The resort boasts fishing and pontoon boats for rent, guided fishing trips, horseback riding, sunset supper rides, and all day horseback trips. Combine horses and fishing on high mountain rides to alpine lakes and streams where the trout are the freshest! In one of the last real wildernesses Colorado has to offer, you'll likely see elk, deer, coyotes, rabbits and numerous other wildlife. Here bald eagles soar over towering peaks and bright wildflowers dot lush meadows where babbling brooks hide rainbow trout.

Mountain cabins are also available. Ask about the complete facilities for groups, seminars, elder hostels and family reunions.

Location: South of Lake City off Highway 149.

Total RV sites: 12	Pull thru sites: 9	Open: 5/1 to 10/1
Full hookup sites: 12	45+ foot long sites: 9	Tom, Midge, Dan & Michelle Murphy
Water & elec. sites: 0	Slideout sites: 12	Lake San Cristobal
Elec. only sites: 0	Licenses sold: Fish & Hunt	PO Box 1000
50 amp sites: 0	LP Gas: None	Lake City, Colorado 81235-1000
Hookup sites open in Fall: 12	Credit Cards: V	970/944-2401
Winter hookup sites: 0	Elevation: 9100	800/456-0170
RV site cost: $		

Within 15 minutes:

At RV Park:

Woodlake Park

Near the Alpine Scenic Loop Backcountry Byway and on the Silver Thread Scenic Byway, Woodlake Park has uncrowded, spacious sites, surrounded by river and mountain vistas. Partially shaded by willow and spruce trees, the sites are grassy and gravel. The full hookup sites are pull thrus with barbecue grills and campfire pits. At 50 feet apart, the sites offer privacy and solitude to each guest. You'll only hear the babble of the Lake Fork of the Gunnison River as it runs its course.

Get the whole family involved in the fun, organized pavilion activities such as line dancing (instruction given). There's no end to the exciting adventures this mountainous area has to offer: bird watching, fishing, hiking, hunting, mountain biking, horseback riding, Jeeping, ATVing and exploring areas of geological interest and old ghost towns. Drive your ATV from Woodlake Park to the San Cristobal Lake Road. ATV without having to go on the highway.

Camper cabins and a luxury cabin are also available.

Location: Two ½ miles South of Lake City on Colorado Highway 149 between mileposts 69 and 70.

Total RV sites: 13	Pull thru sites: 10	Open: 6/15 to 10/1
Full hookup sites: 13	45+ foot long sites: 8	Latellya Smith, Owner
Water & elec. sites: 0	Slideout sites: 13	Hwy 149 South
Elec. only sites: 0	Licenses sold: None	PO Box 400
50 amp sites: 0	LP Gas: None	Lake City, Colorado 81235-0400
Hookup sites open in Fall: 13	Credit Cards: None	970/944-2283
Winter hookup sites: 0	Elevation: 9000	
RV site cost: ¢		

Within 15 minutes:

At RV Park:

Lake George

Map: I-15

Lake George was founded in 1887 when a Boston manufacturer, George Frost, built a dam at the mouth of Eleven Mile Canyon. The town of Lake George was constructed a few miles away. Workers cut ice from Lake George to refrigerate railroad boxcars containing vegetables and fruit. Six miles east, Florissant Fossil Beds National Monument was once a raging volcanic field whose lava and ash preserved insects, leaves and fish. Over a half-million year period, sediment formed shales which mud flows covered and protected until erosion brought about the fossil discovery in 1874. Established in 1969, the monument encompasses ancient Lake Florissant which existed some 26 to 38 million years ago. Learn at the visitors center how to spot the exquisite impressions of dragonflies, beetles, ants, butterflies, spiders, fish and even some mammals and birds in the valley. It is one of the most extensive fossil records of its type in the world. At the nearby 7,000-acre Dome Rock State Wildlife Area, you'll see Rocky Mountain bighorn sheep, deer, elk, bobcats, coyotes, eagles and wild turkeys basking in the shadow of Pikes Peak. Eleven Mile State Recreation Area, 9 ½ miles from Lake George, offers excellent fishing plus boating, sailing, and hunting. Gem hunters can find goethite, amazonite, and smoky quartz in the Tarryall River Valley north of Lake George.

Fun Things to Do

- Eleven Mile State Park (719) 748-3401
- Florissant Fossil Beds National Monument (719) 748-3253
- Florissant Heritage Museum (719) 748-3562
- Gold Belt Scenic Byways Tour (719) 748-3562
- Historic Hornbeck Homestead (719) 748-3253
- Historic Walking Tour, Florissant (719) 748-3252

Travel Port Campground

All the sites at Travel Port are full hookups 20/30 amps with room for slideouts. Several sites are pull thru and some have 50 amp hookups. Most sites have picnic tables, shade from tall ponderosa pines and campfire pits.

Both dogs and horses are welcomed at Travel Port. Hunters will want to make use of the on-site guides during hunting season. Several restaurants are nearby and a swimming pool and museum are within minutes. Anglers will enjoy excellent fishing at close by Eleven Mile Canyon and Reservoir, Wrights Reservoir and Tarryall Reservoir. The Lake George area is also great for horseback riding, mountain biking, and hiking Wilkerson Pass.

A group meeting room is available for family reunions and other gatherings.

Location: On Highway 24, 40 miles West of Colorado Springs near Lake George.

Total RV sites: 0	Pull thru sites: 8	Open: 5/15 to 9/30
Full hookup sites: 25	45+ foot long sites: 6	Bob & Pat Gilley, Owners
Water & elec. sites: 0	Slideout sites: 25	39284 Hwy 24
Elec. only sites: 0	Licenses sold: None	PO Box 544
50 amp sites: 4	LP Gas: None	Lake George, Colorado 80827-0544
Hookup sites open in Fall: 0	Credit Cards: VM	719/748-8191
Winter hookup sites: 0	Elevation: 8300	
RV site cost: ¢–$		

Within 15 minutes:

At RV Park:

Leadville

Map: H-12

Upon arriving in Leadville, at 10,152 feet, you can't miss the awesome Sawatch Mountains (Ute for "blue earth") to the west with two of the highest peaks in Colorado, Mt. Elbert and Mt. Massive, and the grandeur of Mosquito Range to the east. The brilliance of the aspens, green pine forests, and flowers adorn the hills of summer as well as the warm welcome of the citizens will greet you. But what made this town is beneath the surface: gold, silver, zinc, molybdenum (hardens steel), and turquoise. During its boom days, a quarter mile of town was filled with saloons, brothels, wine-theaters and gambling halls. Horace Tabor lived a life of boom and bust just like Leadville. Tabor and his wife, Augusta, came west in 1859 and struck it rich in silver in the mid-1870s. One of the town's first multi-millionaires, Tabor, in a scandal that rocked the country, later divorced Augusta and married "Baby Doe." Tabor lost his fortune when silver crashed in 1893. His and Baby Doe's tragic stories are recaptured in Leadville's museums and no visit is complete without a journey into the town's fascinating past. In the summer, you can fish, hike, mountain bike, four-wheel drive, or horseback ride in the San Isabel National Forest. Golf at the highest course in the United States — where your ball goes farther in the thin air. Mountain bikers should check out the Mining Belt Mountain Bike Trail. Leadville is the hub of the new Top of the Rockies Scenic & Historic Byway.

Fun Things to Do

- Historic Home of H.A.W. Tabor (719) 486-0551
- Leadville Colorado & Southern Railroad (719) 486-3936
- Leadville National Fish Hatchery (719) 486-0189
- Matchless Mine Museum (719) 486-0371
- Mt. Massive Golf Course (719) 486-2176
- National Mining Hall of Fame & Museum (719) 486-1229
- Pa & Ma's Horseback Riding (719) 486-3900
- Tabor Opera House Museum (719) 486-1147
- Twin Lakes Expeditions (800) 288-0497

Leadville RV Corral

Camp in downtown, historic Leadville at the RV Corral where the spacious, grassy sites are all full hookups (20, 30 and 50 amps). The open, level sites are all pull thru with cable TV and phone hookups available. Each site has a picnic table and barbecue grill for your camping convenience. The stark, breathtaking views of unadorned mountain peaks surround the town and the campground.

All the attractions of Leadville, from shops and restaurants to museums and historical tours, are within walking distance. Area activities include four-wheel driving, horseback riding, hiking, mountain biking, fishing and whitewater rafting.

Location: In downtown Leadville near the corner of Harrison and 2nd Street.

Total RV sites: 33
Full hookup sites: 33
Water & elec. sites: 0
Elec. only sites: 0
50 amp sites: 33
Hookup sites open in Fall: 33
Winter hookup sites: 33
RV site cost: Not available

Pull thru sites: 32
45+ foot long sites: 33
Slideout sites: 33
Licenses sold: None
LP Gas: None
Credit Cards: VM
Elevation: 10200

Open: All Year
David & Jeanne Yarberry, Managers
135 W 2nd St.
Leadville, Colorado 80461
719/486-3111

Within 15 minutes:

At RV Park:

Sugar Loafin' Campground

The scenery stretches to the sky and beyond at Sugar Loafin' Campground. Among the lodgepole pines and grass you'll find full hookup (20, 30 and 50 amps) sites with spectacular views. The pull thru sites have cement runners and campfire pits. Watch the sunset cast a rainbow of colors on Mt. Elbert and Mt. Massive, both well over 14,000 feet high, before roasting marshmallows over an open fire.

You can pan for some of that famous Leadville gold right at the campground. Get all your mining supplies and other goodies at the general store. The playground and recreation room with a fireplace, pool table and video games are great for the kids. All the attractions of Leadville, from golfing to many museums, are nearby. Rip roaring raft trips and leisure float trips on the Arkansas River launch are near the campground. Turquoise Lake, brimming with rainbow and mackinaw trout, is less than 1 mile away. Relive the adventures of the old West with a horse-drawn surrey ride or a train ride to timberline. After a day of adventures in the mountains, return to Sugar Loafin' for the nightly ice cream socials and free slide shows.

Ask for the "I Love Camping" discount. The recreation room is also available for large gatherings.

Location: Turn off US Highway 24 South at milepost 177 and go 3 ½ miles Northwest on Road 4.

Total RV sites: 73	Pull thru sites: 14	Open: 5/20 to 9/30
Full hookup sites: 38	45+ foot long sites: 73	Edith Seppi, Owner
Water & elec. sites: 31	Slideout sites: 73	2665 CR 4
Elec. only sites: 1	Licenses sold: Fishing	303 Colorado Hwy 300
50 amp sites: 4	LP Gas: weight	Leadville, Colorado 80461
Hookup sites open in Fall: 0	Credit Cards: VM	719/486-1031
Winter hookup sites: 0	Elevation: 9696	
RV site cost: $		

Within 15 minutes:

At RV Park:

Longmont

Also see Estes Park. Map: D-16

Longmont started as the Chicago-Colorado Colony in 1871 and with good management, irrigation and hard-working colonists it was a success. With a splendid view of Longs Peak at 14,255 feet, the town has several buildings listed in the National Register of Historic Places including the T.M. Callahan House, Dickens Opera House and Empson Cannery. Old Mill Park has original buildings, plantings and artifacts preserved by pioneers. To the west is Estes Park and Rocky Mountain National Park with 415 glacially-carved square miles covered in lakes, wildlife and wild flowers. To the south is the university town of Boulder and the Boulder Reservoir where you can swim, sail and water ski during the summer months. If you decide to visit Boulder, stop in the tiny town of Niwot along the way and browse among the quality antique stores. Hiking and biking trails abound and in the winter downhill and cross-country skiing are readily available.

Fun Things To Do

- Boulder Reservoir (303) 441-3468
- Longmont Pioneer Museum (303) 651-8374
- Rocky Mountain National Park (970) 586-2371

Westwood Inn Campground

Quiet, yet centrally located in town, Westwood Inn Campground has large shade elm trees, picnic tables, a privacy fence and a patio area. The full hookup sites have 20, 30 and 50 amps. TV and phone hookup for monthlies.

The campground is close to all the shops and restaurants in Longmont as well as Estes Park and Rocky Mountain National Park. Stay here while visiting relatives in town or for a peaceful Colorado vacation. Westwood Inn is within a half hour drive of Boulder and the University of Colorado.

Overnight and weekly rates are available. There is also a small motel on the property.

Location: Centrally located in Longmont on Highway 287 at 1550 North Main.

Total RV sites: 16	Pull thru sites: 5	Open: All Year
Full hookup sites: 16	45+ foot long sites: 3	Sandy Hansen, Owner
Water & elec. sites: 0	Slideout sites: 10	Dale & Billie Boss, Managers.
Elec. only sites: 0	Licenses sold: None	1550 N Main
50 amp sites: 6	LP Gas: None	Longmont, Colorado 80501
Hookup sites open in Fall: 16	Credit Cards: VMAD	303/776-2185
Winter hookup sites: 16	Elevation: 5047	
RV site cost: $		

Within 15 minutes:

At RV Park:

Loveland

See also Estes Park. Map: C-16

Nestled at the base of the Big Thompson Canyon, Loveland has become famous for its numerous, nationally renown sculptors whose work can be seen at Benson Park. The town was named for William Austin Hamilton Loveland, the man responsible for bringing the Colorado Central Railroad's line from Cheyenne, Wyoming, through here on its way to Denver. In the early 1900s, Colorado was the leading sugar beet producing state in the country and Loveland became the sight of the first sugar mill in eastern Colorado. The very scenic Big Thompson Canyon provides easy access to Estes Park and spectacular Rocky Mountain National Park. Nearby Carter Lake offers 100 acres of fishing and water sports. The new 38-store factory outlet mall is just west of the junction of US Highway 34 and I-25. Enjoy the easy pace in Loveland, where life moves a little slower in this "Sweetheart City."

Fun Things to Do

- Art Casting of Colorado (970) 667-1114
- Benson Park Sculpture Garden (800) 258-1278
- Boyd Lake State Park (970) 669-1739
- Carter Lake (970) 679-4570
- Cattail Creek Golf Course (970) 663-5310
- Clover Leaf Kennel Club (970) 667-6211
- Crystal Rapids Water Park (970) 663-1492
- Loveland Municipal Golf Course (970) 667-5256
- Loveland Mountain Park (970) 962-2727
- Loveland Museum & Gallery (970) 962-2410
- Loveland Sculpture Works (970) 667-0991
- Marianna Butte Golf Course (970) 669-5800

Carter Valley Campground

Just west of Loveland, on Carter Lake Road (CR N29), this rural campground is nestled in a lush, green valley where big blue skies and quiet are a daily occurrence. The level, terraced sites are full hookups (20, 30 and 50 amps) with picnic tables. At night, sit on log benches around the community fire pit. Carter Valley Campground is a great place to escape the traffic and crowds of the big city RV parks. From your site watch deer graze, coyotes search for food and mountain sheep climb the canyon walls.

Located near the eastern entrance of the Big Thompson Canyon and just south of the main road to Rocky Mountain National Park, from here scenic mountain drives abound. On the three nearby lakes you can boat, swim and fish for trout, Tiger Muskie and bass. Horseback riding and wagon rides are nearby. You'll find plenty of places to goof around, from the horseshoes and the playground to the recreation room. Join in the frequent pot luck suppers and nightly bull sessions on the front porch. Other activities include wood carving demonstrations. A wood carving club meets here every Wednesday all year round.

A meeting room in the main building is available for group gatherings.

Location: Seven miles West of Loveland on US Highway 34, ½ mile South on Carter Lake Road.

Total RV sites: 59	Pull thru sites: 0	Open: All Year
Full hookup sites: 48	45+ foot long sites: 0	Frank & Shirley Ford, Owners
Water & elec. sites: 11	Slideout sites: 48	1326 N Carter Lake Rd
Elec. only sites: 0	Licenses sold: Fish & Hunt	Loveland, Colorado 80537
50 amp sites: 4	LP Gas: None	970/663-3131
Hookup sites open in Fall: 48	Credit Cards: VMD	
Winter hookup sites: 48	Elevation: 5200	
RV site cost: $		

Within 15 minutes:

At RV Park:

Loveland RV Village

With a view of the snow-capped Rocky Mountains, Loveland RV Village has level, shaded sites and mowed lawns in this activity-oriented campground. Many sites are full hookups (20, 30 and 50 amps) with pull thrus and phone hookup. Group camping sites are available and each site has a picnic table, patio and barbecue grill. The emphasis here is on family fun because there's so much you and yours will find to do.

Amenities include a heated swimming pool, kiddie pool, senior area and pet walk. Challenge family and friends to miniature golf, basketball, badminton, horseshoes or volleyball. Fun, planned activities include bingo, ice cream socials, Sunday morning pancake breakfasts, pot luck dinners and more. Every month, from March to October, special events are planned, from the annual Easter Egg Hunt to Father's Day Weekend to the August corn roast. No matter when you vacation here, there's always something going on!

Location: Three miles East of Loveland at US Highway 34 milepost 95, 1 mile West of I-25 Exit 257B.

Total RV sites: 158	Pull thru sites: 130	Open: All Year
Full hookup sites: 130	45+ foot long sites: 130	Reg & Karen Atherton, Owners
Water & elec. sites: 30	Slideout sites: 60	4421 E Hwy 34
Elec. only sites: 0	Licenses sold: None	Loveland, Colorado 80538
50 amp sites: 25	LP Gas: W	970/667-1204
Hookup sites open in Fall: 60	Credit Cards: VMD	
Winter hookup sites: 60	Elevation: 5000	
RV site cost: $–$$		

Within 15 minutes:

At RV Park:

Riverview RV Park & Campground

Snug under big shade trees, the sites at Riverview RV Park are along the pleasant Big Thompson River. The full hookup sites (20, 30 and 50 amps) have phone hookups, picnic tables, campfire pits and fire wood. Group camping sites are available. While relaxing in the cool shade of your site, watch the sunset over the Rocky Mountains which loom to the west of the foothills near Riverview.

With a quarter mile of river frontage boarding the campground, trout fishing is right out your back door. Other camp activities include an arcade in the recreation room, basketball, nightly movies, badminton, horseshoes, volleyball and local tours. The Loveland area has great hiking and mountain biking trails. Bring your horse or rent one nearby and explore the picturesque surroundings.

A camper cabin and trailers are available for rent. The picnic shelter and hall are great for family reunions, club gatherings and square dances. Family challenges can be played out on the huge, open sports field.

Location: Six miles West of Loveland on Highway 34 near milepost 85.

Total RV sites: 128	RV site cost: ¢–$	Open: All Year
Full hookup sites: 128	Pull thru sites: 24	Bill & Ellen Hughes, Owners
Water & elec. sites: 0	45+ foot long sites: 25	7806 W Hwy 34
Elec. only sites: 0	Slideout sites: 120	Loveland, Colorado 80537
50 amp sites: 21	Licenses sold: None	970/667-9910
Hookup sites open in Fall: 128	LP Gas: M	800/447-9910
Winter hookup sites: 128	Credit Cards: None	
	Elevation: 5150	

Within 15 minutes:

At RV Park:

Meeker

Includes Trappers Lake. Map: E-5

Meeker, gateway to White River National Forest and Flattops Wilderness (accessible only by foot or on horseback), attracts many visitors who come for the excellent fishing and hunting. The White River Forest has one of the largest elk herds in Colorado, 111 miles of fishable streams and 780 acres of lakes. Named for Nathan C. Meeker who arrived in 1878 to head White River Indian Agency, the town sits amidst hidden valleys, hot springs and quiet retreats which prompted Utes to call it the *land of shinning mountains*. Meeker is still a ranching community with old brick buildings and relaxed, small-town atmosphere. In 1919, Arthur Carhart, a Forest Service landscape architect working east of Meeker, wanted to create wilderness preserves which would be conserved forever, untouched by man and civilization. His idea was the core of the 1964 Wilderness Act which was fought by most Colorado politicians. Today, however, it's the designated wilderness areas that bring a steady stream of tourists. Wildlife in Piceance Basin includes thousands of animals that pick their way through sagebrush, cedar, piñon-juniper, and Douglas fir. The basin has some 1,200 elk, 350 species of wildlife, 22 species of raptors, ranging from owls to eagles, and even a wild horse herd.

Fun Things to Do

- Dinosaur National Monument (970) 374-2216
- Flattops Wilderness Area (970) 878-4039
- Meeker Golf Course (970) 878-5642
- White River Museum (970) 878-9982

Pollard's Ute Lodge

At the quiet end of the road up the White River Valley near the Scenic Flat Tops Byway, Pollard's Ute Lodge has cool RV sites in a secluded forest of pine and spruce trees. Each site is a full hookup (20 and 50 amps) with a grass lawn, picnic table and barbecue grill for outdoor living at its best.

Pollard's has unlicensed fishing on their private, snow-fed mountain lake. Ask your hosts about the experienced guides and top-quality horses that will take you to drop camps for fishing and hunting trips in the back country. You can mountain bike, horseback ride or hike through the Flat Tops Wilderness Area and the White River National Forest. Ride your horse or take a guided horseback tour to the world's largest aspen tree grove where, in the fall, the shades of ruby red, brilliant yellow and soft amber will amaze you.

Cabins are equipped with handicap facilities. Ask about the discounts for seniors, firemen and policemen.

Location: Thirty miles East of Meeker off Highway 64 on County Road 8 near milepost 28.

Total RV sites: 12
Full hookup sites: 12
Water & elec. sites: 0
Elec. only sites: 0
50 amp sites: 12
Hookup sites open in Fall: 12
Winter hookup sites: 0
RV site cost: $–$$

Pull thru sites: 0
45+ foot long sites: 12
Slideout sites: 12
Licenses sold: None
LP Gas: None
Credit Cards: None
Elevation: 8000

Open: 5/15 to 11/15
Buck & Gloria Pollard, Owners
393 County Rd 75
Meeker, Colorado 81641
970/878-4669
970/878-4669 fax

Within 15 minutes:

At RV Park:

RimRock Campground & Cabins

Your hosts at Rim Rock enjoy "treating others like they like to be treated." Conveniently located on your route to Dinosaur National Monument, the campground is in a scenic Colorado setting of piñon pines, native shrubs and cottonwood trees. The terraced, shaded sites are full hookups (20, 30 and 50 amps) with panoramic views of snow-capped mountains and endless meadows. Group camping sites are available. Warm yourself by the central campfire at night while watching the moon rise. The smooth, red rimrock outcroppings turn the skyline jagged and put you closer to nature.

A gift shop with snacks, RV supplies and ice is in on the premises. RimRock is only a few miles from Meeker which has quaint shops and good restaurants. Anglers can cast for whitefish and trout in the White River, Lake Avery and Rio Blanco Lake. More than 80 percent of this rugged country is prime public land, so you can hike though miles and miles of state and national forest areas. Rent a horse nearby or bring your own to take into the wilderness. Hunt for deer, elk and antelope with a rifle, bow, black powder or a camera.

Housekeeping cabins are also available for rent. The indoor and outdoor meeting areas are great for groups.

Location: West of Meeker, off Highway 64.

Total RV sites: 32	Pull thru sites: 3	Open: 4/1 to 11/15
Full hookup sites: 33	45+ foot long sites: 22	Wes & Linda DuBose, Owners
Water & elec. sites: 0	Slideout sites: 16	73179 Hwy 64
Elec. only sites: 0	Licenses sold: Fish & Hunt	Meeker, Colorado 81641
50 amp sites: 10	LP Gas: metered	970/878-4486
Hookup sites open in Fall: 33	Credit Cards: VMD	
Winter hookup sites: 0	Elevation: 6280	
RV site cost: ¢–$		

Within 15 minutes:

At RV Park:

Stagecoach Campground, RV Park & Lodging

Along the 26-acre, shaded grounds of Stagecoach runs a half mile of the scenic White River. Sites are grassy and in the cool shade. Sites have electricity (20, 30 and 50 amps), water, picnic tables, barbecue grills, and campfire pits. Many sites are full hookup and pull thru. The group camping sites are great for family reunions. At Stagecoach, just sit back, relax, watch the wildflowers grow and listen to the river flow.

If you enjoy games, the camp has horseshoes, volleyball and a playground for the kids. Fish near your site for whitefish, brook and rainbow trout on the rolling White River. The surrounding area also has over 900 acres of lakes and ponds and 200 miles of fishable streams. During the season, take guided hunting trips for large elk and mule deer. Close by, you'll find a challenging golf course, a riding stable and heated swimming pool for more summer fun. Rent a horse or bring your own for unforgettable trips into the high country. The Rio Blanco Ranger District offers 17 trailheads, 250 miles of hiking trails and 280 miles of snowmobile trails. Mountain bikers will find plenty of trails into the wilderness as well.

Housekeeping cabins and motel rooms with kitchenettes are also available. Ask about the outdoor group meeting area.

Location: Two miles West of Meeker at the Junction of Highways 13 and 64.

Total RV sites: 50	Pull thru sites: 28	Open: 4/15 to 12/15
Full hookup sites: 26	45+ foot long sites: 50	Dell & Linda Herring, Owners
Water & elec. sites: 24	Slideout sites: 50	39084 Hwy 13
Elec. only sites: 0	Licenses sold: Fish & Hunt	PO Box 995
50 amp sites: 10	LP Gas: None	Meeker, Colorado 81641-0995
Hookup sites open in Fall: 50	Credit Cards: VMAD	970/878-4334
Winter hookup sites: 0	Elevation: 6000	800/878-4334
RV site cost: ¢–$		

Within 15 minutes:

At RV Park:

Mesa Verde Area

Includes Cortez, Towaoc, Mancos. Also see Dolores and Durango. Map: O-3

The ruins of the Anasazi, a Navajo word meaning "ancient ones," are what bring people to this quiet, sun-drenched area. At Mesa Verde National Park visitors can walk among the incredible cliff dwellings of these prehistoric Pueblo people. The Anasazi culture flourished here from approximately A.D. 1 to 1300 and left behind a priceless legacy of achievements in the famous cliff houses and mesa top villages. The reasons the ancient ones abandoned the area remains an enigma, despite decades of research. At one point, more than 40,000 Anasazi lived here before they disappeared. Ten miles away is Cortez, once called by the Navajo "Tsaya-toh" (rock-water) for its spring. Lowry Indian Ruins, 26 miles north of Cortez, contain the largest and best preserved painted Anasazi kivas in the world: an underground room believed to have been used by men for ceremonies and councils. Hovenweep National Monument, 40 miles west, has its unique Anasazi ruins. Sleeping Ute Mountain is the dominant landmark in Cortez to the southwest and in its shadow is the first tribal casino in Colorado, 11 miles south in Towaoc. Nearby is Four Corners Area Monument, the only place in the United States where four states meet. The monument is located on Ute Mountain in the Ute and Navajo Indian Reservations. Visit the Mesa Verde area and experience Colorado from the beginning where the red canyons of the ancient Anasazi meet the spectacular green forests of the San Juan Mountain Range.

Fun Things To Do

- Conquistador Golf Course, Cortez (970) 565-9208
- Cortez/University of Colorado Center & Cultural Park (970) 565-1151
- Hovenweep National Monument (970) 529-4465
- Lowry Indian Ruins (970) 247-4082
- Mesa Oasis Indian Gift Shop (970) 565-8716
- Mesa Verde National Park (970) 529-4465
- Ute Mountain Tribal Park (970) 565-3751

A & A Mesa Verde RV Resort Park

Camp across from the entrance to Mesa Verde National Park in piñon pine wooded and open sites. The level, full hookup (20 and 30 amps) sites are pull thrus with picnic tables, barbecue grills and fire rings. From your grassy and gravel sites, enjoy views of Mesa Verde and quiet, cool nights.

While the kids have fun on the playground, playing basketball, badminton, volleyball and tetherball, you can swim laps in the heated pool and relax in the spa. For your convenience, the resort has a store with RV supplies, ice, snacks, and Indian art, crafts and gifts. The resort stages country-western music shows for your entertainment. Other campfire programs include ice cream socials and wagon rides. Horses, stabled 500 yards away, are available for high desert trail riding. Hike and bike in the national park or spend your time exploring the famous ruins of the Anasazi cliff houses.

Camper cabins are also available. Ask about the indoor and outdoor group meeting areas and the separate group camping area.

Location: Exit US Highway 160 at Mesa Verde National Park.

Total RV sites: 40	Pull thru sites: 27	Open: 4/1 to 11/1
Full hookup sites: 19	45+ foot long sites: 27	Abe & Alice Saunders, Owners
Water & elec. sites: 21	Slideout sites: 27	34979 Hwy 160
Elec. only sites: 0	Licenses sold: None	Mancos, Colorado 81328-9198
50 amp sites: 0	LP Gas: None	970/565-3517
Hookup sites open in Fall: 40	Credit Cards: VM	800/972-6620
Winter hookup sites: 0	Elevation: 7000	
RV site cost: $		

Within 15 minutes:

At RV Park:

Echo Basin Dude Ranch Resort & RV Park

Formerly a working ranch on more than 600 acres, Echo Basin is lush with meadows, streams and high timber forests. The full hookup (30 amps) sites are nestled in the forest next to the dude ranch and resort complex. Gather your own firewood to toss on the campfire ring during the cool nights.

The ranch has everything you need — a laundromat, a rustic, family-style restaurant, a heated swimming pool and a country store. In between the ranch-sponsored activities like horseback rides, hayrides, weekend rodeos and western cookouts, you can fish on the two stocked lakes or in the swift Mancos River which runs deep and fresh through the ranch. Bring your own horse along for some ranching fun. Hunt in the fall and rent snowmobiles or strap on your cross-country skis during the winter. In spring and summer, tennis, volleyball, basketball and baseball are popular activities. Venture into the San Juan National Forest on foot or by mountain bike on some spectacular trails. Be sure to see the many southwest Colorado landmarks, including Mesa Verde National Park, the mountains around Durango and the southwestern desert.

Deluxe cabins and bunk house rooms are also available. Ask about the lodge for family reunions, weddings, youth camps and company picnics.

Location: Three miles North of Highway 160 near milepost 59 on County Road 44.

Total RV sites: 80	Pull thru sites: 20	Open: All Year
Full hookup sites: 50	45+ foot long sites: 50	Lee & Lori Large, Managers
Water & elec. sites: 30	Slideout sites: 50	43747 Rd M
Elec. only sites: 0	Licenses sold: None	Mancos, Colorado 81328-9214
50 amp sites: 30	LP Gas: None	970/533-7000
Hookup sites open in Fall: 80	Credit Cards: VM	800/426-1890 Reservation
Winter hookup sites: 20	Elevation: 7800	970/533-9103 fax
RV site cost: ¢		

Within 15 minutes:

At RV Park:

Mesa Oasis Campground

On the west side of Mesa Verde, Mesa Oasis Campground has mountain views. The level sites all have electricity (20 amps) and water; several are full hookups with TV and phone hookups available. New, 50 amp, level, pull thru sites with TV hookups have been added. Many sites are open,

grassy and gravel and some are in the shade. A laundromat is provided for your convenience.

Activities include basketball, horseshoes, volleyball and local tours. A game room and a store with groceries, souvenirs and Indian handicrafts bought directly from local Indians, are on-site. RV supplies are always 20 percent off. Nearby, you can fish, four-wheel drive, mountain bike, horseback ride or whitewater raft from late spring to early summer. Guest horses are allowed at Mesa Oasis. Only 8 miles north is the Ute Casino gambling. See the Indian dances and the storytellers perform throughout the summer in nearby Cortez — only 4 miles away.

Ask about the group tent sites, indoor group meeting area and RV storage.

Location: Four miles South of Cortez on Highway 160 near milepost 34.

Total RV sites: 52
Full hookup sites: 17
Water & elec. sites: 35
Elec. only sites: 0
50 amp sites: 30
Hookup sites open in Fall: 52
Winter hookup sites: 52
RV site cost: ¢–$

Pull thru sites: 35
45+ foot long sites: 52
Slideout sites: 52
Licenses sold: None
LP Gas: None
Credit Cards: VMD
Elevation: 6200

Open: All Year
Len Blanton, Owner
5608 Hwy 160
Cortez, Colorado 81321
970/565-8716

Within 15 minutes:

At RV Park:

Mesa Verde Point Kampark

Near the entrance to Mesa Verde National Park, this campground has both open and shady, pull thru sites with full hookups (30 and 50 amps). Each site has a picnic table, barbecue grill and campfire pit and fire wood (charge). Relax in the quiet of your site and contemplate the views of Mesa Verde.

Camp amenities include an arcade, heated swimming pool, indoor and outdoor hot tub, playground, sports fields, horseshoes, and volleyball. The recreation room has a pool table, foosball, video games and a fire place. The camp store has souvenirs, Indian arts and crafts, groceries and firewood. Rent a horse next door for great southwestern style rides. A visit to the ancient ruins of Mesa Verde is a must when vacationing in southwest Colorado. The fascinating Anasazi Heritage Center is just 20 minutes away.

The recreation room is available as an indoor, group meeting area.

Location: ¾ miles East of the junction of Mesa Verde National Park and US Highway 160 near milepost 49.

Total RV sites: 43	Pull thru sites: 21	Open: 4/1 to 10/31
Full hookup sites: 18	45+ foot long sites: 10	Michael & Vietta Wagner, Owners
Water & elec. sites: 18	Slideout sites: 43	35303 Hwy 160
Elec. only sites: 7	Licenses sold: None	Mancos, Colorado 81328-8960
50 amp sites: 4	LP Gas: metered	970/533-7421
Hookup sites open in Fall: 43	Credit Cards: VMD	800/776-7421
Winter hookup sites: 0	Elevation: 7000	
RV site cost: ¢–$		

Within 15 minutes:

At RV Park:

Sleeping Ute RV Park & Campground

Brand new in 1994, Sleeping Ute RV Park is a short drive to Mesa Verde National Park. At the base of Sleeping Ute Mountain and next to the Ute Mountain Casino, this is the closest campground to the Four Corners Monument. Sleeping Ute has 62 long (50-foot) pull thru, full hookup sites (30 and 50 amps) and cable TV hookup with HBO (free).

A restaurant, the Indian Village and the Ute Mountain Pottery Plant are next door to the campground. The indoor pool, kiddie pool and sauna are great for relaxing after a day at the casino or exploring ancient ruins. Send the kids off to the video arcade and playground to work off excess energy.

Ask about the rental teepees.

Location: Eight miles South of Cortez on Highways 160 & 666 on Yellow Hat Drive.

Total RV sites: 62	Pull thru sites: 62	Open: All Year
Full hookup sites: 31	45+ foot long sites: 62	Larry & Deanna Gower, Managers
Water & elec. sites: 31	Slideout sites: 62	Yellow Hat Dr.
Elec. only sites: 0	Licenses sold: None	PO Box 255
50 amp sites: 62	LP Gas: metered	Towaoc, Colorado 81334
Hookup sites open in Fall: 62	Credit Cards: VM	970/565-0651
Winter hookup sites: 62	Elevation: 6220	800/889-5072
RV site cost: $		

Within 15 minutes:

At RV Park:

Ouray Area

Including Ridgway. Map: M-6 and L - 16.

Snug in a small, rocky canyon in the rugged San Juan Mountains rests the little gem of Ouray (pronounced "Your-ray.") known as "The Switzerland of America". Dominated by cliffs that rise up into snow capped peaks, it is located on the Million Dollar Highway, named for the cost to build it in 1883. Ouray is well known for its hot springs, once favored by Ute Indian Chief Ouray, the town's namesake. Silver and gold mining fever embraced Ouray, leaving behind a legacy of abandoned mines and Victorian houses quaintly lining the streets. The wagon roads to old mines now make for great four-wheel driving — backcountry trips on Engineer Pass, Imogene Pass and Black Bear Pass are memorable. Box Canyon Falls and Park, to the southwest of town, has a pedestrian bridge suspended over the 300-foot falls which you walk over to reach the park for a picnic. The nearby Ridgway State Park is centered on a 1,000-acre reservoir which has excellent trout fishing, boating and swimming. Ridgway sits at the crossroads to both the hot springs town of Ouray and the mountain ski town of Telluride.

Fun Things to Do

- Box Canyon Falls and Park (970) 325-4464
- Fairway Pines Golf & Country Club (970) 626-5271
- Ouray Hot Springs Pool (970) 325-4638
- Ouray National Historic District (970) 325-4746
- Ridgway State Park (970) 626-5822
- San Juan Balloon Adventures (970) 626-5495

4J+1+1 RV Park

At the center of the Switzerland of America, this campground is a great home base to some of the best scenery and four-wheel drive trails in Colorado. At 4J+1+1 RV Park you'll find full hookup (20, 30 and 50 amps) sites. Many sites are right beside the Uncompahgre River. Most sites have TV

hookup, picnic tables, patios, barbecue grills, campfire pits, free wood and shade trees. Your site has red mountain cliffs and deep green forests on all sides, and snow-capped peaks in the distance.

On-site activities include basketball and a playground. For your convenience, a large laundromat is on site. Ask your hosts about the local tours. The quaint Ouray business district is within easy walking distance. Take the foot bridge across the churning river to the natural Mineral Hot Springs Pool. Venture into this rugged, majestic countryside on foot, mountain bike or horseback. No matter how you explore it, you'll find Ouray country unbelievably picturesque.

A rustic camper cabin is also available.

Location: In the center of Ouray, exit Highway 550 at milepost 94, 2 blocks West of Main Street on 7th Avenue.

Total RV sites: 85	Pull thru sites: 18	Open: 5/15 to 10/15
Full hookup sites: 50	45+ foot long sites: 20	Jack & Jackie Clark, Owners
Water & elec. sites: 0	Slideout sites: 66	7th Ave
Elec. only sites: 16	Licenses sold: None	Box F
50 amp sites: 5	LP Gas: None	Ouray, Colorado 81427-0079
Hookup sites open in Fall: 66	Credit Cards: VM	970/325-4418
Winter hookup sites: 0	Elevation: 7800	
RV site cost: $		

Within 15 minutes:

At RV Park:

Weber's RV Park

At Weber's RV Park, you'll have a million dollar view of the majestic San Juan Mountains! Although easily accessible from the highway, this campground has a secluded, lower level for RV sites away from the highway. From the open, full hookup (20 and 30 amps) sites with picnic tables, barbecue grills and campfire pits, you'll be camped at the foot of some of the best scenery in the state. Relax in the nice, cool shade of your site.

Your horse can vacation with you or rent one nearby for exploratory trips in the spectacular countryside. Other area activities include fishing, four-wheel driving, mountain biking and hiking. Enjoy the Million Dollar Highway scenic drive to Mesa Verde for an unforgettable day trip. Weber's is near the natural hot springs of Ouray and is the closest campground to picturesque Telluride.

Ask about the daily, weekly and monthly rates.

Location: Two ½miles South of Ridgway, 27 miles South of Montrose, 7 miles North of Ouray, on Highway 550 at milepost 101 ½.

Total RV sites: 30
Full hookup sites: 24
Water & elec. sites: 3
Elec. only sites: 3
50 amp sites: 0
Hookup sites open in Fall: 27
Winter hookup sites: 0
RV site cost: Not available

Pull thru sites: 0
45+ foot long sites: 8
Slideout sites: 8
Licenses sold: None
LP Gas: None
Credit Cards: None
Elevation: 7230

Open: 5/1 to 11/1
Louis & Lena Weber, Owners
20725 Hwy 550
Ridgway, Colorado 81432-9663
970/626-5383

Within 15 minutes:

At RV Park:

Pagosa Springs Area

Includes Chimney Rock and Ignacio. Map: F-9

Pagosa Springs was named by the Utes who called the hot springs "Pagosah," or "healing waters." This little town, surrounded on three sides by the San Juan National Forest, is a good place to get away from it all. Explore the mystery of the only mountain home of the Anasazi at nearby Chimney Rock where these ancient farmers lived some 1,000 years ago. The twin pinnacles were once a scared shrine to the "Ancient Ones". Later, the unusual formations were a landmark for prospectors, missionaries and conquistadores who settled this rugged country. While clambering among the ruins, keep an eye out for the endangered peregrine falcon which nests here. Enjoy the town's hot springs, considered to be the hottest in the world. Windsurf, water ski and sail on Navajo Lake, which extends southward 35 miles into New Mexico. The Weminuche and South San Juan Wilderness Areas' untouched beauty are only accessible on foot or horseback. The nearby Echo Lake Park and Lake Capote are stocked with rainbow and cutthroat trout, large-mouth bass and yellow perch. Other nearby places to go include hiking to Treasure Falls, prospecting on Treasure Mountain, fishing in Williams Creek and visiting the local museums. Let the land of healing waters soothe you and the breath-taking wilderness inspire you.

Fun Things to Do

- Chimney Rock Archeological Area (970) 264-2268
- Fairfield Pagosa Golf Course (970) 731-4141
- Fred Harman Art Museum (970) 731-5785
- Lake Capote (970) 731-5256
- Navajo State Park (970) 883-2208
- Pagosa Chamber of Commerce (800) 252-2204
- Pagosa Ranger District Office (970) 264-2268
- Piedra River Resort & Horse Rides (970) 731-4630
- Rocky Mountain Wildlife Park (970) 264-5546
- San Juan National Forest (970) 247-4874, (970) 264-2268
- San Juan Historical Society & Museum (970) 264-4424
- Wolf Creek Outfitters & Snowmobile Tours (970) 264-5332/2332

Bruce Spruce Ranch

Surrounded by thousands of acres of national forest, Bruce Spruce Ranch is a wonderful retreat in the foothills. The open and shaded sites are full hookups (30 amps) with pull thrus. Group camping sites are available. Each site has a picnic table, patio, and fire ring.

This scenic ranch offers many activities, including volleyball, horseshoes horseback riding, nature hiking and pack trips for trout fishing in lakes, streams and rivers. The private fishing pond on the ranch requires no state license; however, there is a fee ($10/3 fish). During the season, take a hunting pack trip for deer, bear and elk. Guest horses are welcomed. Close by, enjoy the four-wheel drive roads, Mesa Verde and other Indian ruins, narrow-gauge railroad trains, hot mineral baths, wilderness hot springs and more.

Ask about the rustic log cabins, group meeting areas and accommodations for groups up to 30 people.

Location: Sixteen miles Northeast of Pagosa Springs on US Highway 160 near milepost 158, then ¼ miles Northwest on the gravel road.

Total RV sites: 30	Pull thru sites: 8	Open: 5/20 to 10/31
Full hookup sites: 28	45+ foot long sites: 15	Craig & Eugenia Hinger, Owners
Water & elec. sites: 2	Slideout sites: 23	16 miles NE Pagosa Hwy 160
Elec. only sites: 0	Licenses sold: None	PO Box 296
50 amp sites: 0	LP Gas: metered	Pagosa Springs, Colorado 81147-0296
Hookup sites open in Fall: 30	Credit Cards: VM	970/264-5374
Winter hookup sites: 0	Elevation: 8200	
RV site cost: ¢		

Within 15 minutes:

At RV Park:

Elk Meadows Campground

On a beautiful bank overlooking the San Juan River, Elk Meadows is a great base camp for hikers and mountain bikers. The open and shaded, full hookup (20, 30 and 50 amps) sites are level pull thrus with picnic tables, barbecue grills and fire rings. Group camping sites are available.

Pasture your horse on the 22 acres and ride from here on the endless national forest lands. Hunters will find a concentration of wild game: elk, deer, big horn sheep, turkey and grouse. Fish the San Juan River for rainbow, cutthroat, brook and brown trout. Below and behind Elk Meadows, you can swim in the refreshing river. Camp sports include badminton, horseshoes, volleyball and a playground. Watching movies, hiking the trails and participating in the potluck suppers are also popular activities.

Family reunions and large groups are welcomed. Camper cabins are available.

Location: Five miles Northeast of Pagosa Springs on Highway 160 at milepost 149.

Total RV sites: 32	Pull thru sites: 20	Open: 5/1 to 10/31
Full hookup sites: 19	45+ foot long sites: 13	Donald & Barbara Palmer, Owners
Water & elec. sites: 13	Slideout sites: 13	5360 Hwy E 160
Elec. only sites: 0	Licenses sold: None	PO Box 238
50 amp sites: 5	LP Gas: None	Pagosa Springs, Colorado 81147-0238
Hookup sites open in Fall: 32	Credit Cards: VM	970/264-5482
Winter hookup sites: 0	Elevation: 7300	
RV site cost: ¢–$		

Within 15 minutes:

At RV Park:

Lake Capote Park

On the Southern Ute Indian Reservation west of Pagosa Springs and just east of Chimney Rock, Lake Capote Park has spacious RV sites shaded by tall ponderosa pine trees with easy access to picnic tables and barbecue grills. 10 sites have water and electric hookups. The huge bath house has hot showers, flush toilets and is handicap accessible.

Lake Capote is an angler's paradise (no states license required, but you need to buy a permit on site): fish in a pristine, spring-fed 33 acre lake stocked with 4,000 rainbow and cutthroat trout monthly. Rent a rowboat, paddle boat, canoe or pole boat on-site. Other park activities are bird watching and taking nature hikes. The Chimney Rock Archaeological area is just 3 miles south. Be sure and explore the mysteries of the Anasazi while vacationing here.

Location: West of Pagosa Springs at the Junction of Highways 160 and 151.

Total RV sites: 10
Full hookup sites: 0
Water & elec. sites: 10
Elec. only sites: 0
50 amp sites: 0
Hookup sites open in Fall: 10
Winter hookup sites: 0
RV site cost: Not available

Pull thru sites: 5
45+ foot long sites: 5
Slideout sites: 10
Licenses sold: None
LP Gas: None
Credit Cards: VM
Elevation: 6500

Open: 4/1 to 9/30
Chris Ribera, Manager
Intersection of Highways 151 & 160
PO Box 737
Ignacio, Colorado 81137-0737
970/731-5256
970/563-0393 Fax

Within 15 minutes:

At RV Park:

Pagosa Riverside Campground & Camper Cabins

On the scenic, majestic banks of the San Juan River, Pagosa Riverside is a quiet, family run campground off the road. The open and shaded full hookup (20 and 30 amps) sites are under large shade trees. The pull thru sites also have cable TV and phone hookup. Each site has a picnic table, barbecue grill and fire ring. Pick between river and lakeside sites. Either way, the evenings are quiet and cool, the perfect accompaniment to days of sunshine and adventures.

Fish near your site for trout in the river. Camp amenities include paddle boats for cruising the private lake, a game room for the kids, a swimming pool for refreshing dips and a store for your convenience. The store sells firewood, ice, groceries and souvenirs. There's plenty of northern New Mexico and Colorado to see from here: it's only an hour to the famous Durango/Silverton Narrow Gauge Railroad and to the Cumbres & Toltec Scenic Narrow Gauge Railroad. There's great fishing on the San Juan River; indulge in nearby horseback rides; explore the Indian ruins at Chimney Rock or whitewater raft, play tennis, hunt, hike or mountain bike. The therapeutic Pagosa Hot Springs are less than 5 minutes away.

Ask about the camper cabins. Weekly and monthly rates are available.

Location: On US Highway 160, 1 1/3 miles East of Highway 84's milepost 146.

Total RV sites: 52	Pull thru sites: 31	Open: 4/15 to 11/15
Full hookup sites: 36	45+ foot long sites: 34	Ron & Darryl Jones & Julia Lussier
Water & elec. sites: 16	Slideout sites: 34	2270 E Hwy 160
Elec. only sites: 0	Licenses sold: None	PO Box 268
50 amp sites: 0	LP Gas: None	Pagosa Springs, Colorado 81147-0268
Hookup sites open in Fall: 0	Credit Cards: VM	970/264-5874
Winter hookup sites: 0	Elevation: 7100	
RV site cost: Not available		

Within 15 minutes:

At RV Park:

Sportsman's Supply & RV Campground

In the San Juan National Forest north of Pagosa Springs, Sportsman's is far enough from town to feel secluded. The campground is 18 miles north of US Highway 160 on Piedra Road. Camp under the shade of fragrant ponderosa pines where the full hookup (15, 20 and 30 amps) sites also have picnic tables, barbecue grills, fire rings and free wood. Satellite TV and phone hookups and group camping sites are available. You'll find comfort at the edge of the wilderness here.

Join in the weekly pot luck suppers and meet your fellow campers. Satellite TV, video rentals and a recreation hall are among the camp amenities. The campground boasts badminton, horseshoes, hiking trails and volleyball. Anglers will want to try their lines in the nearby Williams Creek Lake or the many nearby rivers and streams, while others may want to hunt in season. Bring your own or rent a horse here for a ride to alpine meadows and beaver ponds. Crazy Horse Outfitters on-site provide high country adventures, guided horseback rides, and fishing and hunting trips into the wilderness. Take time to explore the nearby Weminuche Wilderness where the back country splendor has remained un-tarnished by civilization.

Cabins and a rental travel trailer are available.

Location: In the San Juan National Forest, they are 18 miles North of US Highway 160 on Piedra Road, the first 6 ¼ miles are paved, the rest are gravel.

Total RV sites: 32	Pull thru sites: 2	Open: 5/15 to 11/15
Full hookup sites: 32	45+ foot long sites: 29	Don & Becky Travelstead, Owners
Water & elec. sites: 0	Slideout sites: 32	18 mi N on Piedra Rd
Elec. only sites: 0	Licenses sold: Fish & Hunt	PO Box 70
50 amp sites: 0	LP Gas: metered	Pagosa Springs, Colorado 81147-0070
Hookup sites open in Fall: 32	Credit Cards: VM	970/731-2300
Winter hookup sites: 0	Elevation: 8100	
RV site cost: ¢–$		

Within 15 minutes:

At RV Park:

Wolf Creek Valley Country Store & Campground

Just minutes from the Continental Divide, Wolf Creek Valley Campground has spacious, shaded sites amid spectacular mountain scenery. The full hookup (30 amps) sites are nestled within a forest of large aspen, pine, spruce and fir trees. All sites have Satellite TV hookup, picnic tables, rock fire rings and free wood. Up high in the Rocky Mountains, the nights are cool, the days warm and the humidity low.

The country store on the campground is bursting with groceries, camping, fishing and hunting supplies as well as hand made crafts like quilts, pottery, baskets, and sterling silver jewelry. Within minutes you can be standing on the shores of the San Juan River and Wolf Creek fishing for rainbow, brown, cutthroat and brook trout. Hiking and walking trails branch out from Wolf Creek and into the national forest. Treasure Falls, a mountain waterfall, is a short walk away. Look for the elk, deer and rare bear seen sometimes from the campground. After cooking dinner, play a game of horseshoes or badminton before the sun sets. Be sure to bring along your camera to capture the picturesque views, churning rivers, lush forests and abundant wildlife. You can even hunt for the legendary five million in gold hidden and lost on Treasure Mountain!

Location: At the base of Wolf Creek Pass, 15 miles East of Pagosa Springs, off Highway 160 at milepost 157 ½.

Total RV sites: 19
Full hookup sites: 18
Water & elec. sites: 5
Elec. only sites: 0
50 amp sites: 0
Hookup sites open in Fall: 18
Winter hookup sites: 0
RV site cost: ¢

Pull thru sites: 4
45+ foot long sites: 4
Slideout sites: 19
Licenses sold: Fish & Hunt
LP Gas: None
Credit Cards: VM
Elevation: 8000

Open: 5/1 to 11/15
Donald & Sandra Walker, Owners
13341 E Hwy 160 Unit 5
Pagosa Springs, Colorado 81147
970/264-4853

Within 15 minutes:

At RV Park:

Poudre River Canyon Area

Includes Bellvue. Also see Fort Collins. Map: B-14

Designated Colorado's first National Wild and Scenic River in 1986, the Poudre River Canyon, also known as Cache la Poudre, is in the midst of the Roosevelt National Forest. In 1840, French trappers camped at the mouth of the canyon west of Fort Collins. A heavy snow fell, forcing them to reduce their load, so they buried their gun powder, or "cache la poudre," along the river's banks. In 1879, settlers built a rough road along the river, soon leading to a steady stream of more cabins. With water rushing east from Rocky Mountain National Park, the crashing Poudre River runs along Highway 14 and is teaming with brown and rainbow trout. Some areas of the river are Wild Trout sections where bait fishing is not allowed. Where there are rapids, there is whitewater rafting — the river is a hot spot with both rafters and kayakers. Accessible from the canyon, the Cache La Poudre Wilderness Area ranges in altitude from 6,000 feet to 8,600 feet and its steep, rugged terrain is seldom traveled. Hiking is popular in the Comanche Peak Wilderness, the Rawah Wilderness, the Neota Flat Tops Wilderness and in Roosevelt National Forest. While fishing is the number one draw here, hiking comes in a close second. In the winter, try one of the many cross-country ski trails in the breath-taking high peaks of the Cameron Pass area at 10,276 feet.

Fun Things to Do

- Avery House (970) 221-0533
- City Park Nine Golf Course (970) 221-6650
- Collindale Golf Course (970) 221-6651
- Fort Collins Museum (970) 221-6738
- Glen Echo General Store, Gift Shop & Restaurant (800) 881-2208, (970) 881-2208
- Link-N-Greens (970) 221-4818
- Ptarmigan Golf Course (970) 226-6600
- Southridge Golf Course (970) 226-2828

Glen Echo Resort

In the heart of Roosevelt National Forest, quiet Glen Echo Resort is on the beautiful Poudre River, Colorado's "trout route." The level, shaded sites are full hookups (20, 30 and some 50 amps) with picnic tables and concrete patios; most have barbecue grills. You will relax in this tranquil mountain setting while listening to the murmur of the scenic Cache La Poudre River

Amenities include a picnic pavilion, a casual, non-smoking, family restaurant with tasty home cooking and a general store with fly fishing and other tackle, RV and camping supplies, propane, sporting goods, groceries, souvenirs, and Texaco gasoline. The store also has largest selection of authentic Native American jewelry and crafts in northern Colorado' personally selected by the owners at the Navajo Reservations in Arizona. Be sure and try the restaurant's peanut butter malts and pies. Glen Echo sports a playground, recreational hall and horseshoes. Enjoy fishing on Colorado's only designated wild and scenic river right near your site. It's a short drive to Red Feather Lakes for more alpine fishing, or you can hike the stunning Comanche Peak Wilderness in the Mummy Mountain Range, the Rawah Wilderness or the Neota Flat Tops Wilderness.

Modern cottages, rustic cabins and family mountain homes are also available.

Location: Located in Roosevelt National Forest, 41 miles West of Fort Collins on Highway 14 at milepost 90.

Total RV sites: 50	Pull thru sites: 12	Open: 5/10 to 11/1
Full hookup sites: 50	45+ foot long sites: 8	Sam Shoultz & Ken Matzner, Owners
Water & elec. sites: 0	Slideout sites: 8	31503 Poudre Canyon Dr.
Elec. only sites: 0	Licenses sold: Fish & Hunt	Bellvue, Colorado 80512-9312
50 amp sites: 3	LP Gas: metered	970/881-2208
Hookup sites open in Fall: 50	Credit Cards: VM	800/348-2208 Reservation
Winter hookup sites: 0	Elevation: 7200	970/881-2066 Fax
RV site cost: ¢–$		

Within 15 minutes:

At RV Park:

Home Moraine Trailer Park

The open, level, grassy sites at Home Moraine are next to the roaring Poudre River with mountain views. The full hookup (20 and 30 amps) sites have phone hookups and picnic tables. Pets are not allowed in the park. Enjoy warm days and cool nights in this quiet and peaceful trailer park.

Fish on the scenic river or on the private, stocked pond where no license is required. Home Moraine has horseshoes and hiking trails. Most guests here are seniors who stay by the month or season. With easy access from the highway, you too will find this a restful spot.

Location: 48 miles West of Fort Collins on Highway 14 at milepost 85.

Total RV sites: 32	Pull thru sites: 0	Open: 5/1 to 10/15
Full hookup sites: 32	45+ foot long sites: 6	Jack & Iola Revis, Owners
Water & elec. sites: 0	Slideout sites: 32	37797 Poudre Canyon Drive
Elec. only sites: 0	Licenses sold: None	Bellvue, Colorado 80512-9501
50 amp sites: 2	LP Gas: None	970/881-2356
Hookup sites open in Fall: 32	Credit Cards: None	
Winter hookup sites: 0	Elevation: 7476	
RV site cost: Not available		

Within 15 minutes:

At RV Park:

Poudre River Resort, Inc.

Adjacent to the spectacular Poudre River, high in the Rocky Mountains, the resort has, grassy, full hookup sites with cement patios. Fall asleep under the stars and wake to birds chirping in the trees along the river. You'll find the Poudre a quiet mountain getaway.

For relaxation, soak outdoors in the community hot tub or rent a movie from the on-site video service. For added convenience, there's a grocery store and snack bar. You'll find excellent hiking trails and stocked fishing lakes, both at the resort and in the nearby mountains. If you get tired of camp cooking, dine at one of the local restaurants. In the winter, pristine back country areas are accessible by cross-country skis or snowmobile. Whether you hike it or ski it, Poudre River country is refreshingly un-crowded and the mountainous terrain where pine forests and wildlife abound is Colorado at its best.

Modern cabins are also available.

Location: 45 miles Northwest of Fort Collins on Highway 14 near mileposts 89 and 90.

Total RV sites: 6	Pull thru sites: 5	Open: All Year
Full hookup sites: 6	45+ foot long sites: 5	Janet & Venus, Owners
Water & elec. sites: 0	Slideout sites: 6	33021 Poudre Canyon Dr.
Elec. only sites: 0	Licenses sold: Fish & Hunt	Bellvue, Colorado 80512-9426
50 amp sites: 0	LP Gas: M	970/881-2139
Hookup sites open in Fall: 6	Credit Cards: VMD	
Winter hookup sites: 6	Elevation: 7200	
RV site cost: $		

Within 15 minutes:

At RV Park:

Sportsman's Lodge & Store

Since 1931, Sportsman's Lodge has been an ideal setting for family reunions. The lodge's beautiful location and modest furnishings, many from the 1930s, will make you think time has stood still. The full hookup RV sites are spread out over 5 acres and there's an area for picnicking and a campfire. Sit in the shade along the river and watch rainbow trout jump for flies.

The on-site country store sells licenses, gifts, groceries, camping and fishing supplies and snacks. Located in the Poudre River Canyon, the lodge is within minutes of Poudre Falls, Chambers Lake and Cameron Pass. In the spring and summer, take advantage of river and lake fishing, hiking, whitewater rafting, horseback riding, mountain biking and simple, quiet, relaxing. You'll have ample opportunities to photograph the abundant wildlife, including moose, bighorn sheep, and birds, especially humming birds. Fall brings a color tour of turning aspens and big game hunting. At Sportsman's Lodge, you'll escape to the past where time moved a little more slowly and the wilderness awaited exploration.

Rustic housekeeping cabins are available.

Location: 54 miles West of Fort Collins on Highway 14 between mileposts 78 and 79.

Total RV sites: 10	Pull thru sites: 1	Open: 5/1 to 10/31
Full hookup sites: 10	45+ foot long sites: 0	John & Lee Ann Schenk, Owners
Water & elec. sites: 0	Slideout sites: 10	44174 Poudre Canyon Hwy
Elec. only sites: 0	Licenses sold: Fish & Hunt	Bellvue, Colorado 80512-9604
50 amp sites: 0	LP Gas: None	970/881-2272
Hookup sites open in Fall: 10	Credit Cards: None	
Winter hookup sites: 0	Elevation: 7880	
RV site cost: Not available		

Within 15 minutes:

At RV Park:

Pueblo

Map: K-18

Up until the end of the Mexican War in the 1840s, the Arkansas River, which runs through Pueblo, was the border between Mexico and the United States. That cultural heritage is still evident among the diverse ethnic groups, especially Hispanics, who live here. On the eastern edge of the Rocky Mountains, Pueblo was a natural crossroads for Ute, Cheyenne, Arapaho and Kiowa tribes as well as Spanish troops, mountain men, traders, trappers and gold seekers. In 1806, Capt. Zebulon Pike, who was attempting to map the Arkansas River, built a log fort here — supposedly the first structure built by Americans in Colorado. Eventually miners and the railroads found their way to Pueblo and in the late 1880s the town smelters hired European immigrants, Mexicans and blacks creating a literal melting pot. The Pueblo Reservoir, just to the west, sits on semi-arid plains encircled by limestone cliffs and buttes with mountain vistas to the north of Pikes Peak and to the west of the Wet Mountains. The man-made lake, with its clean, cool water and great fishing along its 60 miles of shore, is ideal for sailing too. Golfers will enjoy the 266 days of sunshine a year in Pueblo. The Colorado State Fair is held here every year.

Fun Things To Do

- City Park Golf Course (719) 561-4946
- Colorado State Fair & Events Center (800) 876-4567
- El Pueblo Museum (719) 583-0453
- Greenway & Nature Center (719) 545-9114
- Hose Co. No. 3 Firehouse Museum (719) 544-4548
- Lake Pueblo State Recreation Area (719) 561-9320
- Pueblo County Historical Museum (719) 543-6772
- Pueblo Nature Center (719) 545-9114
- Pueblo West Golf Course (719) 547-2280
- Pueblo Zoo in City Park (719) 561-9664
- Raptor Rehabilitation Center (719) 545-7117
- Rosemount Victorian House Museum (719) 545-5290
- Walking Stick Golf Course (719) 584-3400
- Weisbrod Aircraft & International B-24 Museum (719) 948-9219

Fort's RV Park

Camp in the quiet under big, shady elm trees at Fort's RV Park. The large, level sites are full hookup (30 and 50 amps) with pull thrus and cement patios. The paved streets mean no dust and the grounds at this edge of town park are kept very clean. The ceramic-tiled restrooms are air con-ditioned.

The state fair grounds are only 4 miles away and boating, fishing, swimming, golfing and the Nature Center are 10 minutes away. During the season, walk to the Greyhound race track. All the modern conveniences of Pueblo, markets, restaurants and shops, are nearby.

Location: Exit I-25 South at mile post 94, go 1 Block West to Lake Avenue and ½ block North.

Total RV sites: 32	Pull thru sites: 16	Open: All Year
Full hookup sites: 32	45+ foot long sites: 6	Gerald & Janet Childress, Owners
Water & elec. sites: 0	Slideout sites: 32	3015 Lake Ave
Elec. only sites: 0	Licenses sold: None	Pueblo, Colorado 81004-3862
50 amp sites: 4	LP Gas: None	719/564-2327
Hookup sites open in Fall: 32	Credit Cards: None	
Winter hookup sites: 32	Elevation: 4700	
RV site cost: Not available		

Within 15 minutes:

At RV Park:

Haggard's RV Campground

At Haggard's, the sites are level and open with scenic views of stunning Pikes Peak and the Sangre de Cristo Mountains. The oversized sites are full hookup (20 and 30 amps), pull thrus with picnic tables. Out in the country with lots of elbow room, near the mountains and national forests, Hag-

gard's is only minutes from the modern city of Pueblo. With easy access off US Highway 50, the campground is located halfway between Pueblo and Cañon City.

Campground amenities include a recreation room with video games, playground, basketball and horseshoes for family challenges. A small convenience store is on-site. Rent a horse nearby or bring your own for a ride in the southern Colorado splendor. Pueblo Reservoir, with its vast acreage and 60 miles of shoreline for fishing, swimming and boating, is about a 15 minute drive away. The Royal Gorge, Pikes Peak, Cripple Creek and Colorado Springs are an easy day trip from here.

Location: Fifteen miles West of Pueblo on US Highway 50 West near milepost 297.

Total RV sites: 80	Pull thru sites: 80	Open: All Year
Full hookup sites: 29	45+ foot long sites: 80	Ginger Haggard & Carmen Garcia, Owners
Water & elec. sites: 50	Slideout sites: 80	7910 W Hwy 50
Elec. only sites: 0	Licenses sold: None	Pueblo, Colorado 81007
50 amp sites: 0	LP Gas: None	719/547-2101
Hookup sites open in Fall: 21	Credit Cards: VM	
Winter hookup sites: 21	Elevation: 5300	
RV site cost: ¢–$		

Within 15 minutes:

At RV Park:

Pueblo KOA

At Pueblo KOA, the long, level pull thru, gravel sites have shade trees and wooden shade shelters for your convenience. The full hookup (20, 30 and 50 amps) sites are in a desert setting with views of the towering Pikes Peak. Sites have picnic tables and barbecue grills. With sunny, dry days and cool, quiet nights, this is desert camping at its best.

The recreation room, arcade and equipped pavilion are great for entertaining large groups. Other amenities include a heated swimming pool, basketball and volleyball courts, badminton, horseshoes, a playground and sports fields. The camp store has groceries, ice, clothing, jewelry, souvenirs and toys. Pueblo KOA is centrally located to the beautiful Pikes Peak area, the stunning Royal Gorge and the gambling casinos of Cripple Creek. Several golf courses and a dog track are also nearby for your leisure-time relaxation. Pueblo Reservoir, only 12 miles away, has fishing, boating, swimming and sun bathing on its beach.

Camper cabins are also available.

Location: Six miles North of Pueblo, exit I-25 at milepost 108.

Total RV sites: 85	Pull thru sites: 58	Open: All Year
Full hookup sites: 22	45+ foot long sites: 60	Rolland & Genet Anderson, Owners
Water & elec. sites: 42	Slideout sites: 60	4131 I-25 North
Elec. only sites: 0	Licenses sold: None	Pueblo, Colorado 81008
50 amp sites: 2	LP Gas: metered	719/542-2273
Hookup sites open in Fall: 14	Credit Cards: VMD	
Winter hookup sites: 14	Elevation: 4695	
RV site cost: $		

Within 15 minutes:

At RV Park:

Pueblo South/Colorado City KOA

Relax at shady (some) sites and enjoy incredible views of the Rocky Mountains from Pueblo South/Colorado City KOA. Many are long, pull thru sites with full hookups, picnic tables and BBQ grills. Vacations in this accommodating campground are peaceful year-round.

Entertain the kids on the playground. Families will enjoy basketball, volleyball and horseshoes on the property. Other amenities include a gift shop and store, and a hot tub for relaxing. Avid golfers will enjoy the 27 holes nearby. Visit the intriguing Bishop's Castle, historic Robbers Roost, and breath-taking Royal Gorge. Spend your days mountain biking, hiking, fishing or just plain resting.

Location: South of Pueblo, on I-25 at Exit 74.

Total RV sites: 50
Full hookup sites: 30
Water & elec. sites: 10
Elec. only sites: 0
50 amp sites: 12
Hookup sites open in Fall: 50
Winter hookup sites: 30
RV site cost: ¢–$

Pull thru sites: 50
45+ foot long sites: 50
Slideout sites: 50
Licenses sold: None
LP Gas: M
Credit Cards: VMD
Elevation: 6000

Open: 3/1 to 11/20
Rich & Roxie Taylor, Owners
9040 I-25 South
Pueblo, Colorado 81004
719/676-3376

Within 15 minutes:

At RV Park:

Salida

Includes Howard. Also see Buena Vista. Map: J-13

Salida grew quickly in the 1880s when the railroad made this a rail hub and smelting and supply center. A rip-roaring town, Salida had a famous madam, Laura Evans, who lived to 90 and ran a bordello in town from 1896 to 1950! Today, it's still a roaring town, roaring with rapids, that is. Salida is the headquarters for the Arkansas River Valley State Park. The town has one of the largest, indoor hot springs in the state. The Arkansas River is a launching point for some of the best whitewater rafting around and is the most boated in the country with rapids ranging from easy to challenging. Take a trip down Brown's Canyon, 8 miles south of Buena Vista, and you'll experience the appeal. If you're looking for a less-adventurous experience, you can fish for trout in specially designated areas or in the multitude of mountain streams and lakes, where you'll find smaller brook, cutthroat and rainbow trout. There's ample opportunity for four-wheel drive trips, hiking and horseback riding. Accessible from Salida are the Rainbow and Colorado trails where mountain bikers and hikers can enjoy the mountain wilderness. In the winter try skiing at the much-praised, less-visited Monarch Ski Resort whose basin traps 300 inches annually of light, fluffy powder.

Fun Things to Do

- Fun Time Jeep Tours (719) 539-2962
- Heart of the Rockies Horseback Riding & Jeeps (800) 496-2245, (719) 539-4051
- Monarch Ski Area (800) 332-3668, (719) 539-3573
- Poncho Springs Museum (719) 539-6882
- River Runners Ltd. Colorado (800) 332-9100, out of state, (800) 525-2081
- Salida Golf Course (719) 539-6373
- Salida Hot Springs (719) 539-6738
- Salida Museum (719) 539-4804

Broken Arrow Cafe, Motel & Campground

From the terraced sites on the gently sloping hillside of Broken Arrow, you'll have outstanding views of the snow-capped Sangre de Cristo mountains. Enjoy warm days and cool nights in this mild climate. The long, level, pull thru sites are full hookups with picnic tables and campfire pits. The open and partially shaded sites are among locust and piñon pine trees.

The cafe opens at 7 am and features daily specials and piping hot *homemade* pies. Dine on hearty breakfasts, hamburgers and American-diner style cuisine. The campground is convenient to rafting, fishing, hiking, four-wheel driving, horseback riding, hunting, mountain biking and viewing the Royal Gorge Bridge.

Motel rooms at reasonable rates are also available.

Location: On US Highway 50, 10 miles East of Salida.

Total RV sites: 13	Pull thru sites: 8	Open: 3/1 to 11/30
Full hookup sites: 13	45+ foot long sites: 8	Bonnie O'Loughlin, Owner
Water & elec. sites: 0	Slideout sites: 8	7528 Hwy 50
Elec. only sites: 0	Licenses sold: None	Howard, Colorado 81233
50 amp sites: 0	LP Gas: weight	719/942-3450
Hookup sites open in Fall: 13	Credit Cards: VM	
Winter hookup sites: 0	Elevation: 6800	
RV site cost: ¢		

Within 15 minutes:

At RV Park:

Four Seasons RV Park

In the heart of the Rockies, Four Seasons has full hookups (20, 30 and 50 amps) on level, grassy sites along the churning Arkansas River. Snug in the shade with views of snow-capped peaks, the sites have picnic tables, phone hookup and free TV hookup. This is truly a year-round Arkansas River campground.

The trout fishing on-site is Gold Medal and the playground and recreation hall are stocked with games. Four Seasons sports shuffleboard, horseshoes and sports fields. Ask about the planned group activities and local tours. Down the road are a heated swimming pool and a golf course. Other nearby activities include horseback riding, four-wheel driving, ghost town tours, whitewater rafting, hiking, hunting and skiing.

Ask about the daily, weekly, monthly rates and the year-round and seasonal storage. Meeting and conference facilities are available.

Location: Two miles East of Salida on Highway 50.

Total RV sites: 65
Full hookup sites: 60
Water & elec. sites: 5
Elec. only sites: 0
50 amp sites: 40
Hookup sites open in Fall: 65
Winter hookup sites: 6
RV site cost: Not available

Pull thru sites: 13
45+ foot long sites: 20
Slideout sites: 60
Licenses sold: None
LP Gas: metered
Credit Cards: VM
Elevation: 7000

Open: All Year
Paul & Candy Draper, Owners
4305 Hwy 50 East
Salida, Colorado 81201-9603
719/539-3084

Within 15 minutes:

At RV Park:

Heart of the Rockies Campground

Nestled at the base of Monarch Pass and the breathtaking Continental Divide, this campground has open and shaded, full hookup (20 and 30 amps) sites. All sites are extra long pull thrus. Each site has a picnic table, barbecue grill and campfire pit.

The store has all the camping supplies and treats needed for your vacation. Heart of the Rockies boasts the area's only campground with an outdoor, heated swimming pool. Kids of all ages will like the arcade room, mini-golf, volleyball, horseshoes and evening movies. The campground's scenic horseback rides, bring your horse or rent one of theirs, are also popular. Exhilarating whitewater raft trips and fantastic four-wheel drive tours on old mining roads to picturesque ghost towns are nearby. There's hundreds of miles of wilderness waiting to be explored on horseback and on foot or with a rental Jeep or mountain bike. Heart of the Rockies is also centrally located to Pikes Peak, the Royal Gorge Bridge, the Black Canyon of the Gunnison National Monument and the Great Sand Dunes.

Groups are welcomed.

Location: On US Highway 50, 11 miles East of Monarch Pass, 5 miles West of US Highway 285 and Poncha Springs.

Total RV sites: 45
Full hookup sites: 25
Water & elec. sites: 0
Elec. only sites: 27
50 amp sites: 0
Hookup sites open in Fall: 52
Winter hookup sites: 52
RV site cost: ¢–$

Pull thru sites: 45
45+ foot long sites: 45
Slideout sites: 45
Licenses sold: Fishing
LP Gas: metered
Credit Cards: VMAD
Elevation: 8200

Open: All Year
Tom & Mary Jo Frazer, Managers
16105 Hwy 50 W
Salida, Colorado 81201-9413
800/496-2245
719/539-4051 fax

Within 15 minutes:

At RV Park:

Pleasant Valley RV Park of Howard

On the north bank of the rolling Arkansas River, Pleasant Valley has beautiful shady and grassy, landscaped sites. Most sites are pull thrus and full hookups (30 and 50 amps) with good TV reception. Phone hookups are also available. Elm, spruce, ponderosa, cottonwood, silver popular, and willow trees abound in this peaceful, quiet campground three tenths of a mile off the highway. From the campground, you'll have majestic views of the snowy tips of the Twin Sister Peaks, the central Rocky Mountains and the Sangre de Cristo mountains. Many sites are rented on an annual/seasonal basis.

On-site activities are horseshoes and a recreational hall. The Upper Arkansas River Valley is famed for whitewater rafting, kayaking and fishing while the surrounding area is a hunter's paradise. This is also an excellent area for mountain biking and several ghost towns are an hour and a half away. You can rent a horse from nearby stables. Four-wheel drive tours and whitewater raft trips are minutes away.

Indoor and outdoor group meeting areas are available.

Location: 1/3 mile off US Highway 50 between mileposts 235 and 236, 35 miles West of the Royal Gorge Bridge and 13 miles East of Salida.

Total RV sites: 57	Pull thru sites: 35	Open: All Year
Full hookup sites: 57	45+ foot long sites: 25	Jerry & Becky Lewis, Owners
Water & elec. sites: 0	Slideout sites: 40	0018 County Road 47
Elec. only sites: 0	Licenses sold: None	Howard, Colorado 81233
50 amp sites: 25	LP Gas: weight	719/942-3484
Hookup sites open in Fall: 57	Credit Cards: None	
Winter hookup sites: 10	Elevation: 6640	
RV site cost: Not available		

Within 15 minutes:

At RV Park:

Sugarbush Campground

Sugarbush is an excellent base camp for seeing south central Colorado. The campground is tucked into tall pines near the Arkansas River with a striking view of the Twin Sister Peaks. Most of the level sites are full hookups (20 amps) and pull thrus with picnic tables, barbecue grills and fire rings. You'll find shady, cool sites and friendly relaxation in a rustic setting.

Amenities include a covered pavilion for group activities and family reunions, a video game room and sports field with horseshoes. In the eclectic and well-stocked general store, you'll find antique tractors on display, fishing equipment, video rentals and a surprising range of unusual collectibles, antiques and souvenirs. Fish and watch the deer along the tumbling Arkansas River. Or relax by the small brook that runs through Sugarbush. Nearby, you'll find excellent rafting, horseback riding and hiking on many of the breathtaking trails.

Rustic, housekeeping cabins are also available.

Location: Twelve miles East of Salida and 35 miles West of Royal Gorge on Highway 50 at milepost 235.

Total RV sites: 32	Pull thru sites: 4	Open: 5/1 to 10/15
Full hookup sites: 14	45+ foot long sites: 2	Bill & Sandy Tunstall, Owners
Water & elec. sites: 18	Slideout sites: 5	9229 Hwy 50
Elec. only sites: 0	Licenses sold: Fish & Hunt	Howard, Colorado 81233
50 amp sites: 0	LP Gas: None	719/942-3363
Hookup sites open in Fall: 32	Credit Cards: VMD	
Winter hookup sites: 0	Elevation: 6910	
RV site cost: ¢		

Within 15 minutes:

At RV Park:

San Luis Valley Area

Includes Alamosa, Blanca, Del Norte, Fort Garland, Monta Vista, Mosca, Saguache and Villa Grove. Map: O-13; O-15; N-11; N-12; N-14

The Spanish word for cottonwood grove, Alamosa sits in the center of the San Luis Valley and is surrounded by the majestic Sangre de Cristo and San Juan mountains. Nestled along the Rio Grande River, at about 7,500 feet, the city where the Southwest meets the Rockies boasts 360 days of sunshine. The Great Sand Dunes National Monument, 32 miles northeast of Alamosa, is one of Colorado's most spectacular, constantly shifting, natural formations. The scenic Los Caminos Antiguos Byway passes Alamosa on its way to Antonito. Bird watchers should be sure to visit the Monte Vista Wildlife Refuge and the Alamosa National Wildlife Refuge, both are a popular stopping places during spring and fall migrations for sandhill cranes, ducks, Canadian geese and occasionally the endangered whooping crane. In the winter, numerous hawks, bald eagles and golden eagles stay at the refuges. Fort Garland, the state's oldest surviving military fort built in 1858, is just down the road. Home to Colorado's oldest rodeo, Monte Vista was an early stage coach stop and trading town. Further west is Del Norte where artifacts of man dating as far back as 8000 B.C. were discovered in the mid-1930s. Today, Del Norte houses the Rio Grand County Museum which has some fine historic relics, including an exhibit of rock art.

Fun Things to Do

- Alamosa National Wildlife Refuge (719) 589-4021
- Cattails Golf Course (719) 589-9515
- Fort Garland Museum (719) 379-3512
- Great Sand Dunes Country Club (719) 378-2357
- Great Sand Dunes National Monument (719) 378-2312
- Monte Vista Historical Society (719) 852-4396
- Monte Vista National Wildlife Refuge (719) 589-4021
- Rio Grande County Museum, Del Norte (719) 657-2487
- Saguache County Museum (719) 655-2557
- San Luis Valley Alligator Farm (719) 589-3032
- Splashland Natural Hot Springs (719) 589-6307

Alamosa KOA

In the San Luis Valley, bordered by the Sangre de Cristo and San Juan mountains, Alamosa KOA offers large, level, pull thrus on grassy, full hookup sites at 7,544 feet above sea level. On the direct route to Mesa Verde and the Grand Canyon. All sites have 50 amp service and are set in sage brush with excellent mountain panoramas. Enjoy the view of Colorado's fourth highest peak, Mt. Blanca, from your site while sitting by a campfire.

The campground has video games, volleyball, horseshoes, and a playground. Horseback rides are also available and guest horses are welcome. Pick up a few snacks at the store before fishing, four-wheel driving or mountain biking at any of the nearby trails. Just down the road is a swimming pool for the kids to play in while you soak up the sunshine.

Location: Three ½ miles East of Alamosa and 20 miles West of historic old Fort Garland on Highway 160.

Total RV sites: 38	Pull thru sites: 38	Open: 4/1 to 11/1
Full hookup sites: 10	45+ foot long sites: 38	Yogi Chaudhry, Owner
Water & elec. sites: 28	Slideout sites: 38	6900 Juniper Lane
Elec. only sites: 0	Licenses sold: None	Alamosa, Colorado 81101
50 amp sites: 38	LP Gas: weight	719/589-9757
Hookup sites open in Fall: 38	Credit Cards: VMD	
Winter hookup sites: 0	Elevation: 7544	
RV site cost: Not available		

Within 15 minutes:

At RV Park:

Blanca RV Park & Campground

With a view toward the gigantic waves of the Great Sand Dunes National Monument, Blanca RV Park offers shaded, grassy sites. The level, spacious pull thrus have full hook-ups (one has 50 amps or 220 volts). Enjoy the serenity of southern Colorado while relaxing under the cool shade of 50-year-old Cottonwood trees.

On the eastern edge of town, the campground's store offers gifts, curiosities and snacks. Anglers will enjoy lake fishing for giant trout at Smith Reservoir and northern pike at Sanchez Reservoir. Horseback riding is minutes away and guest horses are welcome. Be sure to explore the largest, in-land sand dunes in the world which butt up against the Sangre de Cristo Mountains.

Location: 20 miles East of Alamosa on US Highway 160.

Total RV sites: 20	Pull thru sites: 12	Open: All Year
Full hookup sites: 20	45+ foot long sites: 4	Major & Sharon Oringdulph, Owners
Water & elec. sites: 0	Slideout sites: 12	521 Main St.
Elec. only sites: 0	Licenses sold: Fish & Hunt	PO Box 64
50 amp sites: 1	LP Gas: metered	Blanca, Colorado 81123-0064
Hookup sites open in Fall: 20	Credit Cards: VMAD	719/379-3201
Winter hookup sites: 20	Elevation: 7750	
RV site cost: ¢		

Within 15 minutes:

At RV Park:

Great Sand Dunes Oasis

Surrounded on two sides by publicly owned land, the Oasis sits adjacent to and at the entrance of the Great Sand Dunes National Monument. You'll have spectacular views of the dunes and the San Luis Valley from level, gravel, pull thru sites with camp-fires. All sites have full hookups, with 20 and

30 amps available. piñon trees, mule deer, antelope and smaller wildlife abound on the open lands around this Sangre de Cristo mountain campground.

In addition to the gift and grocery store and a full-service cafe open for break-fast, lunch and dinner, the Oasis has its own ½-acre fishing pond, an ice cream social, game room and playground. Daily four-wheel drive tours are available into the hard-to-reach areas of the ever shifting Great Sand Dunes. Explore nature trails where snow-capped peaks provide picturesque vistas. Mountain bike trails and horseback rides are nearby and guest horses are allowed on the property.

Group camping sites, an indoor group meeting area, cabins, motel rooms and rental tipis are also available. Ask about the special group rates.

Location: At the entrance to Great Sand Dunes National Monument on Highway 150.

Total RV sites: 20	Pull thru sites: 20	Open: 4/1 to 10/31
Full hookup sites: 20	45+ foot long sites: 20	Jim & Joyce Kuenkel
Water & elec. sites: 0	Slideout sites: 20	Mike & Patti Vittoria, Owners
Elec. only sites: 0	Licenses sold: None	5400 Hwy 150 North
50 amp sites: 0	LP Gas: metered	Mosca, Colorado 81146
Hookup sites open in Fall: 20	Credit Cards: VMD	719/378-2222
Winter hookup sites: 0	Elevation: 8200	
RV site cost: Not available		

Within 15 minutes:

At RV Park:

Navajo Trail Campground

On the western edge of Alamosa, Navajo Trail Campground is in the valley of cool sunshine at an elevation of 7,600 feet. The level, pull thru, full hookup sites have 20 and 30 amps. Located in the central San Luis Valley, the highest and largest inter-mountain valley in the world, and the closest RV park to Alamosa, Navajo Trails is a great base camp for tourists.

The campground has a playground, miniature golf and gift store. It's convenient to restaurants, stores and shopping. Nearby are areas to fish, four-wheel drive, mountain bike and horseback ride. Walking distance from the campground is Alamosa where you can enjoy all the amenities such as an 18-hole golf course and square dancing.

Location: On the Navajo Trail to Mesa Verde National Park in Alamosa at the West end of Highway 160.

Total RV sites: 46
Full hookup sites: 46
Water & elec. sites: 0
Elec. only sites: 0
50 amp sites: 0
Hookup sites open in Fall: 46
Winter hookup sites: 0
RV site cost: $

Pull thru sites: 20
45+ foot long sites: 20
Slideout sites: 46
Licenses sold: None
LP Gas: metered
Credit Cards: VM
Elevation: 7600

Open: 4/1 to 11/15
Bill & Lina Colston, Owners
7665 West Hwy 160
Alamosa, Colorado 81101
719/589-9460

Within 15 minutes:

At RV Park:

Saguache Creek Lodging & RV Park

Surrounded by mountains, in the center of San Luis Valley, Saguache Creek RV Park offers grassy, full hookup (20 amps) sites with campfire pits. Laundry, restrooms and hot showers are provided. All the RV sites are pull thru and some will accommodate rigs larger than 45 feet.

A moderate drive from the Great Sand Dunes National Monument, Saguache Creek is near hunting, fishing, whitewater rafting, skiing and sight-seeing areas of southern Colorado. On-site, the kids can play in the game room with video and board games. Horses and pets are permitted. A short drive away are museums, golf courses, reservoirs and mountain bike trails.

An old West style motel with some kitchenette rooms are also available. Ask about the banquet room and evening entertainment for your family reunion.

Location: On Highway 285, 1 mile South of Saguache.

Total RV sites: 8
Full hookup sites: 8
Water & elec. sites: 7
Elec. only sites: 7
50 amp sites: 0
Hookup sites open in Fall: 8
Winter hookup sites: 0
RV site cost: ¢–$

Pull thru sites: 8
45+ foot long sites: 4
Slideout sites: 8
Licenses sold: None
LP Gas: None
Credit Cards: VM
Elevation: 7787

Open: 4/15 to 11/15
Glenn Shirley
21495 S Hwy 285
Saguache, Colorado 81149
719/655-2264

Within 15 minutes:

At RV Park:

Southwest Station RV Park & Store

A small, new RV park tucked away at the north end of the beautiful San Luis Valley, Southwest Station RV Park has full hookup sites (20/30 amps). Located in Villa Grove, the park has cool nights and is in the midst of the stunning scenery of the Sangre de Cristo and San Juan mountains.

The gift shop on-site features southwestern handicrafts. Pets are welcomed here. Bonanza, an old mining area, is a 12-mile drive. A swimming pool, four-wheel drive tours, fishing, horseback riding, golfing and museums are within driving distance. Convenient to nearby restaurants, Southwest Station is a good base camp for hunters and those in route to the Great Sand Dunes National Monument.

Location: 20 miles South of Poncha Springs and 17 miles North of Saguache on Highway 285 in Villa Grove.

Total RV sites: 5
Full hookup sites: 5
Water & elec. sites: 0
Elec. only sites: 0
50 amp sites: 0
Hookup sites open in Fall: 5
Winter hookup sites: 0
RV site cost: ¢

Pull thru sites: 0
45+ foot long sites:5
Slideout sites: 5
Licenses sold: None
LP Gas: None
Credit Cards: None
Elevation: 7980

Open: 5/15 to 11/15
Jonni Busche, Owner, & Bill Busche
34056 S Hwy 285
PO Box 265
Villa Grove, Colorado 81155-0265
719/655-2718

Within 15 minutes:

At RV Park:

Ute Creek Campground

Vacationing at Ute Creek Campground in Fort Garland requires only two activities from you: fishing and relaxing. All the open, RV sites are full hook-ups (20 and 30 amps) with campfire pits. TV hookup is available. Picnic in an area cooled by large shade trees or dabble your feet in the mountain

stream running through the campground. Off the main highway on good gravel access roads, you'll find this a quiet campground.

A playground on site and a swimming pool, sauna and volleyball at the nearby community center will exhaust the kids' energy while you practice casting in the stocked pond. The large meadow is great for family gatherings. Re-live the past with a horse drawn carriage ride or take a guided pack hunting and fishing trip to high mountain lakes. Guest horses are permitted here.

Location: Exit Highway 160 at Narcisso, go North 1 block then West on 5th Street.

Total RV sites: 24	Pull thru sites: 24	Open: All Year
Full hookup sites: 24	45+ foot long sites: 20	Frosty & Karen Smith, Owners
Water & elec. sites: 0	Slideout sites: 24	PO Box 188
Elec. only sites: 0	Licenses sold: None	Ft Garland, Colorado 81133-0188
50 amp sites: 0	LP Gas: None	719/379-3238
Hookup sites open in Fall: 24	Credit Cards: None	
Winter hookup sites: 24	Elevation: 8000	
RV site cost: Not available		

Within 15 minutes:

At RV Park:

Woods & River Campground

Situated on the Rio Grande River, this campground follows more than a quarter of a mile of roaring rapids which are ideal for fishing or leisurely strolls along its picturesque banks. The large, grassy, pull thrus have cable TV hookup and shade trees. Woods & River Campground is a clean, friendly, quiet place to put up your feet for a while. All sites are full hookups with campfire pits.

A playground and game room are on-site. Great mountain bike trails are only minutes away. Come for rafting, fishing, relaxin' in cool, clean air and country sunshine. The Del Norte area offers many attractions for the summer and winter vacationer — ghost town exploring, hunting deer and elk, and skiing at Wolf Creek Ski Area.

An indoor, group meeting area is available.

Location: In Del Norte, 7 blocks North of Loaf'N Jug on US Highway 160 or 6 blocks West of State Highway 112.

Total RV sites: 26
Full hookup sites: 26
Water & elec. sites: 0
Elec. only sites: 0
50 amp sites: 0
Hookup sites open in Fall: 26
Winter hookup sites: 0
RV site cost: Not available

Pull thru sites: 26
45+ foot long sites: 26
Slideout sites: 26
Licenses sold: None
LP Gas: None
Credit Cards: None
Elevation: 7800

Open: 5/1 to 10/31
Sam Selters & Sharon Boyce, Owners
25 Cedar
PO Box 62
Del Norte, Colorado 81132-0062
719/657-2820

Within 15 minutes:

At RV Park:

Silverton

Map: M-6

A trip to Silverton is a trip back in time. Designated a National Historic Landmark, the town seems frozen in the last century with its luxurious, many-windowed Grand Imperial Hotel (built in 1882), picturesque Victorian homes and restored miners' cabins. In its heyday, Silverton had as many as 32 gambling halls, saloons and "sporting houses" on Blair Street. Granted exclusively to the Utes in 1868, the treaty was ignored when gold and silver strikes brought miners in by the wagonload. Because of the atmosphere, several Western movies have been filmed here, not only to take advantage of the historic look, but to capture the splendorous mountain magic as well. At 9,303 feet, Silverton is surrounded by four towering peaks and hundreds of miles of the San Juan, Uncompahgre and Rio Grande national forests — no matter which direction you go, you'll find hikes through the high mountains, past raging rivers to abandoned ghost towns. The area is also filled with four-wheel drive trails and roads to other mountain towns like Ouray, Telluride and Lake City — this area has some of the best Jeeping in the world. For a truly memorable vacation, ride the Durango-Silverton Narrow Gauge Railroad, starting in Durango or Silverton, and spend some time in Silverton where history lives.

Fun Things to Do

- Durango-Silverton Narrow Gauge Railroad (970) 247-2733
- Old Hundred Gold Mine Tour (800) 872-3009, (970) 387-5444
- San Juan County Historical Society Museum (970) 387-5838

Red Mountain Lodge & Campground

Adjacent to the lodge, Red Mountain Campground has open sites with a views of the picturesque mountains. The full hookup (20 and 30 amps) sites have cable TV, phone hookups and a picnic table.

Kids will like the playground, sports fields, new miniature golf course, horseshoes, and volleyball. Camp activities include river fishing, motorbike trails, hiking trails and snowmobile trails. There's something for everyone within walking distance: the Durango/Silverton Narrow Gauge Train depot, horseback ride, four-wheel drive tours, and hunting in season.

Motel rooms with kitchenettes are also available.

Location: In Silverton, 1block North of Highway 550 on Highway 110.

Total RV sites: 14	Pull thru sites: 3	Open: 4/15 to 10/15
Full hookup sites: 14	45+ foot long sites: 4	Roger & Gerri Teesdale, Owners
Water & elec. sites: 0	Slideout sites: 14	664 Greene St.
Elec. only sites: 6	Licenses sold: None	PO Box 346
50 amp sites: 0	LP Gas: None	Silverton, Colorado 81433-0346
Hookup sites open in Fall: 14	Credit Cards: VM	970/387-5512
Winter hookup sites: 0	Elevation: 9300	
RV site cost: Not available		

Within 15 minutes:

At RV Park:

Silverton Lakes Campground

Beside the flowing Animas River, in the heart of the extraordinary San Juan Mountains, Silverton Lakes Campground is directly on the San Juan Skyway, a gateway to a fantastic, four-wheel drive alpine loop. The full hookup (20 and 30 amps) sites are level and open pull thrus with picnic tables, barbecue grills, campfire rings and free wood on a 23-acre park. The scenery is spectacular year round, from snow-covered peaks in June to a breathtaking carpet of color in September.

Rent a Jeep here to explore 700 miles of roads to ghost towns and abandoned mines. Or trek into the hills of yesteryear on foot, by mountain bike or with a horse rented from local stables. Hunt for rocks, gems and arrowheads in the mountains where you just might discover an elusive vein of gold! Try casting your line into the stocked trout ponds to catch a tasty, fresh meal to cook over the campfire. All the amenities of the national historic district of Silverton, shops, restaurants and the Durango/Silverton Narrow Gauge Railroad, are minutes away.

Location: Northwest of Silverton, a ½ mile past downtown Silverton off Highway 110 on Kendall Street.

Total RV sites: 50	Pull thru sites: 25	Open: 5/1 to 11/1
Full hookup sites: 35	45+ foot long sites: 15	Jim & Judy Greenfield, Owners
Water & elec. sites: 15	Slideout sites: 15	2100 Kendall St.
Elec. only sites: 0	Licenses sold: Fish & Hunt	PO Box 126
50 amp sites: 0	LP Gas: None	Silverton, Colorado 81433-0126
Hookup sites open in Fall: 0	Credit Cards: VMAD	970/387-5721
Winter hookup sites: 0	Elevation: 9300	
RV site cost: $		

Within 15 minutes:

At RV Park:

Somerset

Map: I-7

Few places offer such a delightful combination of climate, scenery and recreation as the Somerset area. The natural beauty of the countryside, the clean air and the surrounding majestic mountains are the ideal vacation ingredients. The close by West Elk Wilderness is a magnificent place for hiking and hunting. The entire area is a focal point of backroads and trails leading into the wilderness. Take a drive along the West Elk Scenic Byway and record some of this area's uniqueness with your camera. Nearby, in Paonia, you'll find abundant orchards filled with sweet and sour cherries, apricots, peaches, plums, pears, nectarines and a large variety of apples.

Fun Things to Do

- The Bawie School Historical Site (970) 527-4500/4264

Crystal Meadows Ranch, Cabins, RVs & Restaurant

Tucked between two mountain ranges, in a scenic river valley, Crystal Meadows Ranch has shaded sites in the forest along a bubbling mountain creek. Adjacent to the restaurant and cabins, the full hookup (30 amps) sites near the river have picnic tables, barbecue grills, and fire rings. The campground is nestled serenely in the mountains where Anthracite, Coal and Muddy creeks join to form the North Fork of the Gunnison River. At Crystal Meadows, you're surrounded by the sound of cool rushing alpine-fed water and vistas of pine covered peaks.

For your convenience, there is an on-site grocery store with RV supplies, ice, limited groceries, and gasoline. The outdoor pavilion and indoor conference room are great for your retreat or family reunion. The restaurant serves tasty breakfasts, hearty lunches and delectable dinners. Fish in the privately stocked lake or in the snow-fed creeks. Rent horses nearby, or bring your own to ride. Horseback ride, mountain bike, or hike in the nearby West Elk Mountains and the Ragged Mountains, two vast and scenic wilderness areas. Hunters will find abundant deer and elk here in season.

Six cabins and rooms are available for rent.

Location: On the West Elk Loop Scenic Byway, 6 miles East of Somerset on Highway 133 near milepost 24, ½ mile Southeast on County Road 12 (Crested Butte-Kebler Pass Rd).

Total RV sites: 23
Full hookup sites: 23
Water & elec. sites: 0
Elec. only sites: 0
50 amp sites: 0
Hookup sites open in Fall: 23
Winter hookup sites: 0
RV site cost: $

Pull thru sites: 0
45+ foot long sites: 8
Slideout sites: 20
Licenses sold: Fish & Hunt
LP Gas: None
Credit Cards: VMD
Elevation: 6200

Open: 5/28 to 11/13
Bill & Kay Tennison, Owners
30682 County Rd 12
Somerset, Colorado 81434-9625
970/929-5656
970/929-5657 fax

Within 15 minutes:

At RV Park:

South East Plains

Includes Ordway, La Junta and Lamar. Map: L-22; M-23; L-26

On Colorado's eastern plains, Ordway is 5 miles west of Lake Meredith and Lake Henry which offer fishing, boating and water skiing. Olney Springs and Ordway Reservoir, 1 mile north, are regularly stocked for excellent fishing. From La Junta take the Scenic and Historic Byway that follows the Santa Fe Trail along US Highway 50 to Trinidad. During the Civil War this trail was a corridor for soldiers and a turning point for the Northern side in the West. A crossroads of the Santa Fe and Navajo trails, La Junta (Spanish for "the junction") still is the transportation hub of the sunny, scenic, historic lower Arkansas River Valley. Produce and cattle are shipped daily from La Junta by train. Nearby, at the Comanche National Grasslands, you can watch for the 275 species of birds and 40 species of mammals on 400,000 acres of ranch land. Outdoor recreation includes hunting, fishing, sight-seeing and rock-hounding. In town, the reconstructed trading post of Bent's Old Fort used to be a frontier hub where American trade and influence flowed south to Mexico. The Koshare Indian Museum has grown from a 1933 Boy Scout troop project into a nationally known, authentic Indian dance group and museum where you can see Indian dances during the summer. Be sure to stop and buy a variety of locally grown, sun-ripened fruits and vegetables, particularly melons. Visit La Junta and see why locals call it the "Smile High City." Prowers County is known as the goose hunting capital of the world and Lamar is at its center. Located on what was once a 25-mile long grove of huge cottonwood trees known as Big Timbers that provided shade to Indians and other travelers, Lamar has a rich history.

Fun Things To Do

- Bent's Old Fort National Historic Site (719) 384-2596
- Big Timbers Museum, Lamar (719) 336-2472
- Comanche National Grasslands (719) 384-2181
- Koshare Indian Museum (719) 384-4411
- La Junta Golf Club (719) 384-7133
- Otero County Museum (719) 384-7500
- Rocky Ford City Golf Club (719) 254-7528
- Spreading Antlers Golf Course, Lamar (719) 336-5274

Junction Campground, Store & Restaurant

A rural campground with level, open and shaded sites, Junction Campground in Ordway has a restaurant. The shady, full hookup (20 and 30 amps) sites are pull thru with phone hookups and picnic tables. You'll find this a quiet stopover with friendly service.

The recreation room, arcade, and sports fields will keep the kids busy while you take a refreshing dip in the community swimming pool next door. Fish on three nearby lakes where you can also boat and water ski on two of them. Other amenities include the full-service restaurant and large convenience store. The Junction Campground is the perfect place to stay before going into the mountains.

An indoor, group meeting area is also available.

Location: In Ordway at the junction of Colorado Highways 71 and 96.

Total RV sites: 24	Pull thru sites: 24	Open: All Year
Full hookup sites: 12	45+ foot long sites: 24	Shannon & Jeanne Torgler, Managers
Water & elec. sites: 0	Slideout sites: 24	18055 Rd G
Elec. only sites: 0	Licenses sold: Fish & Hunt	PO Box 97
50 amp sites: 0	LP Gas: metered	Ordway, Colorado 81063-0097
Hookup sites open in Fall: 12	Credit Cards: VMD	719/267-3262
Winter hookup sites: 12	Elevation: 4500	
RV site cost: ¢		

Within 15 minutes:

At RV Park:

La Junta KOA

Flat and open with some shade, La Junta KOA is easily accessible from the highway. The grassy and gravel, level, pull thru sites are full hookups with 15, 30 and 50 amps. Located in the lower Arkansas Valley along the historic Santa Fe Trail, La Junta KOA has cool, refreshing evenings in the summertime.

Upon your arrival, your hosts escort you to your site.

While the kids romp in the arcade and on the playground, you can take a leisurely dip in the swimming pool. The two air conditioned recreation rooms have a card table, ping pong, video games, cable TV and a book exchange. Take a historic tour of Bent's Fort. You'll find the nationally known summer Koshare Indian Dances fascinating and entertaining. La Junta KOA is a great stop-over site to or from your trip to the Colorado Rocky Mountains.

Location: From the junction of US Highway 50 and Highway 10, go 1 ½ miles West on US Highway 50.

Total RV sites: 41	Pull thru sites: 30	Open: 3/1 to 11/5
Full hookup sites: 30	45+ foot long sites: 25	Margy & Hank Rogers, Owners
Water & elec. sites: 12	Slideout sites: 30	26680 Hwy 50 West
Elec. only sites: 0	Licenses sold: None	La Junta, Colorado 81050
50 amp sites: 4	LP Gas: metered	719/384-9580
Hookup sites open in Fall: 42	Credit Cards: VMD	
Winter hookup sites: 0	Elevation: 4066	
RV site cost: $		

Within 15 minutes:

At RV Park:

Lamar KOA

Situated on over 10 acres with grassy, pull thru sites and full hookups (30 amps), Lamar KOA is near all the activities of the south eastern Colorado plains. The official Colorado Tourist Information Center is located here and this is a convenient stop for Rocky Mountain-bound vacationers

and hunters. On the historic Santa Fe Trail in the lower Arkansas River Valley, this KOA has good gravel interior roads.

The kids will like the swimming pool and playground. Enjoy a game of 9-hole miniature golf, perfect for kids of all ages. The camp store has groceries, RV supplies, souvenirs and snacks. Tired of cooking? Order a hot pizza or sandwiches on-site and dine in. The Lamar area features outstanding dove, quail, pheasant, antelope, duck and goose hunting so come prepared to explore the outdoors.

Location: On the Sante Fe Trail off Highway 50 at milepost 431.

Total RV sites: 36	Pull thru sites: 36	Open: All Year
Full hookup sites: 11	45+ foot long sites: 36	Bill Rich, Owner
Water & elec. sites: 28	Slideout sites: 36	5385 Hwy 50 & 287
Elec. only sites: 2	Licenses sold: None	Lamar, Colorado 81052
50 amp sites: 0	LP Gas: W	719/336-7625
Hookup sites open in Fall: 36	Credit Cards: VMD	
Winter hookup sites: 11	Elevation: 3615	
RV site cost: ¢–$		

Within 15 minutes:

At RV Park:

South Fork & Wagon Wheel Gap

Also see San Luis Valley Area. Map: N-10

South Fork is situated at the western edge of the San Luis Valley, one of the biggest intermountain valleys in the world. Since the late 1880s, South Fork, at 8,250 feet, has been a logging and lumbering community. The Rio Grande River between South Fork and Del Norte has been designated Gold Medal trout water which means it offers the greatest potential for trophy trout fishing success in Colorado. The town, at the foot of Wolf Creek Pass, is near numerous, year-round recreational possibilities. Whether you hike it or drive it, the surrounding mountains have deer, elk, grouse, ptarmigan, bighorn sheep, snowshoe rabbits, and even an occasional bear, bobcat or cougar! The nearby town of Wagon Wheel Gap was the scene of several early Indian battles and it's said Kit Carson's brother-in-law farmed here in 1840. The town's railroad station is listed on the National Register of Historical Places.

Fun Things to Do

- Blue Creek Restaurant (800) 326-6408, (719) 658-2479
- Chinook Smokehouse (800) 238-6837, (719) 873-9993
- Spruce Lodge Rafting (800) 228-5605, (719) 873-5605
- Wolf Creek Ski Area (719) 264-5629

Aspenridge Cabins & RV Park

The boundless quiet is beautiful at Aspenridge RV Park which sits on the picturesque Silver Thread Scenic Byway. The level, full hookup sites have free cable TV and campfire pits. South Fork is surrounded on three sides by the Rio Grande National Forest and some of the largest, undisturbed wilderness areas in the country — the outdoor activities here are countless.

The game room and the indoor and outdoor, group meeting areas are great for family reunions and the kids. Nearby, the Rio Grande River boasts excellent, gold medal trout fishing or, if you prefer, your hosts can supply you with a map to the many local lakes whose deep, calm waters await your expert casting. Hike into the unusual Wheeler Geologic Area, a haunting landscape of pinnacles, canyons and arches accessible only by foot. Bring your horse or rent one nearby and take an unforgettable trail ride into nature at its finest. You'll find plenty of old logging and mining roads which make for exhilarating four-wheel drive or mountain bike trips. Make Aspenridge your camping and fishing headquarters in Southern Colorado.

Modern cabins are also available.

Location: On the Silver Thread Scenic Byway, ½ mile Northwest of Junction 160 on Highway 149.

Total RV sites: 60
Full hookup sites: 60
Water & elec. sites: 0
Elec. only sites: 0
50 amp sites: 0
Hookup sites open in Fall: 25
Winter hookup sites: 10
RV site cost: ¢

Pull thru sites: 7
45+ foot long sites: 60
Slideout sites: 60
Licenses sold: None
LP Gas: metered
Credit Cards: VMD
Elevation: 8180

Open: All Year
Charles & Brenda Murray, Owners
0710 W Hwy 149
South Fork, Colorado 81154
719/873-5921

Within 15 minutes:

At RV Park:

Blue Creek Lodge, Cabins & Campground

This is a vacationer's paradise — a haven for fishing enthusiasts, hunters, skiers, hikers and photographers. The full hookup (30 and 50 amps) sites have campfire pits.

The lodge offers hospitality with home-cooked meals in the full-service restaurant. Treat yourself at the soda fountain, carouse in the game room and stock up on curios from the gift shop. Have your hair styled at Thressia's Beauty Salon right on the property. In the winter, try tubing, ice skating, snow-mobiling, cross-country or alpine skiing at the Wolf Creek Ski Area. In the spring and summer months, enjoy the high rivers in a raft — you can participate in the yearly raft races during the second weekend in June. If you're planning a tamer vacation, go hiking, rock hounding or fly fishing in the Rio Grande River across the road, or in the many mountain lakes nearby. Bring your own horse or rent one nearby for trips into the back country. In the fall, come hunt in some of the finest elk and deer country in the Rocky Mountains!

Housekeeping cabins, lodge rooms, dorm beds and trailers are also available.

Location: Off Highway 149 between mileposts 11 and 12.

Total RV sites: 34	Pull thru sites: 6	Open: All Year
Full hookup sites: 34	45+ foot long sites: 7	Bill & Thressia Philbern, Owners
Water & elec. sites: 0	Slideout sites: 34	Wagon Wheel Gap Hwy 149
Elec. only sites: 0	Licenses sold: Fish & Hunt	Star Rt 81133
50 amp sites: 17	LP Gas: None	South Fork, Colorado 81154
Hookup sites open in Fall: 34	Credit Cards: None	719/658-2479
Winter hookup sites: 6	Elevation: 8735	800/326-6408
RV site cost: Not available		719/658-2915 fax

Within 15 minutes:

At RV Park:

Chinook Lodge & Smokehouse

Camp beneath tall pine trees in the heart of the Rocky Mountains at Chinook Lodge. The shaded, full hookup sites are 32 feet wide and 50 feet long with picnic tables. Chinook Lodge is easily accessible from the highway.

The small store sells groceries, snacks, hunting and fishing licenses. To whet your appetite, the smokehouse makes tasty smoked ham, turkey, fish and old-fashioned beef jerky. The South Fork area is ideal for fishing, hunting and cross-country and downhill skiing. The nearby gold medal waters of the Rio Grande River and numerous mountain lakes are an angler's dream come true. The roaring Rio Grande is also fun for "blue-water" rafting trips during the summer.

Rustic modern log cabins are also available.

Location: On the East edge of South Fork on the South side of US Highway 160.

Total RV sites: 6	Pull thru sites: 0	Open: 5/15 to 11/1
Full hookup sites: 6	45+ foot long sites: 6	Roy & Barb Pruett, Owners
Water & elec. sites: 0	Slideout sites: 6	29666 Hwy 160 W
Elec. only sites: 0	Licenses sold: Fish & Hunt	PO Box 530
50 amp sites: 6	LP Gas: W	South Fork, Colorado 81154-0530
Hookup sites open in Fall: 6	Credit Cards: VM	719/873-9993
Winter hookup sites: 0	Elevation: 8300	800/238-6837
RV site cost: ¢		

Within 15 minutes:

At RV Park:

Cottonwood Cove Lodge & Cabins

Nestled in thousands of acres of untouched mountains, near the clear, icy waters of the Rio Grande River, Cottonwood Cove has full hookup sites with campfire pits. An authentic, 1940s guest ranch, Cottonwood Cove is in a picture perfect setting, ideal for a refreshing escape from everyday life.

Relax in the cool shade of cottonwood, aspen and pine trees while admiring the view of the surrounding mountains across the way.

The lodge, built in 1945, has a cozy family room, a cafe serving nightly specials, a recreational room and gift shop. Cottonwood Cove provides one or two hour horseback rides. You're sure to catch many gold-medal trout in the Rio Grande and surrounding mountain lakes. Mountain bikers will delight in the close proximity of the Wolf Creek Ski Area, Wheeler Geological Area and hundreds of miles of national forests roads here.

Housekeeping cabins, lodge rooms and dormitory beds are also available.

Location: Northwest of South Fork on Highway 149 and the Silver Thread Scenic Byway.

Total RV sites: 8	Pull thru sites: 2	Open: 5/25 to 10/25
Full hookup sites: 8	45+ foot long sites: 2	Richard & Kathi Small, Managers
Water & elec. sites: 0	Slideout sites: 1	Hwy 149 milepost 13
Elec. only sites: 0	Licenses sold: Fishing	HC 33 Wagon Wheel Gap
50 amp sites: 0	LP Gas: None	South Fork, Colorado 81154
Hookup sites open in Fall: 8	Credit Cards: VMD	719/658-2242
Winter hookup sites: 0	Elevation: 8448	
RV site cost: $–$$		

Within 15 minutes:

At RV Park:

Grandview Cabins & RV

At Grandview Cabins & RV in South Fork, all the sites are full hook-ups (20/30 amps) with TV and phone hookup available. Choose among sites shaded by pine trees or in the open. Many of the sites are extra long with a few pull thrus. Situated near the beautiful Rio Grande River and the national forest,  this campground is close to old mining towns, hiking, mountain biking and four-wheel drive trails.

At the large recreation hall join in the many daily activities from cards and dances to barbecues and relaxing in front of the fire. The game room has board games. Send the kids to the playground and the groups to the indoor meeting area. Call ahead to bring your horse to Grandview, located on a scenic highway. Cast your line into the nearby Rio Grande River. Elk and deer abound here, just 18 miles from the Continental Divide.

Housekeeping cabins with fireplaces are also available.

Location: ¾ mile from Highway 160 on Scenic Byway 149.

Total RV sites: 92
Full hookup sites: 92
Water & elec. sites: 0
Elec. only sites: 0
50 amp sites: 0
Hookup sites open in Fall: 92
Winter hookup sites: 5
RV site cost: ¢

Pull thru sites: 3
45+ foot long sites: 40
Slideout sites: 80
Licenses sold: None
LP Gas: weight
Credit Cards: VM
Elevation: 8200

Open: All Year
Gary & Maria Hodges, Owners
Junction Hwy 149 & 160
PO Box 189
South Fork, Colorado 81154-0189
719/873-5541

Within 15 minutes:

At RV Park:

Riverbend Resort Cabins & RV Park

In a mountain setting on the South Fork of the Rio Grande River, Riverbend Resort has nearly a mile of grassy RV sites overlooking the river. The full hookup (30 amps), pull thru, back in sites have picnic tables, barbecue grills, fire rings and free Satellite TV hookup. Ponderosa, spruce and aspen trees dot the campground.

The resort sports horseshoes, a playground and planned group activities. Fish on the trout-stocked river or in many of the nearby mountain lakes. Riverbend Resort is in the heart of Wolf Creek, which offers fantastic hiking, mountain biking, horseback riding and hunting. While the kids play in the arcade, you can relax in the hot tub after a day of view-filled hiking. The newly opened Kathy's Krafts Shop offers both art supplies, crafts and classes.

Cabins and a triplex bunkhouse are available.

Location: Three miles Southwest of South Fork on US Highway 160 at milepost 183.

Total RV sites: 58	Pull thru sites: 16	Open: All Year
Full hookup sites: 58	45+ foot long sites: 25	33846 West Highway 160
Water & elec. sites: 0	Slideout sites: 25	Box 129
Elec. only sites: 0	Licenses sold: None	South Fork, Colorado 81154-0728
50 amp sites: 0	LP Gas: metered	719/873-5344
Hookup sites open in Fall: 58	Credit Cards: VM	
Winter hookup sites: 0	Elevation: 8300	
RV site cost: ¢		

Within 15 minutes:

At RV Park:

South Fork Campground, RV Resort

The level, fully shaded sites at South Fork Resort are along the Rio Grande River. The full hookup (50 amps) sites are pull thrus with fire rings, barbecue grills, picnic tables and cable TV hookups. Numerous pine and aspen trees surround the grassy sites with views of the Continental Divide.

Kids will like the recreation room, playground, horseshoes and volleyball while avid anglers will appreciate fishing right out their back door on the quarter mile of river frontage. Both a mini country store and Rowena of South Fork Unique Boutique are on-site. Explore the mountainous terrain on foot, horseback, mountain bike or with a four-wheel drive vehicle. Take a local trail or wagon ride in the summer or sleigh rides and sleigh dinners in the winter. Spend the warm months river rafting and gold medal fishing nearby. Check out the close by cross-country trails and the downhill skiing at Wolf Creek Ski Area during the snow season.

Camper cabins and tipis are also available for rent. Ask about the indoor, group meeting area for your family reunion.

Location: Four miles East of South Fork on US Highway 160 at milepost 190.

Total RV sites: 33	Pull thru sites: 13	Open: All Year
Full hookup sites: 23	45+ foot long sites: 16	Rowena & Raleigh Graham, Owners
Water & elec. sites: 10	Slideout sites: 9	26359 W Hwy 160
Elec. only sites: 0	Licenses sold: Fish & Hunt	South Fork, Colorado 81154
50 amp sites: 23	LP Gas: metered	719/873-5500
Hookup sites open in Fall: 33	Credit Cards: VMD	800/237-7322
Winter hookup sites: 23	Elevation: 8130	
RV site cost: Not available		

Within 15 minutes:

At RV Park:

Spruce Lodge, Rafting & RV Park

If you're into mild water rafting, Spruce Lodge is the place to stay. Built in the 1920s, the lodge is a quaint, historic log building that blends modern conveniences with turn-of-the-century charm. The full hookup (15 amps; one with 30 amps) sites adjacent to the lodge and rafting company are open and shaded. Sites have cable TV hookup, picnic tables, and barbecue grills. Gather around the central campfire at night.

A gift shop with local, handmade crafts and souvenirs is right on the property. After a full day of rafting, soothe your tired muscles in the spacious hot tub. Outside, play miniature golf. Ask your hosts about un-guided rafting on the Rio Grande — there are mild, fun family trips for beginners. Other area activities include trout fishing, horseback riding, hiking, hunting and four-wheel driving. Rent a mountain bike and ride the back country trails.

Rustic lodge rooms and modern motel units are also available.

Location: On the North side of US Highway 160 at the East end of South Fork.

Total RV sites: 12	Pull thru sites: 6	Open: 5/1 to 9/30
Full hookup sites: 12	45+ foot long sites: 6	Jim & Marilyn Karlovetz, Owners
Water & elec. sites: 0	Slideout sites: 12	29431 US Highway160
Elec. only sites: 0	Licenses sold: None	PO Box 156
50 amp sites: 0	LP Gas: None	South Fork, Colorado 81154-0156
Hookup sites open in Fall: 12	Credit Cards: VMD	719/873-5605
Winter hookup sites: 0	Elevation: 8400	800/228-5605
RV site cost: ¢		

Within 15 minutes:

At RV Park:

Ute Bluff Lodge, Cabins & RV Park

Everything is within reach of the Ute Bluff RV Park: Wolf Creek Ski Area, Rio Grande River and Rio Grande National Forest. All grassy sites are full hookups (30 amps) with TV and phone hookup. Many of the sites are pull thrus with room for slide outs. Ute Buff is easily accessible with good gravel roads.

Just 2 miles east of South Fork, from Ute Buff Lodge you can fish and raft the Rio Grande River or hike, hunt and mountain bike in the national forest. Whether you spend the day playing in the snow or hiking in the sunshine, at night relax in the outdoor hot tubs under the stars.

Housekeeping cabins and motel rooms are also available.

Location: East of South Fork on Highway 160.

Total RV sites: 45	Pull thru sites: 20	Open: 4/15 to 10/1
Full hookup sites: 45	45+ foot long sites: 0	Ron Vanderploeg & Nancy Hoobler
Water & elec. sites: 45	Slideout sites: 20	US Highway 160
Elec. only sites: 45	Licenses sold: None	Box 160
50 amp sites: 0	LP Gas: None	South Fork, Colorado 81154-0160
Hookup sites open in Fall: 20	Credit Cards: VMAD	719/873-5595
Winter hookup sites: 2	Elevation: 8180	800/473-0595
RV site cost: $		

Within 15 minutes:

At RV Park:

Steamboat Springs Area

Includes Clark. Map: C-9

A famous ski center, Steamboat Springs in the Yampa Valley offers much more than just winter sports. Fish Creek Falls is a breathtaking, 283-foot waterfall and historic bridge. From the falls you have access to hiking and mountain bike trails that lead to the Continental Divide. To the northeast of town is the Mount Zirkel Wilderness Area where the elevation ranges from 7,000 feet to 13,000 feet in a 141,000-acre undeveloped area, ideal for hiking, fishing and hunting. The Yampa River Trail System runs adjacent to downtown. Steamboat Springs was supposedly named in 1865 when French trappers riding through thought they heard the chugging of a steamboat. But it was a hot springs that chugged until 1908 when the railroad blasted out the rock chamber over the springs. Today, for relaxation, you can choose from among the more than 150 hot springs in the area. Northern Utes (the Yamp-satika) summered in the area as early as the 1300s. Be forewarned, according to local legend, the "Yampa Valley Curse" means visitors are cast under a spell that compels them to return again and again.

Fun Things to Do

- Mount Zirkel Wilderness Area (970) 879-1870
- Sheraton Steamboat Golf Course (970) 879-1391
- Stagecoach State Park (970) 736-2436
- Steamboat Springs Golf Course (970) 879-4295
- Strawberry Park Hot Springs (970) 879-0342
- Tread of Pioneers Museum (970) 879-2214

Elk River Guest Ranch

On the upper Elk River, surrounded by Routt National Forest and near the pristine Mount Zirkel Wilderness area, Elk River Guest Ranch is an excellent place to get away from it all. The full hookup sites are encircled by the outstanding scenery of the Elk River Valley all year long. Bring along your camera to capture wildlife, wild flowers, rushing rivers, billowing high country meadows and, in the fall, aspen in all their colorful, golden glory.

The ranch will prepare you for hunting and fishing on Steamboat and Pearl lakes or on the more than 100 mountain lakes and 900 miles of nearby streams. The ranch also offers horseback rides of varying lengths, including a lunch trip to Pearl Lake. Feel free to bring your horse to stay in the corral. In the winter, try cross-country skiing or snowmobiling on the 25 miles of groomed trails or downhill ski in Steamboat Springs. Unwind in the hot tub and join your hosts around the nightly, summer campfires after a day of high country adventures.

Quaint, comfortable cabins are also available.

Location: 20 miles North of Steamboat, West of Clark off Highway 129 on County Road 64.

Total RV sites: 6	Pull thru sites: 0	Open: All Year
Full hookup sites: 6	45+ foot long sites: 6	Pat & Joey Barrett, Owners
Water & elec. sites: 0	Slideout sites: 1	29840 CR 64
Elec. only sites: 0	Licenses sold: None	Clark, Colorado 80428
50 amp sites: 0	LP Gas: None	970/879-6220
Hookup sites open in Fall: 6	Credit Cards: VMD	800/750-6220
Winter hookup sites: 2	Elevation: 7600	
RV site cost: $		

Within 15 minutes:

At RV Park:

Walden

Map: B-12

Walden sits in a basin surrounded by the sharply uplifted peaks of the Medicine Bow Range, Rabbit Ears Range, Never Summer Mountains and the Park Range. The town, in the smallest and most isolated of the three Colorado parks, North Park, opens north to Wyoming and its valley floor is covered in ranches, hay and sagebrush. Up until the 1820s, Utes hunted the North Park area for buffalo and the abundant other wild game. Trappers followed and eventually miners found their way here as well. As mining proved unsuccessful, many turned to ranching which is still the community's mainstay. One mile south is the Arapaho National Wildlife Refuge where you can see elk, moose, deer and numerous waterfowl. With access to Routt National Forest and Mt. Zirkel Wilderness Area, the Big Creek Reservoir is 35 miles northwest of Walden. Two nearby lakes, Cowdrey Lake and Lake John, have excellent fishing and seasonal waterfowl hunting. Try whitewater rafting or a scenic float trip through the Northgate Canyon in the North Platte Wilderness Area. The more adventurous might want to try hiking in the Colorado State Forest where the mountain scenery is unforgettable.

Fun Things To Do

- Arapaho National Forest (970) 887-3331
- Arapaho National Wildlife Refuge (970) 723-8202
- Big Creek Reservoir (970) 723-8204
- Colorado State Forest (970) 723-8366
- North Park Pioneer Museum (970) 723-4711
- North Platte Wilderness Area (970) 369-4632
- Roosevelt National Forest (970) 224-1277
- Routt National Forest (970) 723-8204

Richard's RV Park

On the southern end of picturesque Lake John, Richard's has level, open sites overlooking the deep blue lake. All hookup (30 amps) sites are pull thrus with picnic tables and free wood. Enjoy the relaxed, isolated atmosphere as you breathe in the crisp mountain air and survey the panoramic views of snow-capped peaks in the distance.

Located on a working cattle ranch, Richard's is adjacent to Richard State Wildlife Area. On-site activities include a recreation hall, sports fields, horseshoes and hiking trails. The biggest attraction, 600-acre Lake John, a top trout lake, is accessible by auto. Boat ramps and docks are at both the north and the south ends of the lake. Stop wishing and go fishing along either the lake's 6 miles of shoreline or the nearby North Fork of the North Platte River. Hunt for sage grouse, duck, goose, elk, deer and antelope in season.

Ask about the Stay, Store & Save Plan. Groups, clubs and reunions are welcomed.

Location: On the South end of Lake John, 15 miles Northwest of Walden on County Road 7A.

Total RV sites: 33	Pull thru sites: 33	Open: 5/10 to 10/15
Full hookup sites: 13	45+ foot long sites: 33	Bob & Lois Richard, Owners
Water & elec. sites: 20	Slideout sites: 33	4521 County Rd 7A
Elec. only sites: 0	Licenses sold: None	SR Box 410
50 amp sites: 0	LP Gas: None	Walden, Colorado 80480-0410
Hookup sites open in Fall: 0	Credit Cards: None	970/723-4407
Winter hookup sites: 0	Elevation: 8400	
RV site cost: Not available		

Within 15 minutes:

At RV Park:

Westcliffe

Map: L-15

When silver was king in 1881, the Denver & Rio Grande Railroad expanded from Cañon City west and built Westcliffe just a mile from nearby Silver Cliff which was a legendary wild mining town and once vied to be Colorado's capital! After silver went bust, Silver Cliff crumbled but Westcliffe managed to hang on as a ranching and farming community, though rail service was shut down in 1937. Just north of town is Lake DeWeese, in the bowl of the Wet Mountain Valley, which offers fishing and water sports. Grape Creek, which flows below the reservoir, can be good for rainbow and brown trout. Lakes of the Clouds, at 11,200 feet, are accessible only by four-wheel drive or by hiking in 5 miles. But the trip is worth it as the remote beaver ponds below the lakes have brook and cutthroat trout while the upper lake has rainbow trout. Explore local historical legends or go mountain biking and four-wheel driving by the colorful wildflowers in the surrounding forests.

Fun Things to Do

- Cross D Bar Trout Fishing (719) 783-2544, (719) 783-2227, (303) 733-5577 Denver
- Silver Cliff Museum (719) 783-2394
- St. Andrews/Westcliffe Golf Course (719) 783-2734
- Westcliffe Schoolhouse Museum & History Tours (719) 783-9453

Cross D Bar Trout Ranch & Campground

High in the Wet Mountains, this famous ranch offers family fun, spacious camping and fabulous trout fishing at four scenic, crystal clear lakes. The open and shaded sites in this natural setting have water and electrical (30 amps) hookups. The pull thru sites have picnic tables, barbecue grills, fire rings and free wood. The ranch is in the cool shadows of the spectacular Sangre De Cristo mountain range on 360 acres.

Free fishing instruction is available for novices and fishing equipment, rentals, camp store and snack bar are on-site. Anglers of all skills with enjoy the spring-fed, stocked lakes were no license is required and no limit is set. Catch rainbow, brook, golden, cutthroat and donaldson trout here. There's a separate fly fishing area, a catch and release only lake and a trophy fishing lake. Other activities include horseback riding (guest horse are permitted), mountain biking, hiking and messing around on the playground. Cross D Bar Recreation Foundation is dedicated to providing the disabled and elderly the opportunity to experience the thrills and challenges of fishing, camping and outdoor recreation. Cross D Bar offers a family vacation the whole family can truly enjoy.

The ranch is handicap accessible and groups are welcomed. Ask about the outdoor, group meeting area for your family reunion.

Location: Twelve miles East of Westcliffe on Rosita Road. Turn off between mileposts 12 and 13, 4 miles West at the junction of Highways 96 and 65.

Total RV sites: 20	Pull thru sites: 17	Open: All Year
Full hookup sites: 0	45+ foot long sites: 20	Dick Mandel, Owner
Water & elec. sites: 20	Slideout sites: 20	Lynn & Sandra Attebery, Manager.
Elec. only sites: 0	Licenses sold: None	2299 County Road 347
50 amp sites: 0	LP Gas: None	Westcliffe, Colorado 81252
Hookup sites open in Fall: 20	Credit Cards: VM	719/783-2007
Winter hookup sites: 20	Elevation: 9200	303/733-5577 Denver Metro
RV site cost: Not available		

Within 15 minutes:

At RV Park:

Winter Park

Map: E-14

Located in the beautiful Fraser Valley and enclosed by the Arapaho National Forest, Winter Park is home to numerous activities. Don't be fooled by the name because Winter Park is also a summer playground. You'll discover an exhilarating alpine slide, excellent fishing, breath-taking hiking, fun whitewater rafting and dazzling scenery. There is also an extensive mountain bike trail system covering some 500 miles of mapped trails and 200 miles of marked trails using old logging and ranching roads sure to delight two-wheeler beginners or experts. Drive over the spectacular Berthoud Pass which crosses the Continental Divide at 11,301 feet. Or take the Rollins Pass Road in a four-wheel drive (inquire locally about current conditions before you go), following the original railway over the Divide which was used for 24 years until the Moffat Tunnel was completed in 1927. Anglers will be drawn to both the beautiful settings and the rainbow, brook, mackinaw and cutthroat trout and kokanee salmon in the lakes and rivers of the Arapaho National Forest.

Fun Things to Do

- Alpine Slide (970) 726-5514
- Grand County Historical Museum (970) 725-3939
- Pole Creek Golf Course (970) 726-8847

Snow Mountain Ranch/YMCA of the Rockies

On a vast 4,950 acres near the western entrance to Rocky Mountain National Park, Snow Mountain Ranch has full hookup (15 and 20 amps), pull thru sites. Each site has a barbecue grill, picnic table, fire ring and free firewood. From summer youth programs with craft classes, talent shows and archery lessons, to winter sleigh rides and ice fishing, Snow Mountain is designed for family fun.

For your convenience, the ranch has a grocery store, restaurant, snack bar and library. The ranch can accommodate groups of 1,500 people at its conference facilities — ideal for either a small seminar or a huge family reunion. Stay on site to swim in the indoor pool, play tennis and miniature golf or roller skate in the skating rink. Snow Mountain Ranch sponsors numerous activities, such as family and youth programs, hiking, horseback riding and cross-country skiing. Bring your downhill skis in the winter for trips to nearby Winter Park and Silver Creek ski areas.

Modern housekeeping cabins and lodge rooms are also available.

Location: Between Winter Park and Granby on US Highway 40 at milepost 219.

Total RV sites: 35
Full hookup sites: 9
Water & elec. sites: 17
Elec. only sites: 9
50 amp sites: 0
Hookup sites open in Fall: 0
Winter hookup sites: 0
RV site cost: Not available

Pull thru sites: 0
45+ foot long sites: 0
Slideout sites: 0
Licenses sold: None
LP Gas: None
Credit Cards: None
Elevation: 8800

Open: 5/27 to 9/5
Kent Meyer, Managing DIrector.
PO Box 169
Winter Park, Colorado 80482-0169
303/443-4743 Denver Metro
970/726-4628

Within 15 minutes:

At RV Park:

Indexes

RV Parks in Alphabetical order

Swimming Pool, RV Parks with

Horseback Riding, RV Parks Near

Hot Tub, RV Parks with

Fishing, RV Parks with on Site

Lake or Reservoir, RV Parks Near

Golf Course, RV Parks Near

Raft Trips, RV Parks Near

Mountain Bike Trails, RV Parks Near

50 Amp Sites, RV Parks with

45-Foot or Longer Sites, RV Parks with

Horses (Guest's) Permitted, RV Parks with

Group Meeting Room or Pavillion, RV Parks with

Cabins for Rent, RV Parks with

Winter RV Hookup Sites, RV Parks with

Tell your friends, so they can have their own copy
Check your local bookstore, or use this.

ORDER FORM

COLORADO

CABINS
COTTAGES
& LODGES

Discover Scenic Vacation Hideaways

&

RV PARKS

A Pictorial Guide

TO ORDER, Phone toll-free, or mail this to:
Rocky Mountain Vacation Publishing, Inc.
5101 Pennsylvania Ave, Suite #5, Boulder, CO 80303-2799

Denver Area (303) 499-9385; (800) 886-9343

Cabin book	$12.95	$
RV book	$ 15.95	$
Shipping and handling	$3.50	$
Colo residents add 4.26% tax		$
Total		$

Payment Method

☐ Check or money order is enclosed

Please bill credit card

☐ **VISA**® (13 or 16 digits) ☐ **MasterCard**® (16 digits)

Expiration Date ☐☐ Month ☐☐ Year

Credit Card # ☐☐☐☐☐☐☐☐☐☐☐☐☐☐☐☐

Name _____ Signature _____

U.P.S. Address _____

About the Authors

Having visited more Colorado RV parks and campgrounds for more years than anyone else, Hilton and Jenny Fitt-Peaster are the foremost experts on this subject.

Their experience began in 1965 when Hilton began renting motorhomes with his father near Chicago. (Their lifelong interest in camping and scouting led them into this field.) By 1968 their company was the largest full-service motorhome dealership in the USA. Two years later in 1970, Hilton became a founder and the first executive director of the Recreation Vehicle Dealers Association of America. Since 1977 when Jenny joined Hilton in business, they have served as the executive directors of the Colorado Association of Campgrounds, Cabins & Lodges.

In 1980, they began publishing the annual *Colorado Directory of Camping, Cabins, Lodges, Fun Things To Do,* now in its 16th year. They became licensed real estate professionals in 1983 for the express purpose of marketing campgrounds, cabins and lodges — in 1985, they established Colorado Campground & Cabin Resort Realty, Inc., the only brokerage in Colorado exclusively specializing in these properties statewide. In 1988, the authors founded the Colorado Cabin Resort Association, which merged with the Colorado Campground Association in 1991 to become the Colorado Association of Campgrounds, Cabins & Lodges of today.

In 1993 the Fitt-Peaster's launched Rocky Mountain Vacation Publishing, Inc. with their award-winning first book titled *Colorado Cabins, Cottages and Lodges — Discover Scenic Vacation Hideaways.*

In an industry-wide vote in 1995, Jenny was elected as an inaugural director-at-large of the new Colorado Travel & Tourism Authority.